SERVE NO MASTER

HOW TO ESCAPE THE 9-5, START UP AN ONLINE BUSINESS, FIRE YOUR BOSS AND BECOME A LIFESTYLE ENTREPRENEUR OR DIGITAL NOMAD

JONATHAN GREEN

DRAGON GOD BOOKS

Simultaneously published in United States of America, the UK, India, Germany, France, Italy, Canada, Japan, Spain, and Brazil.

Serve No Master has provided the most accurate information possible. Many of the techniques used in this book are from personal experiences. The author shall not be held liable for any damages resulting from use of this book.

Paperback ISBN 13: 978-1535078009

Paperback ISBN 10: 1535078006

Hardback ISBN 13: 978-1947667006

FOREWARD BY STEVE SCOTT

"There must be a better way to live."

This was a constant thought that I had during my daily commute while fighting bumper-to-bumper traffic in New Jersey.

That was 2002.

But it wasn't until late 2004—more than *two years later*—that I finally did something to change my life.

What did I do?

I quit my job and started an Internet business.

Honestly, not a day goes by that I wish I could go back in time and begin my business those two years earlier in 2002. But at the time, I didn't know how to turn my dream of passive income into a reality.

That's why I'm excited that *you* have taken the first step to replacing your job by checking out the following book, *Serve No Master*.

In the past 13 years, I have run a variety of Internet-based businesses – affiliate marketing, blogging, creating information products, and self-publishing. If there is a way to generate online income, then I've probably tried it at one point.

During this time, I've developed a highly-tuned "B.S. Meter" when it comes to people who teach strategies for generating online income.

It's been my experience that most of the so-called "gurus" have very little practical knowledge about what it takes to build a lasting business.

Jonathan Green is different.

While I've only met him in person one time, I had heard of his work for many years before that. And I can tell you that he's the real deal.

Not only has Jonathan built *multiple* successful online business, he also lives an amazing life with a house in a tropical paradise and the flexibility to always be around his family. Plus, he can grab a surfboard whenever he wants, walk across his front yard, and hop into the water to catch a few waves. To me, this is the perfect example of someone who lives life on his terms.

And in *Serve No Master,* Jonathan provides a blueprint you can use to start a business to live a life on *your* terms.

Don't get me wrong: This book won't show you how to "get rich quick" or anything of that nonsense. If you want to build a *lasting* online business, then you should be prepared to work hard and hustle.

Fortunately, *Serve No Master* shows you how to get started.

There are three reasons why I like (and recommend) this book.

First, Jonathan weaves together a series of short vignettes on how to develop the thinking that's necessary to escape the rat race and become your own boss. This is powerful stuff because in the words of Yoda, "You must unlearn what you have learned."

The harsh truth is that most people believe the lies they've been told about the modern world. The reality (as Jonathan shows) is that your job security is not so secure, the educational environment doesn't teach you the real skills you need to thrive, and that exchanging time for money is a fool's errand.

Next, I like the fact that Jonathan teaches you the core concepts that are critical to creating an income that replaces your job. He does this by covering a few key points:

- How to create a financial plan for an online business by

identifying how much you need to support you and your family.

- A simple strategy for taking that first step online—by leveraging your existing skills and building a business off your existing talents.
- How to find a market for your business and identify the people who will pay money for your product or service.

Finally, I like Jonathan's focus on building a business that serves a need and isn't about cutting corners. Sure, most of this advice isn't sexy or glamorous like what many other books promise, but his advice is exactly what I would recommend to anyone interested in getting started online.

Over a decade ago, I made the faithful decision to life live on *my* terms. At the time, I was told by close friends and family that it was a crazy dream. They said I should be happy with my 9-to-5 job. They said I should be grateful for a steady paycheck. They said that online businesses are nothing more than a scam. And they said that it's not possible to travel the world and make money while doing it.

I'm happy to say that I proved them wrong.

But I could have also failed in spectacular fashion because I didn't have a person or resource to turn to which showed how to build a "real" online business.

The good news is *you* have access to the resource that I never had. In the following pages, you will discover the proven strategies that can help you *Serve No Master*.

Steve Scott

Wall Street Journal Bestselling Author of Habit Stacking.

FREE GIFT

Thank you for your purchase of Serve No Master. As an extra bonus, I want to give you FOUR free gifts.

1. QUIT YOUR JOB CHECKLIST

The “Ready to Retire” checklist that lets you know the exact moment you can fire your boss forever. Mark the moment on your calendar when you can start living a life of freedom.

2. AUTHOR AND ENTREPRENEUR ACCELERATOR - LIFETIME MEMBERSHIP

Get lifetime access to the most powerful group you will ever join. As a permanent member of my private accelerator, you will get free content daily as well as support from thousands of others on the same path.

Every day there are new training videos, stories of success and moments of inspiration…all waiting for you.

3. FIVE DAY BUSINESS CHALLENGE - COMPLIMENTARY TICKET

Each month, I run a challenge with interviews from 25 experts at building an online business. Together we will refine your online dreams and help you focus on the best path for YOUR life. At the end of the challenge, you will know the exact steps to take to break the chains to a job you no longer love.

4. GET MY NEXT BOOK FREE

Members of my tribe get complimentary review and beta reader access to my new books, before anyone else in the world knows. Get a chance to read my next book AND affect the final version with your suggestions and opinions.

You get these bonuses as well as a few surprises, when you enter your best email address below.

Accelerate your success and click the link below to get instant access:

ServeNoMaster.com/quit

1

THE DAY THE EARTH STOOD STILL

It was a couple of days after Christmas, and I'd put my entire life on the line. Months of work, years of preparation and strategy – and seven thousand dollars of my family's money.

I'd invested it all – everything – on one wild idea that I hoped would save my sanity and give me financial freedom. And now the roulette wheel was spinning.

Two days earlier the last of my credit cards was frozen. All of my bank accounts were empty. If the ball didn't land on my number, my life was about to come crashing down around my ears. It sounds like an incredible risk, but I knew that if I didn't do it, I'd go crazy.

What makes a regular guy so desperate?

For years I had been working as a "fixer" for small businesses, selling my time for dollars. Making videos, writing articles, working on code until late at night. If they needed it, I did it. I was a human drone!

I needed to escape that life and move to the next level. My clients had turned into my bosses, and I was desperate to extricate myself from the constant phone calls, emails, and texts that chased me every day.

Sitting in front of my computer that morning, all I had left was hope. If this didn't pay off, I would have to declare bankruptcy. And I didn't exactly have a supportive environment. Everyone around me told me I was a gullible idiot, that I was working on some get-rich-quick scheme, and that I was too lazy to do "real work." But there comes a moment in life when you just have to take that leap of faith and bet on yourself.

10 am, my first product went live – a digital training course explaining everything I did online, and how to build a base of clients. Sure, I was sick of being a "local consultant", but I also knew there were tons of people who'd bend over backward to have what I had.

The first sale came in and I was jumping up and down in my seat like a little kid, so nervous I wanted to throw up. One sale alone wasn't nearly enough to save me – I was almost ten grand in the hole. Each little sale sent me an alert to my phone as the email came in.

You made a sale!

I couldn't believe it. The pennies turned into dollars. The dollars turned into hundreds and then thousands. Was it possible? I could already start to taste success.

Within twenty-four hours I had paid off all of my credit cards. They were way beyond "unfrozen". They were on FIRE. I was in the black, and the sales kept rolling in. My little idea turned into something beyond my wildest expectations. In twenty-four hours there were over one thousand seven hundred sales. After paying off all my debts, over ten thousand dollars in profit was sitting my Paypal account.

From negative seven thousand to plus ten thousand in a single weekend. I couldn't think of a better way to ring in the new year. I went up to Washington, DC to celebrate with one of my buddies. All night my phone kept buzzing in my pocket. Sale after sale continued to rock in while I was rocking in the new year. I was making money faster than I was spending it for the first time in my life.

Even when I was asleep, money continued to pour into my account. And I'd gotten addicted to that little buzzing noise from my cell phone. I could barely nod off before it started up again. With a list of thousands of satisfied customers, my life changed forever. I would never have to drink energy drinks at 5 AM and "grind" at some gig ever again.

I was finally in control of my financial destiny, and I felt my first taste of real freedom.

How was I supposed to know it would get more complicated from there?

2

THE CHAINS THAT BIND YOU

Everybody defines freedom differently.

I can't tell you exactly what freedom is – it's something you've got to decide for yourself. You grabbed this book because you're looking for freedom, and even though I don't know you personally yet, that makes me proud. If you're reading this book, the odds are that right now; you're wrapped in three layers of chains that trap you in a life that doesn't satisfy you. If you've got it in you to break these three layers – changing the way you think about business and life – you've got everything it takes to achieve rapid success. Are these problems that you solve once and forget about? Nope. If you're like me, you'll be improving in these areas all the time. But it gets easier when you aren't struggling for survival with your head barely above water.

The first layer of chains is in your mind. These chains are amazingly powerful and made out of fear. Think about this: they train a circus elephant from birth. They take the baby elephant and tie it to a pole. She will tug and try to break free but is simply not strong enough yet. By the time the elephant is an adult, she will no longer pull on the line. Why? She has been trained to be chained. The amazing thing is that the adult elephant is more than powerful enough to break free. She is no longer tied to the pole with a real chain but instead is held in place by a mental chain. There was a fire at an American circus a long time ago, and none of the elephants survived. Even faced with blistering fire they didn't try to pull on those ropes. They were so convinced that they didn't have the power to escape that they didn't even try.

This is the chain of fear, and it is very strong. Fear is the main force the government uses to maintain control over us. Fear is how they compel us to spend hundreds of thousands of dollars on a college education that doesn't help us get a better job. Fear is what keeps you from quitting your job. We are all afraid because it's around us every single day. Fear is exactly what I felt when I lost my job. When you tell your spouse or your friends that you are going to quit your job, their immediate response is to use fear to keep you enslaved. They will ask what you will do for money, tell you that it's so hard to find a new job now and give you plenty of other reasons that you shouldn't do it. They are all fear-based reasons. I have lived a life less ordinary. I have been told over and over again that I can't do the things that I want to do. That I'm not good enough, skilled enough, rich enough, lucky enough, good looking enough...

We believe in these chains so much that when we see someone walk away from them, it terrifies us. They shatter our reality with their behavior. If he can just walk away from the chains of fear, can I do the same thing? That is an overwhelming question. If you believe in these bonds enough, they become quite real. Every month I have to come up with a project or work on something that I created to generate income. I don't have a steady, single revenue stream like a traditional job. Most people find that shocking and they are more afraid of my freedom than their personal enslavement. Unfortunately, most people believe that working for a large company provides security, but you won't believe how fragile your existence actually is at a large corporation. We are taught over and over again to love our chains and to fear freedom.

The second layer of chains that wrap around you are financial. You just can't afford to quit your job. You need that income stream to pay your rent, feed your family, and cover your medical bills. You need that health insurance in case you get sick. If you leave that job, your life will start to unravel. Eviction notices and collection agencies will start hounding you. These chains are intertwined with fear. Who isn't afraid of getting kicked out of their house and living on the street? You can't leave the prison until you can self-sustain. Financial chains are quite real. They aren't as scary as fear chains but without control of your financial destiny, breaking the fear chain is meaningless.

Bills are real, and we live in a debt based society. More than fifty-five percent of Americans barely break even or spend more than they make. We start out owing a little, and every month our debt continues to increase. Credit cards were only invented a hundred years ago. They turned us from a country of people with savings to a country of people with debt. As long as you have debt hanging over your head, it's impossible to feel true freedom.

The third layer of chains is forged from knowledge. You can't escape the prison without a plan. You need floor plans, a guard schedule, and a getaway vehicle. What use is jumping over the wall if you are just going to be running across a field on foot? Those guys get caught every single time. Without the knowledge of how to change your financial destiny, you don't have any hope of escape. There are a lot of books out there that'll help you with one of these sets of chains, but you need to break through all three at once, or your escape will fail. You'll end up back where you started, even more depressed than before.

Most of us never use what we learned in high school or college. Those schools are designed to churn out factory workers, not leaders. We were trained in obedience more than anything else. We are taught to sit in our seats and stay quiet while we do whatever the teacher tells us to. To move when the bell rings, show up on time, and be quiet. We are trained to obey our prison guards.

But for you, all that is ending right now.

3

I COULD USE A LITTLE HOPE

So imagine this: I'd been injured in a car accident and was staring down a terrifying prospect – years of selling people computers they didn't need at prices they couldn't afford. You've probably been to a "tech store" like this once or twice. They mostly make their money from bilking the elderly.

And when I finally quit, the boss took it as a personal affront. How dare I leave some going-nowhere gig? She told me that nobody would ever hire me again. I was so confused by that – why get so personal, so quickly? I had nightmares for two years after that job and yet they tried to use fear to trap me. She wanted me to feel scared and powerless, to make me easier to control. We are raised to respond to fear, and every institution around us works hard to control our decisions using that power. Why? Because fear works.

Don't believe me? Watch the news at night. Every single story is bad news. People in that business have a saying: "if it bleeds, it leads." The more horrible the story, the more attention it gets. They always play those little snippets during the day - "something innocuous and random in your house is going to kill your children, we'll tell you at eleven." It's a tactic. They use fear just to get you to watch the news. If they wanted to help you, or the danger was real, they would give you the information immediately.

The government uses fear to maintain its power, too. If we aren't hearing about the Russians, it's the Chinese or terrorists. There is always some new existential threat to our way of life. When it's not swarthy foreigners planning our demise, there's something environmental.

When I was a child, I remembered hearing story after story about the hole in the ozone layer that was going to give everyone cancer and kill us all. Let me ask you a serious question: When is the last time you even heard the phrase "hole in the ozone layer?" I bet it's been more than a decade and probably more than two. NASA discovered the hole in the ozone layer a few months before they were about to lose a bunch of funding one year. They got the funding they wanted, and suddenly the "problem" simply disappeared.

What about global warming? Celebrities berate us, and politicians give speeches about how we are so horrible, right before they hop on private jets and burn more fuel than you will in your entire life. The same scientists who started the global warming scare in the 1980s were claiming global cooling just ten years earlier. Aren't you a little suspicious that the same data somehow proves two opposites? The only thing that connects these two conclusions is the desire to use fear to affect your behavior.

The entire Western education system is designed to crush creativity and control you through fear. We are told that if you don't get into a good kindergarten, you'll never get into a good grammar school. Each step along the way you hear how you need to do more activities to improve your little baby resume so that you can build your resume at some other amazing institution.

And by the time you're twenty-five, you have a master's degree that's worth garbage and hundreds of thousands of dollars of debt. Let's do a simple analysis for just a moment to see what your education is worth. Let's just say modestly that your education costs $250,000. That's including room, board, food and every other collegiate and post-graduate expense. And I know that number is far too small if you are thinking about a Ph.D. or law school.

The average small business loan is $25,000. You can go to college or for the same money you can start TEN businesses. If you've read the statistics that the government puts out there to scare you out of starting your own business, you know that eight out of ten small businesses fail. That means you could have taken that college loan, started ten businesses, let eight of them fail and still own two thriving businesses by the time you're in your mid-twenties.

That sounds pretty great to me!

The real problem with college is that most of what they teach you is garbage. It's almost completely worthless in the real world. If you are going to be a doctor or lawyer, then the stuff you learn is useful. My sister has a degree in art history. She then went to law school and became a tier 1 lawyer. She works 100 hours a week. I'm not sure if that's the American Dream for me. How often do you think there is an "art history emergency" in her law office? Where is the value in the undergraduate degree?

All that work and those four years of college have zero effect on her career. Law school could just as easily start at eighteen like it does in most other civilized countries. But then how would these institutions screw you out of hundreds of thousands of dollars?

All that money. Most of what you learn is worthless in the real world. All you learn in the American education system is how to be a drone; our natural desire to learn, grow, and improve ourselves has been commoditized, exploited, and strip-mined. The education-industrial complex stamps out creativity and brilliance with rules, standardized tests, and a host of terrifying narcotics. If I had been just a few years younger, I'm sure my teachers would have used one exotic brand of tranquilizers or another to keep me quiet and drooling.

Most people who graduate from college have degrees in worthless subjects - art history, ancient Greek history, philosophy, communications, leadership, and modern feminist studies. I don't care about the merits of learning those things. What I do know is that none of those give you skills to put food on the table. None of those translates into a real world job.

Rather than admit that they teach you garbage and charge way too much, they pour on the fear. They have to. Their industry depends on it. We hear things like "nobody will hire you without a college degree" all the time. Understand, this isn't sour grapes from a dropout. I have a college degree and a master's. My dissertation for my master's was so good that an educational publishing house picked it up, and it's available in print.

And yet for all that education... that fear driven education; I use less than five percent of the things I learned in college. I use absolutely NOTHING that I learned in my master's course. The main value I get from my education is that I sometimes write in different books, like this one, about how I use nothing I learned in college. And I went to an excellent school.

I graduated at twenty-one with a degree in my fist, and nobody would hire me. I got the same rude awakening most kids these days experience. You walk out of a college that tells you eighty percent of their graduates find a job...only to discover that they include jobs in the fast food industry. They include bottom-level jobs in that statistic. You can get a degree in science and end up stuffing bags at the grocery store, and the university will mark your losing job as a win in their brochures.

We are trapped in a prison of glass walls and invisible guards. The reason you don't ask for that promotion you deserve, quit to start your own business or hop on a plane to start a life in a new country can be boiled down to one single word - FEAR.

This is a book designed to replace fear with reality.

It's unfortunate, but the moment you tell the people around you that you're even thinking about quitting your job or starting your own business, they get in on the game. They give you a host of reasons why it's a foolish idea. And if you're paying attention, you'll see that they're all fear-based reasons. And the fact is - you might not succeed. But that's also what happens if you don't try.

My whole life, I've been driven by the desire to prove people wrong. That's probably my defining characteristic. When people tell me that I can't do something, I have no choice but to prove them wrong. When I cross the finish line, those same doubters shove their heads in the sand and blame my accomplishments on luck. They would rather blame an imaginary force than admit that their fear was wrong.

It's time to break the chains of fear that bind you. If you read this book until the end, you are going to have an exact sequence of steps that you can follow to achieve complete and total financial freedom.

I want to help you. I want to give you hope. Then I want to transform that desire into reality. I've already proven my naysayers wrong with my success. They still blame it on luck or random chance. So now I am going to do the same thing for you. I want us to work together, and stand up to the people who want to manipulate us through fear. I want to prove that my system works for ANYONE.

Your success is going to be my legacy.

4

SHATTER YOUR CHAINS

This book isn't a novel. I didn't write it so that you could furrow your brow and hum to yourself about how nice it is and stick it back on your bookshelf. It's a plan, and it's a simple one. I'm going to help you break through those three layers of chains we talked about earlier. First, we are going to understand exactly where those chains of fear came from, and how to transition your mind into a place where you believe in yourself. A place where you have real confidence in your ability to master your destiny. Without this faith in yourself, you will keep seeking a new master to protect you.

We've already started the process of cracking those fear chains.

I will then help you to formulate a plan. We will design a strategy that allows you to open up new revenue streams. Together we will figure out exactly how much money you need to earn to leave your job behind. To get to that moment where you step through the prison gates and shout at the sun. That moment where you realize nobody can tell you what to do ever again.

We're going to build a plan around who you are as an individual. We will assess what you already know and find a way to leverage that.

The knowledge and skills inside you are the levers we will use to break open the door of your prison. You don't need to learn anything new. You already have the knowledge inside you.

Come with me, and together, we're going to shatter the chains that bind you.

5

WHAT YOU WILL ACHIEVE BY READING THIS BOOK

This book is not designed to make you feel good. To be honest, I don't care about your feelings.

I once worked for a charity in the United Kingdom. Fresh out of college, I got a charity gig teaching DJing at inner city schools and working in a youth cafe. I wasn't paid a penny and had to raise support back in America. On the very first day, all of the volunteers had a little meeting. Everybody started talking in such glowing terms about how important the journey was. They wanted to make sure that we were all great friends at the end of the year. They focused on how we would work together.

I stood up and told them I disagreed. I told the other volunteers that I only care about the destination. What good is working to help those kids without tangible results? My goal was to change lives and give children with no hope something to believe in again.

At the end of my year of charity, everyone I worked with hated my guts. They spread all kinds of false rumors about me. They tried to get me kicked out of a house I had rented. They hated me on a level that... looking back, was really impressive. And yet. Every single kid that came into the cafe loved me. I was the most beloved volunteer. I had many conversations with the kids about religion and hope and the possibility of changing their lives. The rest of the staff combined had zero conversations like that all year. I know this because I asked them directly in the final meeting.

I helped a girl with cerebral palsy believe in herself again, and she ended up becoming an actress on a popular television show. I helped a kid with both parents living on welfare believe that he could break the cycle and become a successful DJ. He did.

I'm not here to tell you how great I am. My philosophy has always been the same. Feelings are secondary to success. My goal is to change your life. Your feelings are secondary to that goal.

Let me be a little more direct.

At the end of this book, I want you to make a bunch of money. That's my only goal. A book, project or website can only have one goal if it wants to succeed. If I were trying to make you feel good and teach you how to make money, I would fail at both. If you need a book that makes you feel good while nothing in your life changes, maybe I'll write a sequel filled with pithy quotes for you.

If you read this book to completion, you will accomplish a few critical things. The first is that you will have a set of financial plans in front of you. Something real, something written down that you can follow. We will set up three financial goals for you. Dialing in exactly how much money you need to make is imperative. People tell me all the time that they want to be rich. That's a lovely word with absolutely no meaning. I deal in specifics. How much money do you need to make every month to live your dream life? That's the goal we're after.

The second thing you are going to design is an actionable plan to profits. We are going to figure out the exact skill or talent that you are going to develop and leverage to start making money FAST. There is something that you are excellent at that other people want to learn. Don't tell me I'm wrong right now. I've done this exercise with hundreds of people in person, and I always find their marketable skill within five minutes. If you don't believe in yourself yet, just shut up and wait until we get to that chapter. Let me make you wealthy, and then you can complain.

The third thing is that you are going to find a market. You are going to know exactly how to find people who want to give you money in exchange for access to your unique skill, talent or knowledge. With a skill and a market, the money will flow into your bank almost like magic. This step is the one that many entrepreneurs struggle with. How many people have a great product that nobody has ever heard of?

My entire life people have been telling me all the things that I can't do. I can't start my own business. Nobody will ever pay me hundreds of dollars just to go out drinking with me for a few hours. I can't live on a tropical island. I'm too young for this and too old for that...

I've proven thousands of people wrong and if right now you think I can't change your financial destiny, then sit down, do the work, and prepare to be proven wrong.

6

MANIFESTING YOUR DREAM

Every human, starting from birth, is driven by two sets of dreams. We have the dreams that are birthed within us, the ones that make our souls sing. And then we have the desires that society has ground into our brains.

Television, teachers, and politicians force-feed us dreams about the kind of car we should drive, the house we should own and the college we should attend. None of those dreams come from within. They don't come from your heart, and they are merely distractions.

What I want you to do is think about what you want for just a moment. Two driving forces should determine every financial decision you make from now on. Do you desire freedom or finances? They are not mutually exclusive, but they are also very different.

I have a lot of freedom. I used to make a lot more money by working a lot more hours. It wasn't making me happy. I'm in the freedom camp. It doesn't matter which camp you're in. There isn't a good one or a bad one. You just have to think about which idea makes you happier.

Would you like to retire in the next five years and live modestly on an island somewhere? Maybe in the mountains where you can go fishing every day or focus on one of your hobbies? Or would you rather have a great house and a luxurious car with the ability to travel five-star every time?

I work with people on both sides of the fence all the time. You should see how I negotiate. When I partner with someone on a project, the first thing I explain is that I'm not interested in being the captain. I'll do a specific amount of work, but I never want that majority share. When you are the boss, you have the responsibility and the stress. I'll just enjoy my smaller percentage from the comfort of my hammock on the beach, thank you very much.

Let's start with a simple, but vital question:

If you never had to work again and nobody would ever judge you, what would you spend the rest of your life doing?

The answer to that question is the first step to finding your core value. It will help you to figure out what drives you. As we dig deeper into this book, we will get more specific with your dream. We will turn your desire into specific numbers. And then we'll develop a plan to hit those financial targets. But for now, I just want you to take a few minutes and let your imagination run free. You know how you used to imagine all the stuff you'd do if you won the lottery, invented something cool, or got that promotion? Get yourself in that kind of mindset as we continue.

7

OUT WITH A WHIMPER

I was twenty-nine, and my career was over.

"You're fired,"

"Hand over your keys and any other company property, and get out of here," my boss said.

I will never forget driving through that snowstorm in February of 2010 on my way home to a brand new apartment in a brand new car - neither of which I could afford anymore.

With a mountain of debt hanging over my head, I walked into that empty apartment... and those words rang in my head over and over again - like the judgment of the totality of me as a person.

To make things even worse, I'd already turned down the only other job opportunity within a hundred miles. The job I spent ten years working toward disappeared in an instant. I started to suspect that I might just be a failure as a human being. My whole life, the years of education, the late nights at work… everything was fading away in front of me. I wanted to die.

I was on trial back at that office, but somehow they forgot the part where you get to defend yourself. Before they said a single word, they'd already reached a verdict. You wouldn't believe the fake reason they invented to fire me. I could tell they'd spent at least a week cooking up something. They decided to fire me, and then they looked for a reason. The sentence was determined before the trial.

And what could I do about it? They had the power, and I didn't.

I thought I was set for life. During the job interview a month earlier they had talked about how we were family now and how people stayed there for ten or twenty years. I would never have to worry about looking for another job again.

It turns out; they were right…

I

WHAT IS JOB SECURITY

People clinging to job security, savings, retirement plans, and other relics will be the ones financially-ravaged from 2010-2020, the most volatile world-changing decade in history.

- Robert Kiyosaki

8

THE LIE OF JOBS FOR LIFE

Do you remember a few decades ago when we started to hear about Japanese companies that gave you a job for life? They used to have a system in Japan where a big company would hire you at eighteen, and you were set until you retired. You could work without the fear of that ax hanging over your head.

So many people drive to work every day laughing at guys like me. They still believe that we have jobs for life in this country, too. There's this idea that if you work for a big enough company, as long as you work hard and make them a lot of dough, you will be protected.

Unfortunately, reality is quite different.

A job interview is a lot like a first date. We make a lot of promises that we have no intention of keeping, and do everything we can to hide the worst parts of our personality. The truth is that your company doesn't care about you. The CEO of your company makes 400 times more than the average worker there. That salary is driven by greed, and if you study economics, those CEO salaries are one of the main reasons the economy has been stalling or shrinking for thirty-five years. That boss isn't going to buy five hundred more pairs of jeans than you are or eat five hundred more meals. And they certainly don't work five hundred times harder than anybody! That money doesn't go back into the economy.

When you come out of college, all bright-eyed and bushy-tailed, you think that if you can just get hired you will be set for life. That getting your foot in the door will be enough. Once you're in there, you can prove yourself. Many people even take jobs as interns. Toiling long hours for a company that makes millions for free! Hoping that six months later you might get offered a job.

That's some Grade A horse manure.

Now, I have to be honest with you for just a moment. I have interns at my company. Every six months or so, I take on a new intern. The reason I have to get a new one every six months is that they keep getting rich. Every one of my previous interns now makes more than ten thousand dollars a month.

What's my secret? I don't teach people how to work for me. What's the fun in that? I teach people how to be rich. That's what I like to brag about. My interns learn so much that I can't afford to hire them anymore. They end up firing me and it's the happiest day of the relationship. I get another intern, and then that one gets rich and moves on. My interns go out and buy houses and start families and quit stupid jobs. I'm changing the world. It makes me so proud when they break free.

That's the reason this book is in your hands right now. I wanted to start scaling up. Instead of helping two people a year, I want to help two million.

When you start working for a company, all of the guarantees are in one direction. You make a lot of promises about behavior, and they promise to pay you a certain amount every month. They don't make any promises about their behavior in return. But we sure do imagine them. "If I treat my company right, they'll return the favor." That's a charming thought – it just has no relation to reality.

Every week we hear about a new company downsizing. That word is so adorable. I just love how they made a fun name for destroying lives. It's a shame that they don't just call it "career murdering" or "future destroying" or simply "soul crushing." Those are closer to the truth. One of my closest friends in the world is also one of the top experts on jobs. He helps thousands of people get back to work every year.

I see a lot of their resumes and what I see there is shocking. These people have resumes that make me shiver with fear. They are twice as educated and ten times as smart as me. They worked for the kinds of companies that blow your mind. And yet each one of them got kicked to the curb because some guy in an office halfway across the country didn't hit a financial projection.

So ten percent of the company had to get the ax. Or twenty percent. The company you work for right now has zero affection for you. They pay you for a service. The moment you think there is an emotional element to the relationship is the moment you are in trouble.

How many people do you know who have worked for the same company for more than ten years? Those days are long gone. If the people aren't jumping from ship to ship, the captains are kicking them off the boat.

9

DOES YOUR BOSS CARE ABOUT YOU?

I know what you are about to say – your boss isn't like that. Your boss is different. Your boss cares about you. Your manager has your back, and he'd do anything for you.

Really? Would he take a pay cut so he could give you a raise?

If you think the answer to that one is yes, then go to work tomorrow and ask him. You better finish this book fast, though, because tomorrow night you are coming home with a cardboard box full of your stuff.

In my twenties, I worked for a host of bosses, and fortunately I had a few great ones. They were the exceptions, not the rule. Most bosses are nice enough people. Plenty of them are incompetent to one degree or another. Most of them like to steal the credit for your work. But overall, they aren't evil.

At the end of the day, it's every man for himself in the office. If your boss has to choose between firing you and quitting, he's going to terminate you every time. Your boss goes to work for one reason - to make money. It's the same reason that you go to work. He's there for himself.

When you start to assume that your boss cares about you on an emotional level, you open yourself up to some serious heartbreak.

When the money stops flowing, it doesn't matter how much he likes you - you're out the door.

It's time to stop thinking of your boss as your life raft or even your lifejacket. If the ship starts sinking, you are going to find out just how cold the Atlantic gets in the winter.

The idea that your loyalty will be repaid is ridiculous. Look at how many people have been fired across the world in the last ten years. These massive companies "downsize" huge swaths of their employees, and then get the ones who still have a job to do twice as much work for the same pay.

Fear is a powerful motivator. As long as a company controls your paycheck, it holds all the power.

10

INCOMPETENTLY PROMOTED

You might still have a sliver of hope for yourself. After all, if you're great at your job, you get promoted. If you're a tireless worker, they'll often put you in charge of two or three other people. And as long as you keep doing great, you will keep moving up the ladder.

But what happens when you reach the point where you can't do a good job anymore? The promotions stop, but you won't get demoted. This is exactly where about ninety percent of managers are right now. They're too incompetent for a promotion because they're too incompetent for the job they have right now.

Most bosses are operating just beyond the level of their ability for this reason. That's why they make mistakes, take credit for your work and limit your creative ideas.

They're grasping for their own survival, doing everything they can to protect their job. One of the most important aspects of that is making sure that his boss doesn't realize that you're better suited for that management position.

11

THE COWORKER WALKOUT

You see this all the time in the movies. The main character's had enough, and he's leaving the terrible company and the incompetent boss he works for. He tells everybody off; he stands up and shouts, "Who's with me?" And everybody is with him – they march right out there with him to start some new company together. Sometimes they roll the credits right after the walkout.

Unfortunately, life doesn't imitate art. People are constantly getting fired these days, not because of personal failures, but because the people driving the company have failed. These leaders buy over-priced companies, make poor investments or simply don't realize that the market is changing. Their failures mean the company needs to cut down costs. So people lose their jobs.

And not one single person who is on the spared list ever walks out with those fired in an act of solidarity. When your boss decides to give you the boot, you will realize just how lonely this world is. Your friends from that company will never follow you out the door. Just like you, they work there for the money and no other reason. If they didn't need the money to pay their bills, take care of their families and support their lifestyles they would have walked out the door by now.

I'm not trying to crush all of your hopes and dreams here. I just want you to realize that when it comes to finances, alliances are very fickle. More than fifty percent of marriages fail. How can we expect the soft alliances we form at work to survive a lifetime?

If your best friend at work was fired tomorrow for a stupid reason, would you quit in solidarity? Would you put your family's financial welfare at risk out of a sense of loyalty? Or would you keep your head down and hope you don't get fired by association?

12

BEGGING FOR A RAISE

Most people have a single revenue stream. We work for the company and take home a check every two weeks. That check or direct deposit is how we pay for our housing, feed our families and use whatever is left over to pay for some entertainment. If you want to increase your income, you have to go back to the same well. The only way you get an extra dime from your labor is to go into your boss's office and beg for a raise.

You can describe that process in whatever way makes you feel good, but you are asking someone in power to give you something. That's my definition of begging. Your entire financial situation is outside of your control. How many times have you seen someone work as hard as they can, always show up on time, work weekends and still the office brownnoser gets the promotion?

Your boss's job is to provide you with the minimum amount of financial incentive to get you to perform your job well. If you will do the job at the same level for eleven dollars as you will for ten dollars an hour, not giving you a raise is the right decision. There is no benefit to him for giving you that raise. Your work won't improve. He has control and can always threaten to fire you. As much as you want a raise, that fear of losing your job is quite powerful. If your fear of losing your job is greater than your desire for a raise, you are trapped. You're in the weaker negotiating position.

I've been in that room asking for a raise before. You are on your knees, and it sucks. I hate that feeling, and I never want you to feel it again. By the end of this book, you are going to be able to open multiple revenue streams. That means you no longer depend on a single source of income. Let's think about this with a little math. Don't worry; I said a LITTLE math.

Let's say you make $1000 a week. You work for one company, and you get that nice fat paycheck every Friday. But then disaster strikes. The company loses a lawsuit and declares bankruptcy. Now you're officially cooked. You've lost your entire revenue stream, and you have to live off your savings while you desperately hunt for a new job. On top of that, your resume is tainted. You worked at a company that collapsed. Future employers will think that you might be bad luck.

That's one way of living.

The alternative is that you live the lifestyle I lead. You believe in multiple revenue streams. You only make $800 a week. But you make it from eight sources. You are making less than at the big job; that's true. But when one of those employers collapses, instead of being broke you still get $700 every week. Instead of trying to find a new job that pays you $1000 a week, you only need to replace $100. Income diversity limits your vulnerability. We want to create multiple revenue streams so that even if one dries up, you are not toast. Instead of begging your boss for a raise when you need more money, you just spend an extra two hours every weekend on your side project. That makes you more money, AND it protects you from single point vulnerability.

13

THE BOSS VERSUS THE TOP EMPLOYEE

My friend works for a very large company in Washington, DC. When it started, it was just him and the boss. He does the majority of the tech work while his boss drives the shop. They started out as just two guys, but now the company has over fifty employees. My friend brings home a six-figure paycheck. That's pretty nice. His paycheck grows arithmetically. That means it grows in a straight line. The longer he works there, the more he makes. That's a pretty good gig. He has a secure job, and he's part of something that grows.

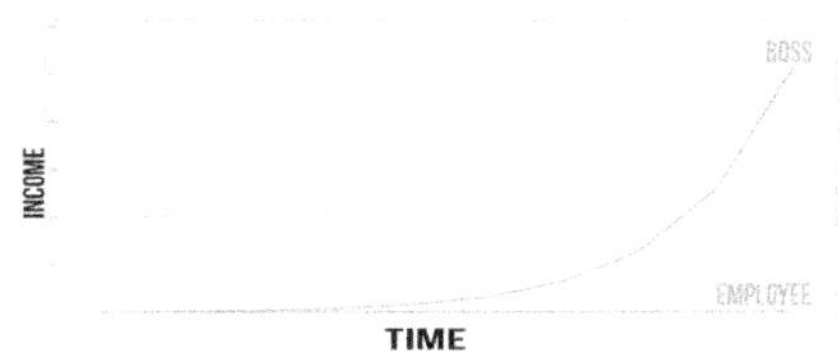

His boss owns the company, and he's now worth deep into eight figures. His financial growth is geometric. Everything the company makes on top of paying this staff, he gets to keep. So his growth looks like a rocket blasting into outer space. While my friend's salary increases by about ten percent every year, his boss is growing by multiplication. It's doubling and tripling.

Every time you talk about starting your own business or doing your own thing, everyone likes to talk about the risk. If you quit your job tomorrow and try to start your own business, you could fail. That's true. That's all that your friends and coworkers will talk about. Fear controls them. But when hope controls you, you get to focus on the reward.

You could quit your job and end up making a LOT more money than you ever imagined. When I was fired from my last job, I was making $2200 a month after taxes. I was twenty-nine, and I had peaked in my career. There were no higher jobs available to me. That's the joy of being in education. Look, that's nothing to sneeze at. It's a decent wage in our country, and the job gave me a huge amount of freedom. When you work in education, you discover that bureaucracy is built on incompetence. They gave me an assignment and told me it would take five to six months. I finished that project and two more in the first week. I spent most of my time taking walks around the campus because I had nothing else to work on. My manager was so incompetent that she performed at around 1% of my level. If I had stayed at that job, I would have gotten better and better at pretending to work. That's how many large organizations work.

I was fired from that position, and I'll tell you exactly why in a moment. I lost that job, and suddenly I had no income. I started working for myself because I never wanted to be that vulnerable again. Within six months I had replaced that income. Within twelve months I started making my old monthly salary every week. I was my own boss and making four times as much money, with no financial vulnerability. That's the power of being your own boss. You get to reap those massive rewards.

The reward is significantly larger than the risk.

14

RISK AND REWARD

Tomorrow, your job could disappear. I can name a million reasons and ways you could be unemployed within twenty-four hours. The owner of your company steals all the money? POOF, you're out of a job. Someone at work misinterprets your comment as sexual harassment? POOF, you're fired. Your company fails to hit its unrealistic financial projections? POOF, you're filling out a welfare application. No matter how good you are at your job, you can lose that job based on someone else's actions. You are not the master of your destiny. If someone else can destroy your income stream, accidentally or on purpose, then you better start preparing.

Any single point of vulnerability is a very serious risk. Would you want to ride in a spaceship with only a single hull? One tiny hole in a window and everyone dies? There is a reason that submariners have those doors that lock between every compartment. If one section floods, the whole crew doesn't have to die. But that's how you are living financially. You have a single income stream. And if anything happens, one tiny crack in a window, it's all gone. Your life is destroyed, and you are back on the old job hunt. Right now that market is crowded. Every day tens of thousands of people who are smarter and more qualified than me get fired.

Sometimes I send in a resume for a job that I'm qualified for just to see what happens. It feels awful. The entire job-search process makes you feel like a peasant cowering before some angry ancient god. I get told all the time I'm not good enough for jobs that pay ten percent of what I make now. I can't get a job, even with a ninety-percent pay cut!

The reason we don't start secondary revenue streams is because of a false sense of security. We are afraid of the responsibility. The thought of being in charge of your financial destiny is scary. But your real fear should be the fact that you are completely and utterly powerless. I had a friend who was a high-level executive vice president at one of the top companies in the world. It doesn't matter where in the world you live; you would know who they are. He lived in a serious mansion, drove a brand new Hummer, and his wife had a beautiful Mercedes. Then one day that company dropped ten percent of the staff. And he was on the chopping block. Within a year he was living in a studio apartment with his wife, and they were struggling to get out from under cars they could no longer afford.

He had a great job making serious money, but it was still a single point of failure. That one point of risk is a problem. It doesn't matter how much money you make at your job; you still have a single point of vulnerability. To me, that is far more terrifying than any other risk. I want to be very clear about something before we go further. I do NOT want you to quit your job tomorrow and start following this book as your new religion because that is the same mistake. If you quit and start a new project, you again are stuck with a single point of vulnerability. What you want to do is keep that job but launch a side project at home for just one to two hours a night. Start small and just focus on replacing your income. Once you are making more money at home than you do at the office, then you can leave that day job. If you follow my method, you will be able to quit your job within the next year. We want to really focus on protecting you from any future financial vulnerabilities.

By keeping your job and just investing a few hours at night to your first project, you get the reward without the risk. You have that primary income stream to support you while you invest time in your financial exit strategy.

II

EDUCATION

Education is what remains after one has forgotten what one has learned in school.

- Albert Einstein

15

YOU WERE TRAINED TO BE A DRONE

If anybody were going to succeed in the American educational system, it would have been me.

I was in the top 1% of students with plenty of brainpower and plenty of opportunities. I took the SAT when I was just 12 years old and scored better than most high school seniors. That test scored my intelligence above 99.97%. In a room with one thousand people, only three will be smarter than me. I'm also a member of MENSA where your IQ has to be in the top 2%. I went to a great college on an academic scholarship and in my late twenties, I completed my master's degree in London. I'm highly intelligent and well educated. The problem is that my entire education was a waste.

I invested around $150,000 in my education. That includes scholarships, loans, money from my parents and my own personal investment. And looking around me, I got out LUCKY. Let's do a little math. My top-of-the-industry job paid me $2200 a month after taxes. At that rate, I could pay off my education in a little under six years...

As long as I didn't eat, drink or need to live anywhere.

That's the discovery that most college graduates are making these days. You graduate with an overpriced garbage degree and the best job you can get sentences you to decades of debt. College only teaches you a single skill. It teaches you how to shut up and be a good little cubicle monkey. Free and creative thought isn't encouraged at these universities anymore. Instead, you are taught to be quiet in class and turn in assignments on time.

That's not how you create a leader – it's how you create an average employee. There are a few majors that lead directly to specific careers, such as engineering, medicine, architecture, and accounting. But if you look at any college booklet, you will see that more than eighty percent of the degrees are basically worthless. You graduate college with massive student loans and no idea what the difference between APY and APR is. You have no idea how to check your credit score, let alone know what it means. You certainly know nothing about starting your own business or controlling your destiny.

All of my education was at top tier institutions. And the only thing I learned was that they screwed me. Every single skill I use in my life, I learned in high school. If you didn't go to college, that's not just fine. It's excellent. Your education is completely irrelevant to me. I have people who work for me, and they all eventually leave me to start their own companies and make six figures. Did any of them go to college? I have no idea! I've never asked. I don't drug test them, we don't go on team building retreats, and I don't care what they do outside of work. Because none of that stuff impacts their performance.

Colleges talk about how they "prepare you for life" which is so ridiculous. It's a meaningless statement. They should be "teaching you how to make money." That's the reason we go to college. Nobody goes to college to learn how to be a man or a great mother or great husband or anything else like that. We go to college because people who go to college are supposed to make more money than people who don't. But it's a lie.

People who start and own companies make hundreds of time more money than their employees. That's what college should prepare you for. But they don't. The bad news is that college tricked you. The good news is that I'm here to fix that problem. I'm not interested in feel-good techniques or keg stands. I'm only interested in specific techniques that will generate income for you. Everything else is a waste.

Here, I'll prove it. First, how much of the time you spent at college gave you knowledge or skills that affect your income? Second, how much did the stuff you learned at college bump your income? Third, how much time and money did you spend at college?

If you're like me, you spent several years and tens or even hundreds of thousands of dollars for a tiny amount of useful information. As for that big pay bump? Let's factor in one other idea. How much money would you have made if you spent those four years working full time? By the time you graduated college, you could have been a manager at a Sears or something. Instead of losing money for four years, you could have been making money, and instead of theory, you would have real-world management experience.

To make matters even worse, most of the people teaching the few valuable courses shouldn't be allowed within five hundred yards of a school. Nobody teaching marketing or business courses has ever made any actual money doing those things. They only know the theory.

Let's try another fun metaphor.

Let's say that in four weeks you have to fight in a mixed martial arts match against some steroid gobbling beast that bounces at a local bar. And if you lose the fight, these mysterious organizers are going to execute your entire family. Yeah, even your lovable Granny Josephine with the bad hip. These guys are serious.

You have two choices of trainers. One is a professor who has read every book on the art of warfare and can even give troop movement orders in Latin. He has studied the videotapes of every great fight and can go into detail on the thoughts and processes of combat. The other choice is a jerk who can't read. At eighteen he didn't graduate high school, and his parents threw him out of the house. He hopped on a plane to Thailand and made a living as a white fighter in Asian basements and parking garages. He has no idea what the rules are for boxing. He doesn't know how to fight fair. He only knows how to win.

If you want to learn from someone who has never done what you need to do, then pick that fancy professor. Your family will die, and you will probably die in the ring too. But at least you received an excellent "education." I'm like that dirty street fighter. I don't know the fancy rules. I don't know the acceptable practices.

I just know how to win.

16

HOW THE AMERICAN EDUCATION SYSTEM HAS FAILED YOU

When you go to the dog track, you get to watch a bunch of greyhounds chasing a fake rabbit in a circle. It's a cool sporting event, and the crowd's got plenty of energy. But it's a little unjust. I mean, the fastest dog might win... but he never actually gets the rabbit.

Welcome to the American educational system.

Most colleges right now brag about their diversity, social programs, and multiculturalism. Those things are great to talk about, and killer copy to stick next to your stock models for the brochure, but none of them gets you one step closer to your goal. They never talk about the average income of their graduates. And they'd rather pole vault off a cliff than tell you how many of their graduates get GOOD jobs.

They keep putting these rabbits in front of you and promising that once you catch the next one, you get to be happy. You work your tail off as a kid to get into the best high school. Then you have to play sports and join as many clubs as possible in high school to get into a good college. And let's dial into that bit of hot garbage for just a moment. Do you think being good at archery is going to help you ten years later when you are trying to find a job? Of course not. All those extracurriculars you have to do in high school are such a waste. Colleges want to pick students who spend time on things that won't affect their income. That right there shows that college is not about income. It's about something else.

You grit your teeth, you get those callouses on your hands from messing with those strings, and you pay your dues. You get into the right college, and you breathe a sigh of relief - finally, you can just focus on graduating and getting into the workforce. But it's a lie. Most good jobs require you to train after college. If you want to be a stock trader you have to take all those courses and get your certifications. Even if you just want to show people houses to buy, you need to go to school and get a real estate license. At the end of college, you're still unqualified for more than ninety percent of the careers in our country. You have to fill your already packed schedule with even more busywork to "separate yourself" from the horde of other "equally qualified" drones-in-training.

But maybe you keep chasing that rabbit because your parents were fooled too. They are convinced that a good education is the key to financial success in our society. And they would have been right – back when Andrew Carnegie was on top of the business world. That correlation no longer exists. Many very wealthy people never went to college. I can tell you right now, that if you didn't go to college...

If instead, you learned a trade - something like laying tile or carpentry or being an electrician - it's far EASIER for me to make you wealthy. That's right. In my experience, lack of education is a significant advantage. At least you didn't learn the wrong way to do everything!

Public education is just abysmal. You aren't allowed to teach the smartest kids; you have to build every class around the laziest ones. And it means that nobody ends up learning anything. Look, it's fine by me if you aren't book smart. You already know that I think most of that stuff is garbage.

If they would separate the kids based on ability and interest, then the system would be so much stronger. Most kids know what path they want by the time they're sixteen. If a kid at sixteen wants to work with his hands, there should be specific options that teach him that. And what I'm saying isn't a novel or ridiculous idea. Many other countries like Japan and England use this type of system. The United States ranks first in hubris, but only 17th in the quality of our educational system. Both of those countries that turn desires into skills that make money are ranked higher.

And the cost of it all is staggering. You pay so much money to walk away with an albatross strapped around your neck. You could start a decent business in your town for less than 35k. Starting the business that I'm going to teach you will cost less than $500. That's all I had to start my company.

Whatever your level of education, the system found some way to screw you. At best, you are an underpaid drone. At worst you didn't even graduate because nothing they were teaching helped you. I'm sorry for that crap experience. Now it's time to turn it around.

17

WHAT YOU SHOULD HAVE LEARNED

There are so many great subjects that college could teach you. They could teach everything that I'm about to cover and so many other great subjects. But I think these are lessons that are sorely missing from high school.

I hate that I didn't get to learn any physical skills in high school. Imagine if you learned "home repair" in high school. This class teaches you how to fix basic wiring problems, how to unclog a severe toilet problem and how to repair the washing machine. None of these are skills you can make money from. But they are skills that we pay other people for all the time. Think about how much money you would save if you had basic home repair skills. Over a lifetime, this ability alone would save you around ten thousand dollars. Not only that but you could graduate high school and find a place to live rent-free because you could be the superintendent.

What about home economics? Whether this is a euphemism for learning how to cook or learning how to balance your checkbook, both are skills you need. Learning how to cook your own food and to shop strategically would cut your food expenses every year by ten to twenty percent. You wouldn't lose as much food to overcooking. You would save the cost of going to restaurants and fast food joints. On top of that, food cooked at home is healthier so everyone in society would live longer.

Imagine if you spent a semester learning about credit - how loans work, what makes a good credit card, the different between APY and APR, and the basics of investing. This knowledge is critical to your financial survival. I can't believe how many people tell me that they own their house. The only way you own your house is if you have no mortgage. If you are paying a mortgage, then you are renting your house from the bank. When you pay double the value, the bank lets you keep it. That's how mortgages work. If you miss a few payments, they take the house away. Do they then give you back all the money you paid? Of course not. Would have been nice to know that when you were eighteen, though!

These are just some of the basics that we could be teaching people instead of trigonometry and history that they will never remember let alone use. We've all seen those shows where they walk up to someone on the street who can't name the Vice President, let alone a Supreme Court justice. Nobody remembers that stuff.

It's unfortunate, but education in our country is a racket. The strongest union in the country is the teachers union. Now if you are part of a different union, I don't mean to hate on your union. But has your union screwed tens of millions of children out of their futures? That's what I thought. When you have ruined an entire generation's hope for the future, then you can brag that your union is as powerful as the teachers union. Teachers in that union can't be fired even if they fall asleep or physically hurt a child. There are teachers in New York who sit in a room all day with each other and get paid. They can't be in the same building as children because they are so dangerous, but they also can't be fired. It takes years to fire a teacher who hurts a student. That's beyond horrifying.

My uncle was a big union guy. He worked on the loading docks. He unloaded and loaded trucks all day long for decades. I understand his union. It's about protecting the workers from dangerous working conditions and being underpaid. That makes sense to me. What do teachers need to unionize about? I used to be a teacher, so I know what I'm talking about. The goal of teachers individually or collectively should be to provide the best education possible to ensure that children have a chance for financial success. But the union doesn't care about that. You can't reward good teachers or punish bad ones. It's a garbage system that I have no intention of subjecting my children to.

18

MEDICATING AWAY CREATIVITY

The worst thing educators have come up with recently is drugging children with powerful psychoactive drugs. Somehow a memo went out, and half the kids on the planet are suddenly diagnosed with ADD. Then they wanted to drug the other half of the students, so they invented ADHD. These "diseases" didn't exist thirty years ago. They were discovered right after big pharmaceutical companies found the cure.

The problem is never that the teacher is boring. That the subject doesn't interest the kid, or that their minds are already buzzing with a thousand better things to do. The problem is that the child is not acting enough like a drone. That is the only purpose of those drugs. To medically force children to act like drones. It stifles creativity, and it's an easy solution that does nothing to deal with the core problem. Do you think that ten percent of the population needs to be on mind control drugs? Do you think humanity evolved through all these thousands of years only to spontaneously get this sick?

It's also interesting that it's almost exclusively boys that get drugged up at school.

I worked as a tutor with a young boy who had "ADD" once. The school told him that he was a moron (their word) with learning problems, who would have to go to high school somewhere else. The parents brought me in because I'm a trigger puller. I find the problem, and I fix it. It took me less than ten minutes to figure out and solve the problem. The kid was a drummer. A very good drummer. He could only think while he was tapping. At school, they wouldn't let him tap his pencils because it annoyed the teacher. So he couldn't learn anything. He needed physical motion to activate his memory. The teachers could have found two rubber soundless sticks and solved the problem in five minutes. But that's not how education works. They wanted to tell him he was mentally challenged and ship him off to a garbage school because it was easier. They said he would fail their high school entrance exam.

At the time I was living with a drummer for the second time in my life. I'm used to people with this need to tap all day long. I can zone it out. I worked with this student for a few months and let him tap away to his heart's content. I learned two things. The first is that teachers seek the easy solution for themselves above all else. The second is that this child was brilliant. He was the greatest natural code breaker I've ever encountered. There was this activity in the prep courses where they would have a complex mathematical code. You have to do all these little math problems on the way to breaking the code. In the seconds it would take me to flip to the back of my book to look up the answer, he would already have it worked out. He was basically the NSA's wet dream. I had to talk to his mom about it and explain that the problem wasn't that he was a moron. He was a genius who couldn't sit still.

I've spent time with people who are great in every field - from Navy SEALs to oil barons. I've spent time with mob lords and professional pit fighters. I have spent time with some of the most brilliant people on the planet, and this kid was so smart it scared me. How do you tell someone that their kid might be the best person on the planet at something?

A few months later he took the high school entrance exam and got the highest score on the test. The school had failed him. His teachers had failed him. They told him that he couldn't pass that test. I told you before that nothing motivates me like being told that I can't do something. On my first day with him, I gave a little speech similar to the one I gave you at the start of this book. I told him never to think about that test again. It's not his job to pass it. It's now mine. His only job was to trust me. Because I'm a trigger puller. That kid went from the worst to the first in a few short months.

I hate the thought of using drugs to crush someone's energy or creativity. Most geniuses are weird. Have you ever met a scientist who wasn't strange or a great doctor who wasn't arrogant? Exactly. That's what you want. Who wants the quiet, nervous doctor? I want the jerk with the terrible personality who always finds the cure. When the teachers want to drug your children, you need to ask yourself if this is good for the child, or just easy for the teacher. I fought for that child. I will fight for my children. And right now I'm fighting for you and your children.

III

THE MINDSET OF THE MASTERLESS

There is nothing outside of yourself that can ever enable you to get better, stronger, richer, quicker, or smarter. Everything is within. Everything exists. Seek nothing outside of yourself.

- Miyamoto Musashi

19

MINDSET

Before we move into our action plan, it's important to find the right frame of mind. Even when you decide to start your side project, fear can cause you to make some bad decisions. The first mistake that many people make is treating it like a hobby or a game. Some people spend tens of thousands of dollars on courses they will never finish, let alone implement. They spend from their entertainment budget, and that is a strategy that guarantees online failure. Most people who try to make money online fail and this is one of the biggest causes. You need to track every single penny you spend. That is a business expense. You cannot consider your business profitable until you have earned back what you spend.

Any money you spend on courses, software, training or coaching - it all needs to be tracked. You can use a spreadsheet or any financial software you choose. I don't care how you track; I just care that you track your money. You have to treat this as a business from day one. If you treat it like a hobby that will be a business when it starts making money, you will fail. I see it over and over again.

The more serious you are about this project, the higher your odds of success. Please don't spend money without being very serious about it. You should start by writing down the cost of this book unless you stole it.

(And if you stole it, please do me the courtesy of buying it once you've made some money using my techniques.)

You also need to keep track of your time. If you spend two hours a night and at the end of the month make an extra $100, you might be really excited. You made money online. But then you will realize that comes out to less than $1.70 an hour. Unless you are living deep in the third world, that is not a great wage. It's wonderful to make that first dollar online. Just remember that you need to improve that ratio so that you are making real money for every hour you invest in your new project. Most new businesses take two or three years to turn a profit. It's not going to take us nearly that long, but you need proper accounting to actually know when you are making enough money.

You need to break free of the fear that you can't go it alone. It's very tempting to jump into bed with a partner simply because you are nervous about all of the responsibility. A great partnership can be very profitable, but most partnerships fail. Until you succeed on your own, don't partner up with anyone. I have been ripped off by a lot of partners. You trust people, and eventually, they decide they want all the pie, and you end up with nothing. Unless you enjoy years of litigation, just believe in yourself. I'm going to give you the path to go it alone.

Taking that big step is scary. You've been trained to be a drone since birth; so breaking free to be a leader is very scary. It's supposed to be scary. That is the whole point of all that programming. Just accept that it's scary and move on.

You are now the CEO of your business. And I'm not going to lie to you; there is a risk of failure. But keeping your current job and treating all expenses of time and money as business expenses will dramatically limit that risk of failure. And if you are out of work right now, that's ok. Just being serious about money and very fastidious will give you a leg up over the majority of people posting on forums about how they can't make any money. Control what you spend and you don't need to earn nearly as much to make it back.

20

STORY OF A COLLECTOR

I have a lot of friends, and I'd like to share a story with you about another one. My friend is a collector. He has a phenomenal collection of knowledge in his apartment. He has a spare bedroom with piles of DVDS and books and courses on how to make money online. He spent north of fifty thousand dollars on the stuff. Most of it is still in the original plastic wrappers. He just has huge disorganized piles. He has all of this knowledge, but the cost is horrifying to me.

Imagine starting your business with fifty thousand dollars of debt. That's like graduating college. It will take my friend a LONG time to break even. The more money you spend at the beginning, the longer it takes you to make a profit. You can spend months or even years trying to fill in that initial financial hole.

Let me be clear for a moment. I'm totally fine with you investing in courses. I even have a few courses that I sell on my website. But the last thing I want you to do is buy ALL of them. Because even though I'll make some money, I know that you will end up failing. When we have too many options in front of us, we lose focus. I wrote the outline for this book a few months ago. I didn't start writing until yesterday. This week I finished three other projects, so now I have the mental bandwidth available to focus on this book until I complete it. I believe in multiple revenue streams, but most people do it all wrong.

I do not mean starting ten businesses online at once. Focus on one project until it's making money and then go on to the next thing. The problem with my friend is that he looks at that room and just sees a bunch of stuff he bought. He doesn't see red ink on a ledger. It's unfortunate because he's very smart, but his flawed mindset has limited him significantly.

21

THIS IS A JOB

I am not unemployed. I am not between jobs. I do think that I'm unhirable. I am unable to take directions or listen to other people anymore. I have been in charge of my destiny for too long. I do not have the ability to bend my neck before another master. I have a job, and that job is sitting in my office and working on different projects.

I have a little office on the beach where I do all my work, including writing this book. I actually have two spots. One is outside on my balcony where I work; inside I have a soundproofed corner of my bedroom where I record my audio. Depending on what I am doing and the position of the sun, those are my two work locations. I never sit there to watch a movie or play games.

You want to have a particular location that you use for work. It's hard to focus when you're in the living room. Sometimes you work in there, and sometimes you watch movies there. That'll mess up your focus. Isolating your body will help you to isolate your minds. Even if you use a laptop, you can play with it somewhere else, but in your office, it's work time.

The more you think of your project as a job, the easier it will be for you to maintain a professional mindset. I have a simple rule for my employees. Having hired and fired a lot of people in the last five years; I finally dialed into the formula that works for me. My employees are not allowed to see me during the day. I don't want to know how many hours a day they work, and I don't want them checking on how many hours a day I work. I give each person on my staff an assignment and tell them how long it should take. Every day they submit their work to me digitally. If they got the job done, I don't care if it took one hour or eight. That is irrelevant to me.

Most companies reward complacency. They pay you and expect you to sit in your job for a certain amount of hours. That trains people to make it look like they are working all day. Excellence and efficiency are punished rather than rewarded. If you finish your assignment in two hours and then go chill in the break room, your boss will yell at you. That's a foolish way to motivate staff.

I want you to focus on efficiency. It's about getting the most amount of work done in the least amount of time. What do you care about more? How long it takes me to write this book or whether it works and helps you open up new revenue streams?

It doesn't matter how many hours you spend in front of the computer. It only matters if your work leads to your financial goals. That's the measurement of success. We want to escape the drone mindset that hours worked is a measure of value. I'm going to write this book once – but guess what? I'm going to sell hundreds of thousands of copies over the next ten years. There is no financial or emotional correlation between hours worked and income received. When you are the boss, that math simply doesn't work.

Your job is to work lean and mean.

22

DECISION

Right now, you've got a decision to make. Are you really serious about changing your life, or are you reading this book to feel good? You can choose either one. After all, you already bought this book, I already got paid, and ultimately, I'm going to be fine no matter what you do. But I'm not here to make you feel good. I don't measure my success in feelings. I measure my success in your income.

You have to decide that you want to start this new job. That you will dedicate time to it and treat it with respect. You have to treat all the money you spend like business expenses. Those are serious decisions. It's fun to play the game "make money online." When you treat it like a game, you are not as emotionally invested in succeeding. That is the same mindset as people who play the lottery. You might win and if you do it's great, but you honestly don't think you will.

People with that mindset spin their wheels for decades trying to make a buck. It stinks because if they lose their job, or there is a medical emergency that will cost a bunch of money, they don't have it. This is not a game.

If I don't work, my children won't eat. I'm not here to shovel a bunch of garbage that I only work ten minutes a day. The people preaching that stuff all work more than they're saying.

I have total control over my schedule and a huge amount of freedom. I work fewer hours than most people. But I always work enough hours to hit my financial goals. That's the mindset your decision creates. If you are willing to take the plunge and you are tired of leaving your financial destiny in someone else's hands then we can move forward together.

This book is called Serve No Master for a reason. I want you to be in a financial position to never have to take crap from anyone else ever again.

23

SETTING 3 FINANCIAL GOALS

We need to get into some real numbers here. You might stink at personal accounting. I know that I do. That's something that you have to work on a lot. You need to start by figuring out your cost of living. How much money do you need to make every month to maintain your current lifestyle? It might be 100% of your paycheck. But it might also be 110% of that paycheck. If you don't know what you spend, you'll never know what your financial goal is.

Before you go any further in this book, you need to work on this chapter and get your answers written down. Your first target is simple; how much money do you need to make to supplement your lifestyle? If you're living like many Americans, you spend about ten percent more than you make. So your first goal is ten percent of your current income. If you generated that in profit every month, you could stop hemorrhaging so much debt. This number is your first goal. This is a specific number that you want to earn from a second revenue stream on top of your current paycheck.

Your second goal is even more exciting: How much money do you need to make to quit your job? That number might not be the same as your paycheck. You need to look at some other numbers before you write this one down. When you quit your job, you're going to lose access to retirement benefits and medical insurance and a bunch of other side benefits. How much will it cost to get insurance separate from your company? Add that expense needs to your projections. You might want to add in anything that is going to stock options right now as well. I know this all sounds intense, but I already told you that this is serious business. If you do these numbers correctly right now, hitting these goals will become easy.

Your third goal is based on your dream lifestyle. How much money do you need to make to live your dreams? Later on, I will talk a lot about travel and ways to control your spending. I live on a tropical island for less than people pay to live in a dangerous neighborhood in New York City. This book is about much more than making money. It's also about how to be smarter with your costs.

For right now, just write down a number that you could make every month and retire while living the life you've always dreamed of. How much money do you need if you are living on a tropical beach and no longer paying off a mortgage or car bills? I don't own a car anymore. Where I live, all I need is a scooter. I only use it about once a week. By removing that car, I got rid of car payments, gasoline costs, car insurance and maintenance costs. A car is many things, but it is NOT a financial asset.

For now just, put a big number there that covers all your costs of living plus your dreams. How much money do you need if you are still determined to send your kids to college? It's super expensive, and the price goes up every year. Maybe that number is ten or twenty thousand dollars a month. Maybe it's a hundred thousand dollars a month. I don't care. Just be honest. If you are honest with me right now we can hit that goal. It just has to be a real number that you feel connected with. If you write down a number that is low, then you won't feel properly motivated, and you will put a glass ceiling in front of your progress. If you put a number that is super high, then you won't feel like it's realistic and you'll never hit it. Be serious before you go on to the next chapter.

24

FINANCIAL MISTAKES - CONTROL COSTS

There is nothing more important when starting a business than controlling your costs. We have already talked about blowing all your money on courses and stuff like that. That's one financial mistake. Another one is not paying attention to the actual costs of running your business. Every website name you own costs around a dollar a month. Not a big deal, until you go hog wild and own one hundred names. That's twelve hundred bucks a year on the expense side of your balance sheet.

That's enough money to buy traffic for one of those websites and make ten times your investment back. These little things add up.

I don't want you to go too far in the other direction and cheap out. For example, you don't want to set up your first website on someone else's domain. Like jonathan.wordpress.org or something. Yes, that's an excellent way to save pennies, but advertising I'M A HUGE CHEAPSKATE on something your customers will see is too far in the wrong direction.

There is a balance. Every time you spend money, just analyze if you think it's a sound financial decision. Is this cost necessary to maintaining your business? Will this investment pay for itself? If you spend ten dollars now, how long will it take to earn that money back?

Often we spend money on things that are shiny but offer a terrible return on investment.

Have a little talk with yourself before you spend any money. Decide if paying someone else to do it is cheaper in the long run than trying to do it yourself. Sometimes spending time is a better decision than spending money. And sometimes it goes the other way.

I'm a big believer in waiting to spend money. Make some money first and then spend from the profits. That has always been my mind-set, and it helps me control my money. The more money you have leaving your account, the more money you need marching in to make up for it.

25

FOCUS MISTAKES

Buying a lot of courses is more than just a financial mistake. It's also a focus mistake, and that is about ten times worse. Here is your new philosophy:

> I work on a project until it is making money. Only then can I try something else.

Most of us buy an online course and go through a few modules. We try the idea for a few weeks, and it doesn't work right away. So we quit and then buy the next new course we see that makes even bigger promises. We end up on the customer hamster wheel and never break free.

There are thousands of great systems for making money online out there. Many of them work. But you have to pick one and stick with it until you experience success. Otherwise, you are trapped in a failure cycle. It's impossible to focus on three things at once. There are a few ways that I'm going to share with you throughout this book. I'm going to make you pick one. If you change your mind later, well...

please just don't do that. If I let you change your mind once, you'll do it again and again and then you won't make any money. You will break my philosophy and then blame me that you failed.

Failure of focus destroys most people trying to make money in the wild west of the Internet. They hop from idea to idea because they are all exciting. People come to me with phenomenal ideas for making money online all the time. When it's outside my knowledge or experience, I turn them down. I'll tell you right now. I have no idea how to sell physical things. I have no idea how to sell bicycles online. I hate that type of business because you have to buy parts or stock, and it's sitting in a warehouse somewhere until someone buys it. I don't like spending money in the hopes that later on, it makes me money. That honestly scares me. I like a business that I can scale infinitely. This book is digital. It doesn't exist. Yes, you can buy the print version. But that version is print on demand. Amazon only prints it after you order it. There is no musty bookstore or warehouse with boxes of copies.

Now, that doesn't mean you can't go down that path. If you are determined to sell physical things, then I can point you to a friend of mine who teaches that. He's an expert and has helped a lot of people. But if you go down that path, you can't change your mind in six weeks when you realize it's not as glamorous as you imagined.

You don't have to get all your training from me. Once you get through this book, you'll have the pieces you need to make money online. I don't care if you then choose someone else's method. I just want you to only choose one method and stick with it until you are profitable.

Show me that you can focus. Finishing this book would be an excellent way to demonstrate that!

26

LETTING FEAR HOLD YOU BACK

Most people live fear-based lives. They tell you that you can't start your own business. You're not smart enough to write a book. You're too ugly to put videos online. If you move to another country, you'll get stabbed a thousand times before you leave the airport. They live disappointing lives and use fear to keep everyone else down.

I suggest that for now, you keep your mouth shut about what you're doing. I know, I know, if you tell your friends how awesome and exciting this book is I will probably sell more copies. Yay for me! But then a lot of your friends will start to give you reasons why this book won't work, and it only takes one or two of those to ruin your day.

They are terrified that if you follow this book, you will get rich and become truly free. Then they will be trapped. Either they have to break free too or admit that they have chosen to remain a serf.

Most people don't want to admit that their lives are a result of their actions. We live in a society based on victimhood. Everyone blames everyone else for the things that their lives lack. When you start your project, you don't have the option of blaming other people. You have to take responsibility for your destiny. No master is looking out for you and feeding you scraps from his table for being a good little doggy. When you go out into the wild, that is gone from your life.

Most people secretly enjoy their financial slavery. They like having a boss that makes them feel safe and warm. And they love it so much that they'll react violently if someone tells them there's a better way.

Rather than telling the people around you how you are about to change your life, just keep your mouth shut, keep your head down, and do the work. That way they can't give you a fresh dose of fear. Fear and lack of faith are mind killers. They're the reason that I live on a tropical island, and you don't. When you let go of fear and focus on action, you become limitless.

27

YOUR FRIENDS ARE YOUR ENEMIES

You are the average of the five people you spend the most time with. If you take your five closest buddies and add up their income, then divide it by five, the number will be pretty close to your salary. The people around us affect us, and we have a tendency as humans to average out. If you have five friends who make less than you, you will never ask your boss for a raise. You're already an outlier.

When I started my own business, a lot of my friends told me how I was going to fail. They told me the same stuff when I decided to move across the world. I'm used to hearing it. Every time I hung out with them, they would pour more negativity into my ear. They didn't have the same goals as me.

And so, we started to drift apart. It happens. I don't want to give you bad news, but when your friends notice your success, they will NOT be cheering. Most of your friends will want to hold you back because they are afraid of you changing. They have this idea that once you succeed you will leave them behind. By the way, they'll be the same friends who will ask to borrow money when you succeed and then never pay it back saying, "You don't need the money anyways."

I left a lot of my friends behind. I loved them, but they hated seeing me happy. It was a hard lesson to learn. My success cast a light onto their lives, and they didn't like what they saw.

When you want to succeed at something, it's better to surround yourself with people on the same path. If you want to run a marathon, you don't hang out with a bunch of couch potatoes. That's not going to work. Every time you say you are going for a run, they will give you reasons not to. Then they will try to make you feel bad for running. Like you're working out just to make them feel guilty for being fat.

When you tell your buddy that you can't go out Friday because you have to work on your new project, he will do the same thing. He will give you a million reasons to skip your project for just one night. What is missing a few hours going to hurt?

Of course, he's willing to destroy your destiny for a few hours of fun. People who don't believe in your future don't care about ruining it. This is how friends keep you from quitting smoking and make sure your diet fails. What will one little dessert hurt things?

And if you're able to resist their charms, they start in about how you think you're better than them. I want a good life for my family. I don't wish ill on anyone around me. But I do choose to limit the time I spend with people who are slaves. I don't like hanging out with drones. It's like aliens came and sucked out their personalities. They are both afraid of and hate freedom.

Let me give you a specific example. I give people ideas for businesses all the time. I have a natural ability to turn someone's skills into money. This is my basic drone test: I say here is what you could do to make ten times more money than you do right now and break free. Drones then respond with hundreds of reasons why my idea is a bad one. They've never started a business and have zero knowledge about how it works, but they sure seem to know all the things that will make my business fail. I'm like King Midas. Every project I touch turns to money. And yet drones have an unending list of reasons why I don't know what I'm talking about.

They take the winning lottery ticket that I've just handed them and rip it into shreds. Then they head back to their cubicle.

Does the guy who gave up crime spend time with guys that are still on the bad side of the law? Nope. He understands that if he spends time with them, he will end up back in jail.

28

THE PEOPLE AROUND YOU

I know I sound like a real killjoy right now, but I'm not telling you to throw your friends away and move into some deep dark cave that happens to have Wi-Fi access.

That's not what I'm about – I want you to enjoy your life, and the memories you share with people are a big part of that. What I'm saying is team up with people who are on your path, or at least respect it. If your friends cheer you on, that's great. But if they want to stop you, then you need to find other champions.

Connect with other people you find online or in person that are on the same path. People that get the sacrifice and understand that you are dedicated to creating an awesome future. My social circle is filled with people who make a lot of money online. The more time I spend with people like that, the more money I make. It's the positive version of that five friends effect.

You want to ally with two types of people. People on the same path as you and people further up the mountain. I'm further up the mountain so I can be your guide and trailblazer. I can show you the footholds that worked for me and help you to avoid the places where I slipped. You also want people at the same level so you can feel a sense of shared victory as you achieve things together. These are the two types of people that you want to invest the most time in right now.

Over time you will notice that some of the people beside you will fall off the mountain. They'll quit, and you have to find new people. This still happens to me. I had a friend who was learning the Amazon game with me at the same time last year. He made a poor decision and fell off the mountain. In that moment his entire mindset changed. I offered to work together on one of my projects, but he turned me down. That was about six months ago. He isn't making any money anymore, and he's back in drone town. It stinks but it's reality.

Now I have different people I talk to about my projects. I surround myself with people who are good at what I want to work on next. Once I master that skill and make money from it, I look for people with the next thing I want to learn. I'm always growing, but I only learn one thing at a time. The people I invest time in change all the time, but it doesn't mean I don't like them. I just don't invest my time in people that bring negativity into my life.

I don't want to hear about reasons why something won't work. I want to hear ways to overcome that challenge. That's the world that I believe in. If you surround yourself with other freedom seekers, then you have a much better chance at finding actual freedom.

IV

THE ART OF THE FAVOR

The person who receives the most favors is the one who knows how to return them.

- Publilius Syrus

29

ELITE WEAPON

We just talked a great deal about mindset, but we ended that section talking about friends. I want to teach you how I leverage all my relationships. This section will show you a path that you never knew existed.

Most people have abysmal social skills. If you read this chapter and apply it, there is an excellent chance you could become my new best friend. This technique works on everyone - including me.

I leave my island very rarely. But when I do, I go to conferences. Sometimes I'm a speaker, and sometimes I'm just networking or working on a project there. People recognize me. My face is everywhere on my website, and I use my real name for everything. Someone will recognize me and walk up to me. People approach a lot more when I speak at the event, but that's normal.

They walk up and just start dumping questions on me. I'm at this conference to connect with people to grow my business and income. But they don't see that. They are completely unaware that I have motivations and desires. They don't see me as a human. They simply see me as a knowledge repository. They ask questions, and I'll answer some for a few minutes... but then a few bad things start happening all at once. First of all, most people keep asking stuff until you make them leave. I answered one question and then three more. How many do I have to answer before you feel that I have fulfilled my social obligation to a stranger?

Every once in a while, I meet someone on my level. I meet a real social assassin, and I love it. If you read my blog and read this book you know all the things that I like. I talk about them all the time. If you walk up to me and offer value first, then you get a lot of time with me. If you research me and find out what I like, then you can offer me something that interests me FIRST.

I like when a guy walks up and goes "I'm a big fan, can I buy you a drink?" - Now he's in the game. How often do men get free drinks? I'm not a beautiful lady, so it happens very rarely. When a guy orders a White Russian, then I know he's researched me. That's how a professional handles it, and I like it. If you can see the other person as a human being and approach them correctly, people will give you amazing things for free.

Another great move is to buy a coaching session. You can buy an hour of my time from my website. You can get me on the phone that way. Once we've connected, we have a relationship. I'm way more likely to respond to your emails because you've shown you believe in me. That counts for a lot. I know a lot of guys who meet their heroes that way. They buy some coaching and use that to form a relationship.

You can also just purchase a course from someone and leverage that. This works on ANYONE. Imagine what happens if you walk up to me and tell me that you bought my bestseller course, and it was incredible, and now you'd like to shoot a video testimonial for me. Guess what? That's a lot of value. Now you are willing to help my business grow? You are in the inner circle immediately. That's a way you can add value and offer something to someone who you feel is way up the mountain from you.

Just think about how that person is a human and try to give them something of value.

If you approach like a fan, then that's where you get trapped.

30

JAR OF DEBT

Let's talk about a little jar that every stingy person owns.

Most people in the world have a jar sitting on their emotional shelf where they store favors. They look at it and remember every person they have ever helped. When someone does something nice for them, they look for the fastest way to repay that favor to escape any emotional debt.

They're so busy tracking this favor ledger that they miss the way the world works. Living like that is extremely stressful and it makes people wary around you. It takes a lot of mental energy to track the favors you've put out into the world. All of that effort could be better spent in so many ways. By treating favors as a finite resource you are limiting yourself.

I don't own one of those jars, and you shouldn't either. Instead, I want to share with you something that a millionaire shared with me. He taught me this secret, and it's one of the reasons, if not the ONLY reason, that I am so financially successful.

31

FAVORS ARE A MUSCLE

Favors are not a finite resource. You can do favors until the cows come home, and you'll never run out. If you switch to the muscle mindset, something cool happens. You become free.

Instead of worrying about favors and tracking numbers all the time, you just do as many favors as humanly possible. You put all of this positive energy into the world, and it comes back tenfold. The more favors you do, the stronger that muscle becomes. People who see favors this way tend to cling together. When you switch to the muscle mindset, you will naturally fit in with the elites wherever you go.

This is how I broke through with my business. I am not an island of a man. I work and interact with people every single day. I just do it digitally. People ask me for favors and introductions all the time, and I do it. Everyone knows that if they ask me for something I'll do everything in my power to help them. This is a strength, not a weakness. They don't have to worry that I'll hit their phones a few weeks later demanding an equivalent favor. How do you even measure the value of favors? Even worse, some people will run away from the relationship when they realize they can't "pay back" the value of a favor. I have had people disappear from my life like ghosts because I did something nice for them. Sounds crazy, but it's true.

I don't remember who I have done a favor for. I don't waste the mental bandwidth. I just help the people around me, and they return the favor. This is a great way to feel free. You no longer have to track the energy that you put into the world or the return. This is one of the reasons being my friend is awesome. I'll always help you out without expecting anything in return.

The mindset is not that I gave a favor to that guy or to that gal. I think about each favor as something I put out into the universe. It's kind of how I view the concept of karma. I put favors out into the world and then the world sends favors back. I don't have to track the favors I have done for any one individual.

Now I know what you're thinking. Some jerks are going to take advantage. That's true. Some people are just value vampires. They take as many favors as they can get before you notice. I encounter one of these vampires now and then. It takes me a while to notice that someone is a garbage human being. They ask for a ton of favors and then when I ask for something small in return they say no. When that happens I just cut them out of my life, let the people around me know that the individual is a value vampire, and then I move on. They get socially ostracized, and that's the end of it.

I don't think about it or worry about it. Their bad behavior determines their fate, but I'm not going to let it affect mine.

32

THE SECRET OF THE ELITE

Truly elite people congregate with each other, and they dwell in a place where favors are the norm. The secret to connecting with someone who has something you desire follows a simple formula.

As humans, we all seek value. First, we seek the necessities - air, water, food, and a place to sleep tonight. Once those higher order needs are met, we focus on immediate value. If you're thinking about buying a new car, you'll notice that brand everywhere around you. How are those cars running, what do the drivers look like on the road? You're thinking about it; you're seeking that value. When you are trying to find a good school for your kids, whenever you hear people talking about schools, your ears perk up.

The moment you sign up your child for school, those conversations become unimportant again. You made the decision, so you no longer think about schools.

When you want to connect with someone who is further up the mountain, the biggest mistake you can make is offering value in an area where they are already strong. Offering a dollar to a billionaire has no meaning. You have given him something in an area where he is already strong. What you want to do instead is find out his passion and desires. Find out what he LIKES to talk about.

I know an online marketer who makes a lot of money. He is very successful, and everybody comes up to him all the time looking for advice. I met him before I made my first dollar online and had no idea what I was doing, but I never talked to him about work. Instead, I found out that he has a passion for amateur archeology. He goes on a dig every summer. It's his real passion. He makes money to support his family and fund his archeology habit. He always has a fossil in his pocket. Whenever I see him, that's what we talk about. Instead of following everyone else's path I follow my own. I found out what he'd rather be talking about. And it's fine by me. I think it's really interesting.

Every time I meet someone on my level I find out what they are into, and what they are seeking. I give them the value they are seeking through introductions, and I connect with them by talking about the stuff they love.

Let me try another example. Where I live, everybody surfs. That's the reason most people come here. Most of these guys have been surfing for decades. I only started last year. I never have anyone to hang with because they always leave me behind. Then these same guys want business advice. Why would I want to invest time in someone that focuses solely on their needs?

When a guy hangs with me and surfs at my level, even though I'm not very good, that builds up goodwill. If that guy asks for advice, I'm much happier giving it. Because I like spending time with him. He met me at my need level. It's not something that I do consciously. I only just realized it as I was writing this chapter.

Everyone here is a great surfer, so they all use short boards. I am early stages and still need to ride a monster. It's hard to find longboards on my island. In fact, it took me six months to find mine, and I had to get it mailed to me from another island. The shipping cost about half as much as the board. If you were to approach me and mention that you can get longboards to me, that would capture my attention. I would be interested in that because it's a challenge in my life right now.

When you want to connect with someone who is at the top of the mountain; you don't focus on their strengths. That's what everyone else does, and it never works. Focus on your strengths and their desires. This concept is vital because we are going to build on your strengths and knowledge to create your online business.

33

THE ULTIMATE VALUE

A single motivation drives all human behavior – the desire for good feelings. People want to enjoy life. Think about how much of our time is spent working towards having good feelings. All the money you spend on parties, cocktails, movies and music fits into this category. We spend money on those things because they make us feel good.

The only reason we work is to make enough money to pay for our leisure activities. The people who do love to work, love work for a reason! They get good feelings from their craft. I feel that way about my work, but I didn't always. I have had jobs I hated, and my only motivation was making enough money to buy the things I wanted.

If you can give people good feelings, they will want to spend a lot of time with you.

Think about the people you like to spend the most time with. How do they make you feel? We all want to be around that one person who is the life of the party. Their energy is infectious. The reason that we like them so much is that they give us good feelings. And we LIKE feeling good. It's our primary motivation.

The secret to being the life of the party is to be without intent. If you try to be the life of the party just to make people like you, it will never work. There is a simple strategy to do this correctly.

First, you want to focus internally. You want to make yourself feel good. Be energetic and have fun because it makes you feel good. Then those around you will get pulled into your good time. And they will like being around you.

Your focus is having so much fun that other people can't resist joining in with you. That's the real secret to popularity and happiness.

34

GO TO WHERE THE PEOPLE ARE

There are two ways to get ahead in business and work.

The method most people practice is to get to work early, stay late, lock yourself in your office, avoid human communication and let your work speak for itself. This is a GREAT strategy if you want to spend your life as a drone. If you have no desire for a management position at work. If you aren't interested in anything other than minor pay raises and meaningless promotions.

But if you want to be in charge of people and make the big money, you have to go with the second strategy.

You put in the hours at work, but you take the time to make connections with your coworkers. You find out about their friends and families. You spend time outside of work with them. You make them trust and depend on you. They LIKE you.

It's a fact of life; popularity leads to success in business.

Sometimes you can spend weeks or months building up the groundwork, and it all comes down to one conversation with a superior. Because you've spent the time to developing your social skills and social network in the office, more opportunities will come your way.

If you aren't going to where your coworkers and industry insiders are hanging out, how are you ever going to meet them? You need to start developing commonalities with the people around you. Find out where they like to hang out, what they like to do and what they like to talk about.

I hate football. But when my co-workers were into football, I started watching it. It gave me something to talk to them about at work. Go to social functions. Head out for drinks after work. I did a lot of this when I was working for other companies, and it paid off in so many ways.

It's a lot easier for a supervisor to give you a promotion when your coworkers don't hate you and won't be bitter about it.

Every industry has tons of conferences, and in the world of startups and entrepreneurs, these events are CRUCIAL. If you think building a social network is important when you work for a big company, it's life or death when you are a company of one.

Remember, you can always move around between different companies in your industry. I'm not saying to actively look for a new job at conferences, but these connections are going to be imperative when your boss downsizes you, or there is a corporate restructure. It is better to have a social network that you don't need, than to need one you don't have.

I used to go to conferences ALL the time. It's how I built my business, and it's how I make connections. You can also join forums and connect with people on LinkedIn and Facebook. I have some industry friends who do all their networking online. They build up a reputation, and everyone likes what they have to say online.

If you never go out with people from work, you will never build real relationships.

I got into Internet marketing and working online because I wanted more freedom. I wanted to travel the world and have total control of my schedule. I started working for myself, so I could live the dream and work from home, but I didn't start making money until I started going to events and making connections and building up a social circle of people who are trying to grow in the same way.

If you don't build relationships with people, then they won't want to do business with you. When people like you, trust you and consider you a friend they will do AMAZING things for you to help you grow your business.

Just going to events isn't enough of course. You have to do it in the RIGHT way.

Whether you are working for yourself or an organization, you can use your social networking skills to get ahead and succeed.

35

PROJECT THE RIGHT IDENTITY

When you introduce me to your friend, you already know who your friend is. You know why you are friends with them. You know what makes them cool, awesome or interesting. You should know the same information about yourself.

Now that I'm well known at the events I attend, I have my circle of business friends and partners. My plan is to invest my time with them and build those relationships with them. If you walk up to me, I'm only going to give you a few minutes of my time. That's how most people are who have a lot going on.

The people you want to connect with the most are only going to give you a few minutes of their time. Not because they think they are better than you, but they just don't know you, and they want to see their friends. You need to be able to demonstrate that you are worth their time in just a few minutes or less.

There are two main reasons people want to talk to you at a conference; either you are fun or you can make them a lot of money. And the truth is that even if you can make them money, they still probably won't be interested right away.

I've never successfully pitched a business idea to someone the moment I met them. I see people try it all the time, and I hate it. The only time I let people get away with pitching an idea right away is if they already have a big reputation in the industry. So don't do that.

You want to focus on being fun and bringing value. Start thinking about what makes you unique. Are you funny? Do you play an instrument? We are all unique in different ways.

Focus on sharing your value without becoming pretentious. I have met people who have one interesting thing about them that I want to learn about. Sometimes they have a technical skill that I'm interested in or a product that I promoted.

I can remember one time when I tried to talk to a guy who had made a Wordpress theme I liked. The guy did not like me and was extremely unpleasant. He avoided answering my questions. I was interested in doing a big promotion for his product and seeing how our businesses could interact.

My company makes almost twenty times as much money as his does, and I could have helped him grow massively. But he was more focused on being a jerk instead of being friendly to me. I haven't heard anyone mention one of his products in over two years. So don't get too full of yourself, you never really know who you are talking to.

They might just mention you in a book some day.

Take the time to think about what makes you unique, special and interesting. At my first event, I met a guy who was a former professional baseball player. He'd only played in six games, but I thought that was cool. His career in baseball had totally fizzled out, but when people found out about his past, they thought it was great.

You never know who you are going to meet when you are at conferences and events. Some of the most unassuming people you meet might have the most going on. Guys who have their lives together don't spend all their time showing off. They let their work speak for itself.

You don't have to act flashy or try to be the master networker. Just be yourself and have fun and people will be drawn to you.

When you meet each person, just focus on bringing the fun into the conversation first. That will give you enough time to talk about business stuff later. And then they will know you and have invested time in you so they will be more interested.

36

STRENGTHS AND WEAKNESSES

I am excellent at some things and atrocious at other things.

When I first got into online marketing, I was really good at getting websites to appear at the top of Google search results. I ran a little business that would help local businesses get Google rankings and therefore more customers. It's how I made a living, and I'd often share tips and tricks with people who would ask me for advice about how to do this themselves. I used to give away knowledge about getting more customers to give value to people.

I have other skills as well. I'm superb at writing and can write more than two thousand words an hour. It takes most people a week to write what I can in just one hour. I can put together in two days what takes most people a month. I've written almost this entire book in less time than you could imagine. All while running my company and taking the time to swim in my pool at my villa and practice guitar and get ocean time.

I'm also talented at putting teams together, forming alliances and creating products.

Those are my top strengths. There are TONS of areas where I struggle. There are a lot of areas that I just haven't delved into yet.

When I meet people at events, I keep my eyes peeled for people who ARE good at those things that I'm not.

A lot of people that I meet at events want to pretend that they are awesome at everything. It takes a martial artist a lifetime to master one weapon, so when someone says they are a master at every single way to make money online, I know it's impossible. I have friends who are experts at Facebook and friends who are experts at Google and friends who are experts at designing sales processes, but I don't know anyone who is an expert at everything.

It's one of the secrets to the upper circles of networking. We can tell when someone is pretending that they have something going on, and the biggest tell is when they act like they are good at everything.

Don't act like you don't know anything and don't act like you are good at everything. You want to demonstrate your value without coming across as a liar. That will massively boost your performance at events.

Even if you stop reading this book right now, you will see an increase in your networking results with what you just learned here.

37

EVENT MINDSET

People can always tell when someone wants something from them, and it's horrible. It's exactly how a woman feels when you tell her you to want to sleep with her before you've even met her. You are ignoring her personality and only judging one aspect of her. Cringe. Embarrassing. Horrible. People want to feel like more than their net worth and business value.

So when you go to marketing events, industry conferences or even out for drinks with your coworkers you need to approach these times with the right mindset.

You aren't there to suck the knowledge out of them because that will make them turn against you. You need to start the process by GIVING value. Focus on sharing good times, fun, your knowledge and everything else that makes you unique. That is one of the big secrets to doing well when you first meet people.

You want to focus on having a good time and sharing your value - even if your value is just a round of drinks. I can't tell you how many millionaires I know that will trade twenty minutes of their time for a drink.

Last year I got HOURS of alone time with a major billionaire just because I threw a good party with cool people. And if you are smart you will use this time to form a connection and get a way of contacting them in the future.

In just a few minutes you can get a phone number, email address or Skype contact, rather than blowing your opportunity and asking them for business advice in the first meeting.

Start building a social network around you. My business network is around five hundred people, but I only have about ten people in my inner circle of friends. Thirty people are in the next ring. Then a hundred around that. The rest are people that kind of know people in my circle.

The bigger your network of friends and connections, the more likely you are to get invited to the secret parties. I will tell you a big secret about conferences. Everyone sneaks up to someone's room to smoke. Even if you don't like to get down, this is where the baller deals happen. It's not my scene anymore.

But one of my friends will be slipping upstairs and invite me along. I go up and suddenly I'm chilling with the biggest people at the event. One connection gets me into the room with ten powerful connections. There is something about being naughty together that brings people together.

Now if you're the kind of person who's going to stand in the corner and judge everyone, don't go up. But if you can at least seem chill, then this is your MASSIVE opportunity to meet people. Once you get a reputation as someone that doesn't smoke people will stop inviting you and your business will suffer.

I have this business friend who is the most unlikely guy for everyone at these secret meetings to be friends with. He's been married for almost a decade and got a ton of kids. He just doesn't seem like the cool bad boy type. He doesn't really do anything bad, but he hangs with us when we hang out.

I never feel like he's judging me when I'm throwing back drinks in a club in Vegas or a T.G.I. Friday's in Orlando. I feel like he's living vicariously through me. I don't know if he really feels that way or if I just project it, but I promote all of his products to my customers when he releases them.

Focus on getting along with everyone.

There is one other beginner mistake that you want to avoid. Don't only talk to beginners or just to people on your level. Usually, at big events, there are three groups of people. There are the power brokers in their circle, there are the beginners in their circle, and there are the people in the middle who kind of have their own thing going on.

The problem with only talking to other new people in the business is that they are a closed network. You are unlikely to get through one of them and into the power brokers circle. They are all doing the same thing as you - meeting the easiest people at the event.

Remember your goal is to build a big network. Try to ignore the rules of the circles. Most of the big players that I know, I thought were idiots when I first met them. I can't really tell if someone has something going on or nothing going on until I've talked to someone for at least fifteen minutes - unless they say something really needy.

You want to build alliances so try to connect with people that have something going on. Try to focus on connecting with other people that don't seem needy. Even if they don't have a lot going on NOW, they are the ones who will have it going on down the line.

If you're focused on giving value, and you talk about anything OTHER than asking for business advice, people will enjoy your company. Whether they are the CEO of a company that competes with yours or a billionaire entrepreneur. Everybody's the same on the inside.

Just give value and they'll like you.

38

BE SOCIALLY SAVVY

So now you're going to events or hanging out after work, and you know who you are. You have some basic strategy about the kinds of people you want to meet and how to approach them and seem like a chill person.

It's time to take it to the next level.

The first thing you want to do is realize there is more going on than most people notice. I can tell you right now that most speakers don't watch each other's talks at conferences. So where are they? Most likely they are in the bar or someone's room.

There is a lot you can learn from listening to all the talks at the event. You can apply a little strategy in advance, though. First, you make a list of all the speakers and players who are going to be at an event. You can even find all of their pictures online.

Then make a cheat sheet, so you know a little something about each of them. You can even look up their latest blog posts or buy one of their products. Now you know who you are looking for, and you have something to talk about on their favorite subject – themselves.

When people come up to me and want to talk about one of my blog posts or products that they liked I just love it - unless they want to complain. Then I hate them.

I have been deciding if I would share this advanced tactic with you or not. It's crazy powerful and will take what I just taught you and turbocharge it.

Pick someone you want to connect with who is going to be at an event. Buy one of their products. When you talk to them at the event, be like hey X product that's yours right? They'll be like Oh yeah I made that! Then you tell them you loved the product and would be happy to do a video testimonial for them if they have a video camera handy.

AND BOOM!

Dude, that's like solid gold for me. If you walk up to me after reading this and tell me that you have a ton of new friends or your business blew up because of one of my products AND you want to shoot a video testimonial for me. I will absolutely love you.

Here is a secret about all great marketers: We want our products to work for you. I love when someone emails me and says they found their soulmate using my book. That's why I do what I do. I love helping people.

So take the time to buy one of my products. Implement it. Then tell me about the results when you see me around.

If you want to shortcut that process, you can even separate yourself from the crowd. Lots of people leave written reviews, and I appreciate every one of them. But when I read that review I'm not going to really know you. You can record a video talking about how this book is awesome and changed your life. That video with your face will stick in my mind forever. This works on any Amazon product. People always read their reviews, but the videos get remembered.

I'm easy to find because I use my real picture and my real name and I am usually drinking a White Russian.

There are a few pitfalls you want to avoid while you're networking and meeting the higher-level people you want to connect with. The first pitfall you want to avoid is social anchors.

That baseball guy I met a few years ago was cool at first, but I ended up spending ALL my time at that event with him and his wife. He unintentionally kept me from meeting more people. I only invested in that one relationship. His business didn't really go anywhere, leaving me with one connection on the way down rather than the way up. Foolishly, I went all-in on that connection. I was too busy making friends to remember that I wanted to build a business - and that takes a lot of connections.

I know one guy who is obsessed with going to bed by 9 pm. He always says he needs to get his beauty sleep and then disappears early. He misses all the parties, late night drunk talk, and connections that happen at night. His priority at events is all wrong.

You want to make a lot of connections, and you need to realize that most of them happen in the dark of the night. You would be surprised at the people who like to party the hardest. I don't want to name names in this section, but there are a LOT of married, small town guys who rage with me under the table at events. And the scariest thing is when they bring their wives to events.

One of my friends is like the most Middle America guy of all time, but he likes to party. And his wife can drink everyone I know under the table. Don't miss out on the drinking. Even if you don't drink that's fine; you can be a designated driver. To people like me, that's solid gold.

That's a GREAT way to bring value to an event. Now you've raged with me AND done me a favor? Of course, I'll give you more of my time now, plus you have a captive audience when we are in the car together.

You might feel like I've lost you a little bit because not everyone goes to Internet marketing conferences. These are key principals that apply to other industries, networking events, and even your regular after-work drinks. If you're a total cubicle guy right now, that's ok. You can go to meetup.com events and practice networking there. Or try the local Rotary club or chamber of commerce. There are TONS of networking opportunities for you no matter what your current industry.

39

PURCHASE STREET CRED

Here is something that a lot of my customers completely miss out on. Every once in a while, I will have a big bill coming up so I'll decide to offer coaching for some quick cash. Usually, a week later I'm like "what was I thinking I hate selling my time!"

The last time I did this I put together a crazy offer for 5k. Now that's a lot of money, but it was a whole program where you were guaranteed to make 20k. I would work with you until you did. I only got two replies, and they both sucked so I didn't take on a student. But listen: this isn't a story about me trying to sell you coaching! It's about the fact that if you buy my high-level coaching, you get to party with me at events.

I was once speaking at an event in Las Vegas, and I offered a bonus to anyone who bought a ticket through me. The tickets were only around $100. If you bought through me I would bring you to a private party I was throwing in VIP at a club the night before the event.

All the people going were millionaire business owners who were going to have everyone at the event fighting for their time the next day. This was the chance of a lifetime. I can tell you right now that we spent over 5k in the club, but nobody bought a ticket through me. My customer base completely missed that opportunity. If just one person had purchased a ticket through me, they would have had access to the ultimate inner circle.

Instead, one person emailed my friend to complain that I talked about being drunk in my email. It's funny. The best opportunities I mail out to over 7,000 customers never get any takers, but when for the same price I promote some training course or piece of software I sell a LOT. Because these people don't see the offer behind the offer.

Friendship with me basically guarantees you business success, because my friends and I all take care of each other. I can't recommend buying small one-on-one coaching packages enough. When I was first starting out, I hired a coach to help me grow my business. He was expensive, but when I went to an event with him I was able to drop his name all day long, and it opened doors for me to people that I'm still close with almost a decade later.

If I take on a one-on-one coaching client, I tend to stay in contact with them for years. If you had purchased that big coaching program, I just offered a while ago. One where you were GUARANTEED to quadruple your money, I would have introduced you to everyone I know at the next event where I saw you.

These days I make people fill out an application before I even discuss long-term coaching. You can still grab an hour of phone time with me now for five hundred dollars, but that offer is going to disappear very soon. I'm just doing some research and want to connect with readers like you.

This isn't just about buying coaching from me. This is about seeing the value in buying coaching from all the amazing people out there that you admire. This is a principle that works to connect you with a lot of amazing people. If you want to grow your business, finding a mentor can help you. This is one of the easiest ways to find one.

40

BUILD A RELATIONSHIP

Have you ever read one of those OKCupid dating profiles where they say they like to have fun?

It seems like such a nothing statement. Everyone has a different definition of fun, and each person will interpret fun in a different way. You want to give people the kind of fun that they like.

Try to bring fun and positive energy and good vibes into your relationships. It's not that hard to stand out at a conference filled with super boring dweebs. You don't have to be cool because you can get away with just not being boring. I know a TON of people who do that.

The most important thing is not to judge people and not to talk down to anyone.

Some people meet me and ignore me until they realize who I am or who my partners are. This doesn't exactly endear them to me.

If you start out just focused on having fun and finding people you like to chill with, you are going to dominate at events. When you are interacting with people, just focus on listening to them and building a relationship.

I know this guy whose dad is a famous marketer. I don't really know who his dad is, but when I was talking to him, all these people walked up to us and kind of ignored us until they found out his last name. Then they started kissing his butt, and he got really upset. I totally understand why.

It sucks when people don't care who you are until they realize what you can do for them. You don't always have to talk about business. I talked to him about TED talks and golf, which he was actually interested in.

People just want to be heard and treated like they matter as people.

It's amazing how many people don't get that. I'm not my bank account, and I'm not my latest product. I really hate it when I talk to someone, and they have no interest in my personal life. That really annoys me. I tell someone I'm dating a great woman who is really special, and two minutes later they want to talk about a product or something. If you let me ramble on about my kids, then I'll really like you. It might be boring to you (hopefully not, my kids are usually doing cool stuff!) but you are building up goodwill.

I always make sure to connect with other people's wives. They like me because most people ignore them. One of my partners is a super religious Mormon. He got married when he was quite young and has four children with his awesome wife. I made sure that I talked to her right away and told her what I'm really about. I wanted her to get a chance to judge me for my actual philosophies and who I am as a person.

A lot of times people hear that I write dating books and immediately that gets a bad vibe. So I spent twenty minutes telling her how I believe in true love and how honesty is one of my core relationship principles. I told her how I write books for women to help them find the man of their dreams and explained the science and research that went into those books. I have helped thousands of women find true love.

This lady is really cool, and I like when I get to talk to her. She's such a nice woman, but I also know that if she and her husband are on the drive home, and she tells him she isn't comfortable with my products – any project I want to do with him dead in the water.

I hope I'm clear here.

This isn't about manipulation. It's about treating people right. If someone brings their wife to an event, talk to her!

And do you know what married women at boring business conferences love to talk about? Anything other than business. I have two nieces and two nephews that I love, in addition to my kids. They are all awesome. So I like to talk to wives about their children and then I show pictures of my kids and nieces and nephews when they show pictures of theirs.

Now I have an advocate when I'm not around. She'll tell her husband that I'm a nice guy - and that's a good thing. Most business is built upon trust and people liking you. If someone's wife likes you, then that's a very good thing.

Now sometimes the wife is the marketer, so I talk to the bored husband. He's got a life and a career and is interesting in his own way. Sometimes he just wants to swap pictures of his kids too, and if not – well, I didn't watch all that football for nothing.

Most importantly, when you are talking to people at events, or anywhere in life, listen to them. Close your mouth until they ask you about your stuff. I try to do only twenty percent of the talking when I first meet someone. Give people the room to let you know what THEY want to talk about.

If you just listen to people, they will usually tell you exactly how to build a friendship with them.

41

FROM FAVORS TO NETWORKING

I know all these lessons about favors seemed like a strange detour. How can we turn this idea of favors and giving value into a real business? Well, when I go to an event, I always have a plan. I figure out what the top people want rather than what they have. I start meeting people and as soon as I meet two people who can help each other I introduce them. Connecting people is very valuable. People I have connected have generated tens of millions of dollars from those introductions. Do you think they forgot about the guy that brought them together? No way.

You want to build up a network of connections so that if something comes up you can offer them value. When you have a giant network of connections, you can leverage it for access to resources. You never have to pay for software or training. You find out about sweet deals and discounts. You get to join that inner circle.

I have a whole video course I made on advanced networking, and I could talk about it for hours, but just understanding the basics is enough for now.

When you give people value, they want to spend time with you and return the favor. Giving a favor without wanting anything in return is the best way to form that connection. Removing ulterior motives means that successful people will like you.

If you give value, treat people with respect, and give everyone a good time, you'll soar in business.

V

TURNING RELATIONSHIPS INTO MONEY

I've always loved the experience of working together with other people toward an artistic goal.

- Trey Anastasio

42

TURN YOUR RELATIONSHIP INTO MONEY

We've made it this far, and I love that it has been an epic journey. There is a lot more book left, and you're doing great. You're going to events and business functions. You have built connections with power brokers and chill newbies. You've even treated their significant others like real people.

This is all great, but let's be honest, you grabbed this book because you want to be rich. And I think that's awesome.

Always do favors first. Anytime there is a way you can help people, connect people or in any other way do people a favor do it. You don't need to ask for anything in return because they will remember you.

Take the time to make people feel good - buy a round of drinks. Tell people you liked their blog post. Offer to give people testimonials and positive reviews.

I have this friend, who does everyone favors. He undercharges for coaching and always helps people in any way that he can. He doesn't focus on his business as much as he focuses on helping people around him. He's a really good dude. I met his girlfriend a few months ago, and I told her he was a badass and how lucky she is to be with him. It's all true, but I took the time because he's been there for me.

You just never know how someone is going to pay you back.

So put a lot of favors into the world. It's kind of like throwing messages in bottles into the ocean. You never know where or when it's going to land, but you can be assured that something cool will happen because of it.

You will be astounded by the favors that people remember months or even years later. They will find the most amazing and thoughtful ways to pay you back. And remember. You don't do favors hoping for something back. You are without intent.

43

SHARE RESOURCES

You have resources in your life that other people would love access too. It might be something you never thought about before. The ability to do carpentry is something that's quite valuable to me right now. With all the salt in the air from the ocean where I live, wood repairs are pretty constant.

Something you might not have thought was valuable, really is to me. Pooling and sharing resources is an excellent way to form strong connections. Maybe you and a buddy pay for coaching together. I've certainly done this in the past. You can even go in on a course together and then work through it as a team. I see no harm in that. I think it's awesome.

You have things in your life that are easy for you, and maybe you haven't even realized that there is value there. Think about the ways you can help people get through life. When I was younger, people that could cut hair or do piercings were super valuable connections. Do you know someone who can get a discount on car rentals?

We will talk more and more about the skills you can use to build your business. That unique knowledge that people want online, they also want in person. It might take a little creativity for you to realize the great resources you have access to.

Maybe you have a high-speed Internet connection, and your friend has a great computer. Combined you can suddenly do much more than either of you could alone.

44

SHARE OPPORTUNITIES

I love when one of my friends tells me about a good offer I can promote. There is nothing like making a bunch of money on a tip. You think I forget people who make me money? Don't be insane.

If you know about something that's doing well or a cool event coming up, don't keep that stuff to yourself. I do side projects with partners all the time. Sometimes, people I don't know come to me with a product and ask if I'll release it with them under my brand and I almost always do it. If the product is good and helps people, then I'm happy to help them get sales and share all the spoils.

When I want to work with someone, I prepare a little strategy in advance. I pour a ton of value on them, but I don't do it in a weird way. I invite them to exclusive events I have access to and introduce them to people that they want to meet. Most people don't want to be treated like celebrities or something special. They just want to be treated like a normal person.

I can tell you the one thing in common with all the big players in my industry I meet. I don't treat any of them special. I just treat them like cool normal people.

This entire section is how I approach people without a big tactical strategy. If you can approach the big names you want to meet and be cool with them and not act like a fan, they are probably going to like you.

This is the plan that I implement over and over again. I give value and introduce them to other people that I think can help their company before I ever mention the idea of something that we could do together. I ask if they have something I can write about on my blog before I ask them to do something for me.

Give a lot of value first. Later on, when you mention your idea, they will be receptive. The great thing about this plan is that it's not sinister. It's basically "be nice to people and then, later on, mention an idea."

It's hard to pretend you enjoy giving value. I know some people who saw what I do and thought that they could just repeat my motions. They said the same things and followed my steps, but people could tell it wasn't genuine. That's why I talked about favors as a muscle first. You have to master and implement that first.

Don't make it something you do, make it someone you are.

VI

HOW RELATIONSHIPS MADE ME RICH

The glue that holds all relationships together--including the relationship between the leader and the led--is trust, and trust is based on integrity.
- Brian Tracy

45

THE GOOD LIFE

At a net worth of $75 billion dollars, Bill Gates is the richest man in the world, and I'm not him.

I'm not a super big shot or some international guru. What I do have is an excellent life packed with interesting people. A lot of what makes that life awesome is building projects with the right people.

It's very tempting to lean on people when you're just getting your start in business – you want to trust that people with more experience will give you a hand up, and it's always fun to work in a team environment. But you don't want to start out in partnerships. Trust me; I learned this in the hardest of ways. You want to get your act together on your own before you go down this path. The book you're reading right now is one hundred percent me. Serve No Master is my main project in life now, and there is only room for one captain on this ship.

I like writing, and one of the fastest ways to get more books out there is to find partners and publishers to handle that part of the game. I have a great life living on a tropical island, so I know a little bit about what I'm doing.

When I first got started, I partnered with the wrong guy and paid for it in some serious ways. I learned my lesson by going solo for a while so that I would know the entire process. That's important if you want a sustainable business.

Instead of telling you all the sob stories, I want to share a few stories about my most exciting, most successful partnerships, so that you can see how partnerships can help when you're ready to take them on.

46

MY BIG SOLO PROJECT

Remember that dramatic, fist-pumping success story at the opening of this book? It was the result of a smart partnership.

I used to sell a lot of products teaching people how to build their businesses on a forum for people who want to make money online. When you sell a product there, they call it a Warrior Special Offer or WSO. I wanted to shift from selling services to selling products. I approached this transition strategically. I knew how to get to the top of Google fast and cheap, so I created a course teaching people how to do this.

I hired a coach who was an expert at breaking into this market. I paid him two thousand bucks to coach me. It was a back-breaking investment, but he was a cool kid that I had met at a conference. If you can afford it, I think it's always good to pay people for their time or products, even if they offer them for free. He never made that offer, but it was worth every penny.

He gave me a step-by-step plan to implement. I had to spend a LOT of money hiring copywriters and graphics people, to make what I was selling look and sound professional. I put in a lot of hard work, and it paid off. The offer did well, and I appeared as a blip on a lot of radars for people in that market.

My name on the forum isn't my real name, so there's no need to go searching around just yet. I had this course that had done well and a new list of over 1600 customers. I started promoting all these products that I thought were good by people that I only knew by reputation.

When I started going to more and more events people would meet me and not even realize that I had made them money, and the truth is that I often forgot myself. I would go to these events and have fun and party and buy people drinks. And then on top of that, they would realize that I had ALREADY made them money, so of course, they loved me.

I invest a lot in my relationships. Here's an example - right now, two Seriously Big Deal marketers I know are dating and will probably get married. At one point the girl was thinking of pulling away, and I talked her into pursuing the relationship. Now they are both super happy. I gave their relationship a little support when it needed it the most.

The more value you give, the more people will respond with love, affection, and even finances.

47

GIRL GETS RING

For about a year my dating blog was #1 on Google for the phrase "get a girlfriend." This gave my website a lot of visibility.

It ALSO meant I was swarmed with emails from people who wanted me to promote terrible dating offers and products that wouldn't ever help anyone. A lot of these people were just obvious grifters who peddled creepy junk and didn't care whether the advice worked or not.

One day I got an email from this guy Ben. He was the manager for a product I'd heard of that helps people get back with their exes. I know that people love that type of product, and I think healing relationships is wonderful. I told him at the time that most of my readers were interested in getting over that bad breakup rather than going back, but I would give it a shot because he seemed like a good guy.

Sadly, my prediction was correct – it was a nice idea, but it didn't meet the needs of my audience. Even though the promotion flopped, we kept in touch. And that one little seed of personal contact blossomed into something amazing.

Even though my customers weren't interested, that product already had a huge audience. Having sold over 100,000 copies, it's one of the most successful relationship products of all time. When we talked, Ben said that most people he approached online were pretty rude to him.

With one email to his customers, he can change a small business into something majestic and people treat him like garbage? I was pretty surprised. When he first approached me, I had no idea he had so much going on. I just thought he was a great guy, so we emailed back and forth a few times.

A few weeks later he asked me if I would write a book that his company would publish. They loved my writing style and could see a great opportunity there. Most people who meet me and find out about that relationship expect a much more exciting story. Like I rushed into a burning building and saved someone's life.

But it didn't take something that dramatic – it never does. All I did was treat someone with respect and courtesy. I've made more in royalties from that one book than I would have in two years of working full time for the university that fired me.

48

GIRLFRIEND IN A WEEK

When I mention the name of my second publisher at any party, I don't have to pay for my drinks the rest of the night. He's one of the biggest publishers in the online world; people try to be friends with me hoping they can become friends with him. I've never felt more like a roadie than I do when I'm hanging around him. Allow me to tell you the story of how we became friends.

I met him on a marketing cruise. I knew his name because I'd purchased products from him in the past, but I didn't recognize him the first time we met. I was waiting for a girl I knew to get a haircut when I looked outside and saw one of my friends talking to some people. I walked over and joined the conversation without realizing just who my friend was talking to. My friend left, and this titan of industry asked me about what I was up to, and I told him about my book, "Girl Gets Ring." I'd been working on the project for more than a year with my first publisher. We were a week from launch, and I was so excited to finally see that first dollar. I was so excited to be at the end of that journey that my enthusiasm was infectious. While we were talking, people would continually interrupt our conversations to pitch ideas to him. It was like the speed round on Shark Tank (or Dragon's

Den if you live in England.) Everyone was just asking him for things. They had ideas that might have made him money, but they didn't invest in talking to him like a normal person. They kept walking up and interrupting our conversation with these ideas, where he could get in on the ground floor.

He finally stopped one of these people in the middle of their pitch, turned to me and asked if I was exclusive with my publisher. And I sort of was. Our agreement was that I was exclusive, but just for female-targeted products. He immediately asked if I'd be willing to do a product for men with him. Somebody, who everyone else was throwing projects at, turned and pitched an idea to me.

It was awesome, and I made sure to meet his wife on the cruise and let her get to know me (remember, I talked about how important that is!) This is how I started another great relationship that has led to more and more. All I did was talk to someone at a conference and share my passion and excitement without asking for anything in return.

I'm not suggesting you walk up to people and just talk about your current projects, but if it's your PASSION, then people will like hearing about that way more than amazing business opportunity.

49

THE UNIVERSITY JOB

It was the most overwhelmed and under qualified I'd ever been. Before I got canned from my position at one of the top universities in America, I was hired. At twenty-nine years old, I was running a small department with several teachers and managing a multimillion-dollar program.

I wasn't ready for that kind of job, but I knew I could figure it out along the way.

I cold-called the head of the English department one day and asked if they had any openings for new teachers. They had an opening for an administrator position that they weren't advertising anymore. It wasn't teaching, but instead, it was being in **charge** of a group of teachers.

I went into that interview and used all the techniques from the networking sections earlier.

My new boss absolutely loved me offered me the position on the spot. She told me the salary range the university was offering for this position. I asked for a number higher than this range, and she immediately gave it to me. Using my simple networking techniques, I was offered a job and salary bump in just one interview.

Implementing the correct social skills works in any industry - even the wrong one.

You don't have to be an entrepreneur to get ahead using the tactics in this book. I first used them to leapfrog ahead in my career as an employee long before I ever thought of going out on my own.

These principles can help you even if you stick with your current career.

50

DOLLARS TO DONUTS

I know that not everyone who reads this book is going to shove a resignation letter down the boss's throat tomorrow. And I don't want you to do that just yet! First of all, it's a little rude. Second of all, you shouldn't make any big moves until you have a secondary revenue stream in place. While you're there, you might as well get better at the game, get a raise, get a promotion. These networking and favor techniques can make that happen.

The ability to form connections and alliances with people is extremely valuable. It works in social situations as well as the corporate world.

From here on out, we are going to unleash your potential, so that you can build something amazing on your own.

VII

LET'S MAKE MONEY

When I was young I thought that money was the most important thing in life; now that I am old I know that it is.

- Oscar Wilde

51

PASSIVE INCOME

When you're an hourly employee, figuring out your hourly wage is very simple. For every hour you work you get paid a certain amount. If you work more than forty hours per week, you make more money per hour as a reward for working overtime. Even teenagers understand how this system works.

Let's say you're rocking the minimum wage game. You're making $15 an hour. If you work forty hours per week, that's $600 for you to live off of, before taxes come into play and start eating away at your income. Most places pay time and a half for overtime. So that means for hour forty-one you are going to get paid $22.50. When I was working hourly, I would have killed to make that kind of money. I only got paid seven dollars an hour when I first entered the world of employment!

That $22.50 might be the only way you are going to make ends meet. You are trapped, though. You can only increase your income by working more hours at this point. Unfortunately, there are only 168 hours in each week. Assuming that you never sleep, take breaks or go to the bathroom, your maximum theoretical income is $2880 for that overtime. You can make a maximum of $3480 per week including your base forty hours and 128 hours of overtime. That seems like a pretty good chunk of change, except it's an impossible number, partially because most places aren't open 24 hours a day, but mostly because if you don't sleep, you'll die.

When you are on salary, it's a pretty similar experience. Instead of saying you get paid per hour, your boss pays you per week. That means that even if you work sixty hours per week your salary doesn't change. There's no overtime bump. You receive more benefits, such as medical insurance, but there is no chance to make extra money by working overtime. If you don't work enough hours in the week, you lose your job, and your income drops back to zero.

The majority of our population operates under that pay structure.

You exchange time for money.

That's the basic formula for life as an employee. The game is rigged against you because there are only so many hours you can labor and keep your health and sanity.

There's a different way to live, and it's a life worth fighting for. It's a life based on passive income. I will write this book only once, but each time someone buys a copy I will get paid. Even when I'm asleep, I will make money, and that's the key to my financial success.

Breaking the connection between time and money will unlock the freedom you have always desired.

This type of project comes with risk and it's a risk I'm sure your spouse, kids, or incredibly nosy neighbor will want to jump in and point out. If nobody buys this book, I don't make any money. No matter how hard you work on a project, you can still make nothing when you're the boss. I have worked on projects that died before they became financially successful. It happens. That's why I am diversified.

Writing this book is taking a lot of my time. I'm not working on any projects while this is in development. I finished three projects earlier this week that will continue to pay me for years, so I can afford to invest the time. I can take a month off anytime I want. Despite the risks, passive and recurring income is the key to true financial freedom. Look at the life of any successful person that isn't working a surgeon's insane schedule, and I can promise you it relies on passive income, whether it comes from owning a store, playing the stock market, or writing books. It's about working once and getting paid over and over, disconnecting the connection between time and income.

It's the best way to remove the shackles from your life. We want to start projects together that continue to make money, even when you're working on something else.

I'm not going to lie to you; initially, the ratio will be low. You'll be putting in a LOT of time for very little financial return. That's simply how this game starts. Over time, you will continue to improve that ratio. Here's a simple example. Following my system for releasing books on Amazon, there is a baseline. For each book you put on Amazon you'll make at least $100 a month. So the first month you work hard and release a book and make your $100. I know that sounds low.

But let's think about it. The first time will take the longest because you are learning the system. The second month takes you only 60% of the time, and you make $200. Your ratio has just massively improved. Month three you work even faster and at the end of the month, you take home $300. Month four you work on something else, and you STILL make that $300. If you put out a book a month, you'll be making $1200 a month in a year. Over time, because it is residual income, the ratio continues to improve. That first month of work will generate more than $2400 over the next two years. That's not so bad for a month of effort. And believe me, I'm not talking about 40 hours a week to make that happen either.

We want to move in this direction. But before I jump into the different methods of making money, I need to learn a little bit more about you.

52

ASSESSMENT

We need to take an honest look in the mirror and assess exactly where you are right now. Take out a notebook and get ready to do some writing. This is a book about making money, and that requires action. The temptation to breeze through this section quite casually will be high. I know that! But I need you to understand something.

If you skip steps this early in the book, your odds of actually succeeding drop to below 10%. My system doesn't work for slackers. It only works for trigger pullers. I have no idea how to help you make money if you do nothing. So I'm sorry to inform you, but your action is required. No one is watching you; I certainly can't check your work. School is over; there's not some guy peering over your shoulder here. To succeed when you are the CEO and the master of your destiny requires self-motivation.

The first thing you need to do is assess your current financial situation. You started this process earlier in the book when we set out your financial goals, and that's wonderful. Now we want to dig a little deeper so that we can establish some budgets.

How much money do you have in the bank? How much debt do you currently have? For most people, that second number is larger than the first. We can work with that. We also want to look at all your current revenue streams. Maybe you have a job and get a little extra money from alimony, a lawsuit, or you even won a little something in the lottery. Wherever you have money coming in, you want to just write it down. You want to know your current financial situation. If your financial position is not secure, then you shouldn't invest a ton of money into courses and technology. For you, time is a better resource to use than money.

Either path can lead to success, but we don't want to spend the wrong resource for your situation. The method I teach in this book and most of my courses uses time as your primary currency. You can then accelerate the process by adding money.

I prefer to spend money out of profits to grow a project, but if your time is more valuable, then you can easily hire people to replace certain steps in this process. Whatever your situation is, I've got you covered.

You need to create a budget for your business. How much money can you spend every month without hurting your overall financial situation? There are only a few fixed costs you need pay to get started. You need a computer and an Internet connection. Please don't try to start a business with a tablet, that's super hard, and I doubt that will succeed.

If you can't afford an Internet connection right now, then you need to start doing some research. There are tons of places everywhere in the world with free high-speed Internet. Why do you think there are so many hipsters that spend twelve hours a day in coffee shops?

For recurring costs, you need at least fifty bucks a month. That's enough to get into the game. I know most businesses require massive amounts of money to get going, but that isn't useful for most people. When it comes to cash, I think like a street fighter – I want to turn dirt into dollars.

This is why I hate physical businesses. Want to sell sugar water on a corner somewhere? Get ready to take out a bank loan. Did you know that most physical businesses try to see a 3-5% profit annually?

Unless you've got enough capital to start and successfully run a half dozen places, those numbers are pathetic! I do things a little differently. If I invest $10 in a project, I want to make $100 back. No exaggeration here, I look for a ten-fold return on my Investment.

Now that we have a bit of baseline for your financial situation, we want to consider your value as a human being. By the way, I promise this will be a lot less depressing than the financial assessment, okay?

Let's start with your hobbies. What do you enjoy doing in your spare time? For each of your hobbies, even if it's only one, measure your expertise and passion levels. You can make a living quite comfortably just talking about something you love, something that you're great at.

Pay special attention to things you're great at, but other people aren't – "watching Netflix" probably isn't a great hobby because anyone can do that. This is the area where many people leave millions of dollars on the table. I have a relative who is magnificent at woodworking. This is something I'm super terrible at. I can't build anything with my hands. It's a skill that I and most of the population lack, so I came to him with a business idea. My idea was to make a blog with videos of him building different toys with his kids. I'm talking about tree houses, wagons, and other great classic wooden toys. I did some research and realized that by building a wagon for your kids with parts from a hardware store, you could knock up to seventy percent off the cost of buying one from a store. And that's just for a wagon. We would target dads who couldn't afford expensive toys and wanted to spend more time with their kids.

We would let them watch him building each project with the kids, so they would see how awesome it was to have that connection with your children. We would then sell the plans to each project for a very low price below the video. The dad gets to spend time with his kids and save, even factoring the cost of plans from us. It was a brilliant idea. When I came to him, my relative told me that this was a stupid idea, nobody would want something like that and that it would never make any money. He felt that his skill had no value.

A few years later a guy named Ted came up with the same idea. You can find out more about it at http://servenomaster.com/book

This guy Ted has woodworking plans for everything, not just stuff you build with your kids. He is making between ten and fifty thousand dollars a day. Because my relative thought his skill had no value and he decided to shut down my idea, he left somewhere in the range of ten million dollars on the table for someone else to make. Now, I'm not saying Ted stole my idea. He just had the same brilliant idea and had the guts to go for it.

Don't decide that other people don't want access to your skills. I've had conversations like that with a lot of people over the years who insist my idea is stupid right until someone swoops in and makes seven figures. I want you not to be selfish right here. If you are good at something manual or something unique, then don't throw it away. Maybe you're a brainiac rather than a hands-on type of guy. I had another friend who was a lawyer and a master of passing the Bar Exam. I wanted to put together a video course in that niche. He said no. Someone else is now a millionaire. Even smart people can make horrible financial mistakes and leave millions on the table.

Lawyers are just like anyone else. They get paid for the time they work. Why do you think they are always talking about billable hours? Most lawyers have to fill in a form every day explaining what they were doing for each three-minute block of the day. That doesn't sound like any fun to me.

Whatever skills and specialized knowledge you have should go onto your assessment sheet. We want to see what you can offer people that you are already good at. That's a great place to start.

The next thing we need to talk about is looks. I know it's something we all want to avoid, but if you have a face made for radio, then we need to know that now. On the flip side, you might be really attractive. That's part of the looks category. More of it is that you match the look of your project. What stereotypes do people think when they see you. It can be nerd, scientist or criminal. The answer won't affect my ability to help you make money. It will only affect the path we select. Right now is about honest assessment, not judgment. I get a lot of hate mail telling me how fat I am. I'm no Prince Charming. I just accept that reality, and I adapt to grow my business. As I said at the top, this isn't about anybody's feelings. My only goal is to shorten the path between you and freedom.

Let's talk about personality. Are you friendly and likable? Or are you more quiet and reserved? The idea here is to figure out if you should be doing videos or podcasts - or if you are better just using the written word. Take the time to listen to a few of my podcast episodes to see if that is something that appeals to you. (It is also called Serve No Master)

Your personality will color your project, and we want to make sure your identity is one that appeals to the audience you target. You may need to create a character or a more extreme version of yourself if you want to go down the audio or video route. Keep that in mind as you fill out this section.

The final part of your assessment is about equipment and resources. This includes software and even stuff you can borrow from a friend. Do you have any video cameras or lighting? How about sound equipment and microphones? Whatever you have that you can use for an online project should go onto your list.

Now we know what your baseline is. We can move forward and build a strategy with this information. I'm getting excited!

53

GARBAGE IN - GARBAGE OUT

Before we start talking about the business you are going to build, it's important to understand that the quality of your effort will directly impact the quality of your financial returns for a very long time to come. If you decide to start a blog about a topic you hate, then your dislike is going to crash the quality of your work across the board. Why would you want to start a new career that you hate? If you're reading this, the odds are that chasing an extra few bucks with something that "sounded good" is what got you here in the first place!

I only do projects that I enjoy. I thought of the name of this book a few years ago. I had the name locked down, but it took me a while to decide how I wanted to build the project. I was always excited about it, and I was waiting for the right moment. That moment is now. The stars have aligned. And here we are together. If I didn't want to write about creating an amazing lifestyle of financial freedom, then writing this book would be a nightmare. I would hate going onto my website to write new blog posts. Because I am working on something I like, the effort is not a problem. Passion is the first crucial element.

You also need to focus on the actual quality of your product. I make a wide range of products for myself and other publishers. You can always tell when I've worked on a project because the quality is at least 10% better than anyone else. When I make a video course, I spend as much time picking the tiny icons that appear next to each bullet point as I do recording the actual videos. That minor detail is important to me. When you buy something I've touched, I want your first thought to be that you underpaid. I want to give you WAY more value than you expected. This applies to both content and presentation.

Whatever direction you want to go in, please start with the mindset that you will not cut corners. There are a lot of places on the Internet where you can buy PLR. This is where you can buy a book someone else wrote and slap your name on the cover. Then you can start selling it all over town. The problem here is that the book is going to be low quality. Now, that's not to say I'm a zealot about the issue. You can use good PLR material as an excellent foundation if you completely rewrite the content. But most people won't do that. If you try to shortcut the product-creation process this way, you end up selling some trash written by someone who doesn't even speak native-quality English and your customer ends up with something that doesn't help them.

Your goal should always be to provide the most useful content possible – it's easier to sell! Eventually, every single topic in this book will end up on my blog. I have no desire to hide my knowledge behind a pay wall. That's not a mindset for success. The reason you bought this book or grabbed it on Kindle Unlimited is because I organized the content into a usable structure. I arranged the book this way to give you a LOT of value. Also, I will not copy and paste between my blog and this book. I will write everything in a different way, for a different medium.

Even my free content I try to make as excellent as possible. That's my goal and approach towards business and life. Everything that you create, sell or release into the universe is your legacy. The Internet never forgets. You might be tempted to cut corners as you are going through this process. The important thing is to learn what corners you can cut that don't affect the experience of your customer. It takes a long time to figure out what they are. Perhaps you are familiar with the eighty-twenty rule. You will spend eighty percent of your time working on stuff that generates twenty percent of your income. It's hard not to get pulled down rabbit holes. As long as you are limiting yourself to one project at a time, you protect yourself from going down a rabbit hole that leads to nowhere.

The book you've got in your hands right now is my legacy. People will be able to talk to my children about this book. That's how I gain immortality. Every time someone reads this book, remembers me, or says my name, I extend my life a little bit. It is the only true way to live beyond the human lifespan. That's why I'll never sell or promote a product that doesn't work. I will eventually recommend some resources in this book just like I do on my website, but I only recommend the stuff that I use.

There are some tempting alternatives that will pay me 10-20 times more for pointing you in their direction. But I don't use them. How can I tell you to use something that I don't trust with my own business? My mindset is based on integrity, because I don't want you to buy one product from me. I want you to join my tribe and stick with me as you build your business and become successful. I want you to post comments on my blog about your success and tell your friends about how I helped you. I want you to trust me because I put your best interests in front of my personal financial gain. I want us to travel this road together for the next ten or twenty years.

You should treat your customers the same way. And it might help if you call your customers clients. That word seems to make the connection feel stronger. You want to think of the people who give you their hard earned money as something important. The more you care about them, the more they will come back for more and more. You want to put the best material you can assemble into your blog or podcast or radio show or whatever project you start. Even before you are making money, make sure your content has quality.

Now let's be clear – when I talk about quality, I don't mean spending 80% of your time on making things look pretty because you're nervous that someone won't like your work. When I say quality, I mean solving people's problems in an entertaining and emotionally satisfying way. It's ok if your website is ugly as long as the words have value. You can focus on making your site prettier after it's generating income.

Integrity is rare in this world, and that's an unfortunate thing. Hype and lies are profitable in this world – if I told you that you could push a magic button on your computer that would make you a millionaire, this book would fly off the shelves. Most people hate the idea of making money, especially if hard work is involved. I would rather help a smaller group of people succeed than make a large group of people feel excited for twenty minutes while they read a book they will never implement. I'm interested in building a tribe of people who can succeed around me. That's what gets me excited, and I hope you have the same ideas in your heart.

54

TURNING YOUR ASSETS AND SKILLS INTO INCOME

At this point, you might be tempted to say that no one cares what you have to say about your hobby. Just like my relative who told me no one wants to build stuff at home anymore. Or my friend who said nobody wants help passing the Bar Exam.

We are at the point in the book where your mindset is everything. It's where the rubber meets the road. It's where we separate the people who are serious about making drastic changes to their life from the dreamers and the excuse makers. If you decide that your knowledge or skills have no value, then you should stop reading this book. Fold it closed, hit the power button, throw your Kindle in the fireplace, because absolutely nothing I can do matters anymore.

If you are stuck right here, you can jump back to the beginning of this book and accept the gift I offered you. When you do that, I'll send you an email. That email will be from my real account. You can reply with your assessment sheet, and I'll give you an idea that you can use to move forward.

Hopefully, I have shared enough with you by now that you are getting a feel for things that people would be interested in. Later on, I'll get technical with the exact steps you can take to generate income. But let's start with the big picture plan. You start by figuring out what you want to talk and teach about. Then you do some research to find your audience.

What do the people you want in your tribe like doing? Do they spend their time on Facebook or forums? Do they respond to video or blog posts? The more you understand your target audience, the better. Read reviews, read message boards, and listen to the words people use when praising a book or magazine on the topic. You should also pay attention to headlines and bullet points for video courses and blogs. What kind of benefits are they advertising? What kind of promises are they making? Are they things you'd be interested in buying yourself?

Before releasing this book, I did lots of research on Amazon. I found where you were hiding. The cover of this book, the length and the description were all designed based on your desires. I researched what you wanted to learn about and created a book that met your needs. I could have written something that is about ten times more technical. But you would have found it too convoluted and overwhelming. Rather than throw you into the deep end I'm starting slow so that you can follow the process and achieve real success.

Once you have found your audience and the medium they respond to, you can start to put together something that meets their need. You start with a blog or a podcast that is all about their needs and desires. You provide content that is both interesting and informative. You start by creating your first piece of property. A place where they can listen to what you have to say. The more you entertain or inform them, the more time they will spend with you. This is the start of the relationship. Over time their trust will increase, and you can then sell things to them. It might only take an hour to move through that spectrum of trust. It all depends on how the new client found you.

You want to create and sell products that help them. Do the research and make sure your training will work. This is where you start to generate income. If you are purely in the entertainment space, then you may focus on recommending stuff that you think is cool. That's totally fine. That is how the majority of websites make their money. It's the business model of every news site out there. They don't sell anything directly.

You might be a real technical expert, and your expertise lies more in the realm of converting visitors into customers. You might be wonderful at statistics or web design. If you have a skill in this arena, your strategy is more about implementing that skill rather than teaching it to other people. You can get into the service game where you let people pay you for your help. Even though you are getting paid for time, you now get to choose your projects and control your pricing. You can give yourself a raise whenever you like. My first online endeavor was helping people to rank their websites on Google so that customers could find them. I charged a flat monthly fee for my efforts. With each client, I simply doubled my price. I discovered that excellent results allow you to charge whatever number pops into your head.

There are thousands of ways to make money online and to include all of them in this book would make it tens of thousands of pages long. I'm sticking with what I know and what has worked for me over and over again. If you are interested in learning something that I don't cover in this book, you can check out my blog at ServeNoMaster.com, and I probably talk about it there. You can also reach out to me via email, and I will help you find the mentor that meets your needs.

55

CONNECTING YOUR PASSION TO PROFITS

Let's say you spent an entire day at your job – sweating, hands cramping, working like a pack mule. If you get home, and you have the choice of working on a blog that you don't like that much or watching a movie with your family, you will probably watch that movie. But if that blog is instead about your favorite topic, then you will enjoy working on it. I like writing this book. That's why it's so long, and I'm writing so fast. I'm pumped to put it out into the universe and get it into your hands – and that kind of enthusiasm is infectious. That's why you want to start with a passion-based idea.

There are many ways to turn your passion into profits, and we're going to talk about them in the next section. You can start a blog, sell books on Amazon, start a podcast, or sell training and services. There are a lot of ways to make money online, and we are going to find the best path for you to follow in the next section. For now, just trust me that the more you like what you are doing, the more money you will make. That's the easiest path to success.

56

BUILDING NEW SKILLS

You can also consider mastering a specific skill that you can leverage online. Some of those skills are:

- Ranking websites on Google
- Ranking books on Amazon
- Designing websites
- Recording voice overs
- Creating beautiful videos
- Writing words that sell
- Ghost writing
- Media buying
- Analyzing data to improve website performance

People are and will pay money hand over fist for people who know how to do this stuff, and you can use these skills to build your own business, too. Once you reach any level of expertise, you can release training to people further down the mountain than you. One of the most valuable skills you can develop is copywriting. The ability to write words that sell is a timeless skill and will be the subject of my next book. You can learn how to master copywriting without spending a penny on the bonus page for this book:

ServeNoMaster.com/book

This page has loads of additional content about each of the skills in this section as well as loads of tutorials. There is so much content that it crashed my server, and I had to split it into two pages! You can find links to my blog post and podcast episodes teaching how to learn copywriting and make serious money in less than six months without spending a penny.

When you develop one of these skills, you can leverage your way into some amazing partnerships. I use my ability to create Amazon bestsellers to forge new business relationships all the time. I have over thirty bestsellers on Amazon, all written under different pen names. I have a track record with this specific skill, and that is a value I bring to many new projects. It allows me to connect with people who would otherwise ignore me.

I'm a big believer in making money while you learn. I started building my first online business by selling services. The greatest thing about selling services is that you get paid up front. When I started selling my Google ranking service, I had no idea what to do. I used the first paycheck to buy the training and software that I needed to deliver on my promises. I provided amazing results and from there the clients started rolling in. It's a great way to start; a few clients at the beginning can help fund your education if you are light on cash.

If you want to learn any of the skills from this list, there is a ton of information on my book page dedicated to helping you figure out the right skill for you and to help you find the best expertise. I can't be everything to everyone, but I'm more than happy to help you along your path and find someone that can help you.

57

WHAT IS YOUR TIME WORTH?

We know how much money you want to make to hit each of your three primary goals. Now we want to work on that money to time ratio. At your job right now you get paid a certain amount of money per hour. If you are on a salary, you can pretend that you don't get paid for hours worked, but we can still get a pretty solid number. Just take how much money you earned last month and divide by the number of hours you worked. That will tell you at least how much your boss thinks an hour of your time is worth.

But ultimately, there's a brand new you, and you need to set your new rates. The problem is, you need to decide what the "new you" is going to sell time for, and I don't have any easy answers for you here. Depending on the project I'm working on my price changes. If it's a new project and I want to garner some testimonials, I'll lower my price. My level of expertise also determines where I price myself. Right now, I'd hop on the phone for about a hundred bucks an hour to talk about stuff from this book. If my phone starts ringing off the hook, I will keep raising the price. Depending on my desire to provide a service, I sometimes raise my price until no one wants to buy it.

As you noticed when I talked about my success using relationships, I've written some of the most successful dating books in the world.

My book for women has sold so many copies that I no longer try to count. I just check out that royalty direct deposit every Wednesday with a smile. For a long time, I provided a great deal of private coaching in the relationship space. I don't want to coach more than 3-4 people a year at most. So I charge $25,000 for me to fly out for a weekend and help someone where they live. My price used to be lower, but people kept paying it. I was totally booked, flying all over the place every weekend and getting worn out. My price reflects the value of my private coaching combined with my desire to stay at home now.

You want to determine how you value your time before you work on anything. That is how you'll find out if you should do something or if you should pay someone else to do it. This is not a hard and fast rule because learning how to do something yourself is often very valuable and hard to calculate. You also want to decide what you want to sell any services for. A common mistake is setting a price for something without factoring in how much of your time it will take. Over time, you will get better at this, but I just wanted to give you some rough numbers to get you started.

VIII

WAYS TO MAKE MONEY ONLINE

Don't let making a living prevent you from making a life.
- John Wooden

58

FREELANCER

The first way you can quickly make money online is by selling your services to the highest bidder. Whatever your expertise, there are people who will pay for it all day long, and as you build up a reputation, you can get the fee you want.

Depending on the nature of your expertise you may sell it entirely online, or you might find customers online and then help them in person. One of the best places to get started is UpWork. I hire people from this site all the time. You set up a profile and post a portfolio. Then you just start bidding on the jobs that people post. I hire people off there all the time for projects.

The great thing here is that the money is in escrow, so you never have to worry about the client not paying you. The money is already out of their account before you get started. Before you jump at this, please remember that it's hard to get picked for jobs when you first get started. You will have no experience and no reviews on there. Nobody wants to be your first client. So you want to find customers using other methods and then get them to hire you via UpWork. This is a way to get that profile started, and you can get some amazing gigs on there. The best part is that you only work when you want to.

Another great place to setup is on Fiverr. This site charges five bucks for everything. Well, that's how it started, but now you can post all sorts of add-ons and packages for services. I have seen plenty of offers on there that cost more than one hundred bucks. The correct way to use this site is to build a customer base. You do a good job on something small for five bucks, and then you can do larger projects for more. This allows you to grow and grow. Yes, you start small, but there are plenty of people making six figures as vendors on this site.

At the next level, you can leverage. You sell a service for a high price, and you pay someone else to do it for a lower price. This is often called arbitrage, and we'll discuss how to get into this game a little later.

I personally always sold my services directly to clients. I posted great ads on Craigslist and found clients all day long. You can find resources for finding clients and building your online resume fast at ServeNoMaster.com/book

59

SELL SERVICES

Everything I do involves some degree of risk, and ultimately, my success depends on managing my fears and controlling as many risk elements as possible. Selling services can be very daunting at first, and if you're used to getting paid per hour, you're going to have to do a lot of new things to build your business.

Selling directly has more reward, but there's also more risk. You deal directly with the client, which means you have to collect payment yourself. Small business owners are always trying to stay in the black and paying your bills will not be a priority. If you don't setup your systems in advance, you can end up spending weeks chasing checks, and some clients will stiff you.

When I first got started, I let some people pay me at the end of the month. When you are an employee, you get paid after you work, so this is how I acted when I was working independently.

It took me a while to learn that you always get the client to pay at the start of the month, with automated billing. There are a few great tools for this. You can get a little dongle you plug into your smartphone that will swipe credit cards. You can also setup recurring payments. You take the credit card information once, and the software charges them every month until they cancel.

I much prefer my client having to act to stop paying me, rather than have to take action to pay me. That means that a lazy client will keep paying for another month or two. It's a vast improvement over driving all over town to get them to write you a check. As you build up a reputation, people will write enormous checks within fifteen minutes of meeting you. It's a heady feeling, but this is where integrity comes into play. Do not take the money if you can't deliver the goods.

The difficulty with selling services is that you aren't fully in control of your destiny. Eventually, you reach the top of your market, and you can't raise your price anymore. The market won't bear infinite price raising. So you will inevitably hit that wall. For some of those types of services that wall is around $25k a month for others, it is closer to 10k. But I find that most people can live pretty comfortably on three hundred grand a year. It just really depends on how high on the hog you need to live. Remember that sheet you made a couple of chapters ago? Look at it closely, and don't get greedy. Not yet, anyway.

Selling services starts out with a lot of client chasing, but eventually the situation flips, and clients are begging you to take their money. So you'll eventually take back a lot of power, but you're still allowing other individuals to control and affect your revenue stream. If you go down this path, try to have at least ten clients on your roster at all times, as this diversity protects you from market shocks. If you lose one client only 10% of your revenue is gone – a blow to be sure, but one you can survive.

There are a lot of ways to sell services beyond the technical. I mentioned earlier that I'd chat to you on the phone for an hour for a hundred bucks. To be honest, I know that in a month, I'm going to have to re-edit this book and push that number through the roof, but that's how I'm feeling today. And even though it doesn't sound life or death, it literally is. I'm selling an hour of my lifeforce for $100.

If we hop on the phone, our conversation will directly affect the course I take in my business.

Here's an example of what I mean. If you ask me about writing email headlines, I'll write a blog post to answer some of your questions – I might even record an entire podcast episode on the subject. The odds are good that if one person is asking me a question in person, a dozen people are thinking the same thing. I think of customer support as a type of a focus group.

Once you get good with coaching one-on-one, you can expand into group settings. For my Kindle Bestseller Mastermind, I have a coaching call every single Monday at 8 PM EST. That software can handle up to 1,000 people at a time. In that situation, I can charge each person $1 and still make ten times more than I would on a one-on-one call. Obviously, that's not the actual price, and I would never have that many people on a call, but I want you to get a feel for how dramatic the advantages of scaling in this type of service can be.

Let's do a bit of math together. You are going to get in the coaching game. That's the service you want to sell. You like the sound of my numbers, so you're going to charge $100 an hour for a private session. If you were to coach clients for forty hours a week, you'd be making four grand a week. Now, please don't run off and do this – if you schedule that many clients we'll have to break you out of an insane asylum a few weeks from now. Remember that you need to put breaks in between your clients or you'll burn out in the first week. New people often forget to put in breaks for eating and going to the bathroom and stretching their legs. But let's just say we stay theoretical, and you're making that four grand a week, which is pretty impressive. If you were to get into group coaching, when you notice that many people have similar questions, you could offer a two-hour session for just one dollar per person. You can now effect one thousand people an hour rather than just forty people a week. If you do four group sessions a week, you make the same as you did working full-time!

Now we both know that people won't pay $1 for a coaching session. The price is too low. You will probably have to charge ten bucks for group coaching and a hundred bucks for a one-on-one.

All the math aside, if you can help a group of people at the same time, you can make more money while charging a lower price. That's the power of scaling. When you are making over five hundred dollars for an hour of group coaching, you'll want to reassess what you charge for a one-on-one. You will end up raising your rates because your time has become more valuable. This is how you can make more and more money very quickly.

Some services simply don't work in the group environment, and that's ok. Over time you can continue to raise your prices and even take on some staff to handle the volume. Something glorious happens around that moment; you become the boss, and you're working the least while making the most. It takes time to get there, but it feels pretty good to be at the top of the pile.

60

SELL TRAINING

Want to predict the success you'll have in business? Add together the number of people you help and the amount you effect them. That's the reason why I sell a combination of training and services. With training, you can help a lot of people a little bit, and with services you can help a few people a lot. I like to have a mix in my business model.

Let's say you start with selling a service. You might notice that people keep asking you to help them with the same thing. It doesn't matter if you are helping people to study, train their dog or fix clogged toilets. Each of these services is something you can then convert into a product. You already know what people ask about the most because they have been asking you.

So you start with services and then develop the ideal product. You can make a booklet on how to unclog a toilet like a professional plumber using tools found around the house. When someone contacts you with a clogged toilet, you can now offer them two choices. You can email the pamphlet immediately for a small fee, or they can wait however long it takes you to drive over and pay a lot more. This is the basic idea of selling training in addition to a service.

There are several ways to provide training. They can read it, listen to it, or watch it. This book comes in two modalities. You can read it, or you can listen to it. There is not a video version, although I might try and figure out a way to do that on Amazon just to see if it's possible. If you were to buy my Kindle training course on my website, you would get access to all three methods of learning. You get a video, an audio version, a worksheet, and even a transcript. I know that people learn in different ways, and I try to meet my customers at the point of their need. That's also why that course is more expensive. The quality of the content and the quality of the delivery method will determine how much you can charge for something.

One of the early mistakes people make when selling knowledge is overpricing. We decide that what we know is so valuable that we want to charge what we think it is worth. Instead, we need to realize the value of a large customer base and pay more attention to what the market will bear. I can sell infinite copies of this book through different mediums. I can sell my ideas for a low price and make my profit with volume.

Structure a product business like a pyramid. As people work their way up the pyramid, they get an increasing amount of access to you. At the very bottom of the pyramid, you have free stuff you give away - blog posts, small reports, and podcast episodes. At this level, they get some basic information, but you don't talk to them directly. A level above that you have your low-ticket offers. These are training courses that you sell for anywhere from five to one hundred dollars.

Different markets require different prices. In some sectors, if you charge too little, people won't trust you. Would you like to buy a Mercedes from me for ten bucks? Your first thought is that that I'm hiding something or trying to trick you because the price is too low. You want to research your market and competition as you are setting prices.

As you work your way up the pyramid, you move from ebook products up to video courses and monthly group coaching calls. As you move up the pyramid, the number of clients goes down while the price goes up. Even though fewer customers step up to each higher level, the increase in price more than covers the difference.

You might give away a thousand copies of your free report. From that, ten people buy your book for seven bucks. Then out of those ten people, only one buys your course for ninety-seven dollars.

At this point, it's all math. How many people do you need entering the pyramid at the bottom to generate the numbers you desire at the top. You can have multiple products at each level as your business grows.

At the very top, you're offering your time in the form of private coaching. I know people in the finance sector who sell coaching for over $100,000 a year. How are they getting away with it? They're selling people access and increasingly valuable knowledge.

This is the structure that most online businesses take, and it's the exact structure of my own business. You just grabbed this book for less than ten bucks. A select few people might have even gotten it for free during a promotion. At the time of this writing, I have no idea what you paid for the audio edition - Amazon sets the price only after the whole thing has been recorded, so I can't put it here.

Right now, you are at the bottom of my pyramid. You might decide that this book doesn't fit what you are looking for. If you want to learn the technical aspects of running Facebook ads or setting up payment buttons, then this is not the right book for you. Many people want to learn things about marketing online that this book doesn't cover. Hopefully, you knew what you were getting into, and this book meets your need.

61

ENTERTAINMENT

You can make a great living online just by being entertaining. Most of the time I'm online, I visit sites that entertain me. I read one news blog, a few lifestyle blogs and then I hit up a few comic sites that I like. Those are all entertainment. That's how most people approach the Internet; they are looking to be entertained. All those people at work with managers who track time rather than results have to fill their days, right?

If your main thing is video games, you can blog about that big time. Whenever I get stuck in a game, I hop online and do a quick search to find a solution. There's opportunity in blogging about games or in writing guides. You can make blog posts, videos, or podcasts about anything you like. You can even record yourself talking while playing your favorite games. This is a new industry that has created quite a few millionaires in the last few years.

When you follow the entertainment approach, the path to money is a little different. Often you can't create something that your followers want to buy. But in the world of the Internet, nothing is more valuable than traffic, and if you can get people to see what you are doing, you can sell that traffic to sponsors. This is exactly what television shows do with product placements and commercials. As long as you don't recommend stuff you don't believe in, you can be very successful here.

62

AFFILIATE

The odds are pretty good that you know how affiliate marketing works, even if you've never actually heard the term before. Have you ever recommended a movie to a friend? What about a car or a book? Well, that's affiliate marketing – suggesting something you trust to someone you know. It's just that in the past, you've been doing it for free! There are plenty of people who will pay you cold hard cash for telling people about something that you believe in.

The most common form of this is Google AdWords. You put some code on your website, and Google shows ads that relate to your topics. You don't have to do anything else, and you get paid each time someone clicks on one of those ads. The payment depends on your market of course – a blog about life insurance will make more money than a blog about your favorite musician - but you make a penny here, and a penny there and it can add up to something quite nice.

You don't have any control over the ads because Google shows what it decides is relevant. You don't have to spend a lot of time researching the right products to promote. All you have to worry about is making the content and getting paid. Google has a ton of rules for advertisers, so you don't have to worry about shady people making garbage and dumping it on your site. The downside is that you might be "sponsored" by stuff you don't like.

Let's say you posted a review of an office chair, and you didn't like it. Too clunky, too ugly, a total nightmare for your back. You post a brutal review, saying it was garbage. Google might stick a link to an Amazon sales page for that chair next to your article. That's because their software only tracks the words on your page, and can't tell that your review is negative.

That's the problem with automation. Computers still aren't that smart. When you are getting started, this can be a good way to make a bit of money. AdWords isn't the best way to monetize your website long-term, but it is an excellent way to make that first dollar. The first time you actually make real money is a wonderful feeling. The sooner that happens, the likelier you are to stay the course and build something amazing.

There are a lot of networks that run on this type of automated system. Many of the networks use visual ads rather than the pure text links that Google provides. You can find a network that you like and tell them the type of ads that fit your online presence.

As you become more active in your advertising, you can lease commercial space on your website. You can charge a price per month for someone to put their banner ad on your site. It's the same as reading a commercial at the start a radio show. Many people do this as a way to generate income from a free podcast.

If you want a serious piece of the action, become a true affiliate. You get paid based on actions rather than just sending traffic. There are two markets for this. One is called cost per action (CPA). You send someone to a page that asks for some information. I used to have a KILLER website offering people free gift cards. I was doing great until Walmart sent me a cease and desist for outranking their website.

As soon as people entered their name and zip code, I got paid around a dollar. If I wanted to play higher stakes, there was a second page that asked for the full mailing address. If people filled that out, I got paid four bucks. The deeper the action, the higher the commission. Filling out an insurance form will get you around 50 bucks while just getting a zip code might give you one.

In the CPA game, you get paid for leads, not sales. Most of these offers pay you for getting them a new email address. They know their numbers, so they have a whole plan. They will send that person a bunch of different emails that eventually get the person to buy something. They know how many leads it takes to get one customer. They also know what that customer will pay them over the lifetime of their relationship. They do a bunch of math, and then decide what they will pay you for that lead. Most people that operate in this space are doing arbitrage. They buy traffic from one place and resell it somewhere else. That game is all about volume, but if you have a job that pays you well, and you're looking for more freedom, you can dabble there for sure, and you'll take off fast once you can sell traffic for more than you pay for it.

I do a lot of affiliate marketing myself, but I work under a pay per sale system. I send you a hundred customers, and I get a commission. There are some great places to find reliable products to promote – that have a refined sales message, testimonials, and proof, and are just exciting to talk about! Clickbank is where I sell a lot of products.

You can find stuff in any niche, check it out, and then promote it to your fans. They send you a direct deposit every Wednesday, and that's pretty nice.

The best way to make money here is not to send people directly to someone else's website. Instead, you want to get someone's email address and establish a relationship. The most valuable asset you can have online is an active mailing list. You want to give your readers a lot of value and only promote things that will improve their lives and fit their needs.

The idea of being an affiliate is that you sell someone else's product and get paid a piece of the action. I tend to do a mix of selling my products and promoting other people's things. When you are starting out, it's a lot easier to promote someone else's products until you have time to create your own. They've got a lot of proof, slick production, and can be an excellent way to get your foot in the door with your audience. Affiliate marketing is a powerful way to leverage your audience, and it doesn't require you to make anything to sell them.

63

BORN IN FEAR

I wasn't born with a sense for business. For a long time, I was TERRIFIED of the thought of starting my own business. I'm a natural entrepreneur, and yet the chains of fear we talked about earlier had a vice grip on my psyche.

By the time I was in my late twenties, I was near the peak of my career. I was living in London, and I was chasing two careers at once. During the day I would teach at a university, and at night I would help men talk to women in the hopes of finding true love.

I was making several times more money at night, and I helped tens of thousands of people, but the thought of financial "instability" terrified me. I wanted a respectable job, the kind of thing that my parents could be proud of.

I stuck with my educational career. I loved teaching at first, but after a while, it just became so boring. You have to teach the same lessons over and over and over again. It starts to feel like you are trapped in this weird Groundhog Day scenario, living the same day over and over again. I'm sure plenty of great teachers don't feel that way, but that's what started happening to me.

As a teacher, you're trapped by dozens of rules. Things you can't talk about, words you can't use and methods you have to follow. You have to follow a curriculum set by someone thousands of miles away, who has never even heard of your school, let alone met your students. I felt like a puppet, dancing on a very long set of strings.

I had an anonymous blog at the time about my dating life. I set it up and just wrote about my experiences. I never used anyone's real name and after a few years, I was shocked to realize that I was getting a LOT of traffic.

I had no idea people would be interested in what I thought was my personal journal. It became popular, so I wrote a little dating guide to help people get the courage to talk to each other. I think I sold like ten copies. That was pretty cool, but it certainly wasn't enough money to be a real career. I found a few private coaching clients through word of mouth, and that was a lot more successful. Using the Internet to make money still baffled me.

When my visa ran out, I returned to America with a brand new master's degree and fresh experience from a university with an impressive name in London. I cold-called a local community college to ask for a job teaching. I can't explain exactly what happened. I went in for a job interview, and they gave me a work schedule. I was already hired. I also cold-called the local elite university. It's one of the top twenty universities in America according to those magazines that make lists. They didn't have a job opening, but I talked them into meeting with me. At the interview, they offered me a job that wasn't even advertised anywhere. They said the job would pay a decent wage, and I would be running a small department with six teachers.

Did I have any experience in administration? Nope, but I sure knew how to fake it. All that time I'd put in dating helped me to develop some great social skills, and I know how to appear confident even when I'm way outside my comfort zone. I immediately told my new boss that I needed more money than they offered and a whole new office setup. They gave me the salary that I asked for and a new desk chair and even a brand new computer.

Everyone else in the department was envious. I already had another job, so I was able to negotiate without fear.

The things I have shared with you before about mindsets and

favors are the techniques I used in that negotiation. That is why I covered that material first. You now have the ability to get yourself a raise at work or negotiate if you jump to another company. Even if you don't want to break free of all your chains, I want to help you!

I was twenty-nine years old. I was the only person from my graduate program to get a job in higher education. And I wasn't just a teacher; I was running a program worth over $1.5m. That was shocking to me. I used the job offer letter to get a new apartment and buy a car. I accepted these long-term financial chains because my "dream job" was secured.

And then I lived happily ever after, right? Wrong. Within a week I realized that the job was nothing like I imagined. Assignments that were supposed to last for months took me hours. I don't have that natural bureaucratic skill of doing nothing while it looks like I'm doing something.

One of the assignments was to get the students in my department some amazing field trips. I was supposed to come up with something amazing with a budget of zero. They had messed up the money or something before I came on board and every dollar was already allocated for other stuff. A big oil company funded the program. That was all the information I had the first day I sat at my desk.

Within six hours, I had two amazing trips locked in. The first one was to a bottling plant that didn't even give tours! I did some research and found a new method of making bottling caps from oil. So when I approached the plant manager, I explained that the funding for my project came from an oil company, so it would be a perfect fit and great way for them to earn some goodwill from a vendor. He went from skeptical to excited. As I already taught you, I approached him by offering value first. I found a way this tour would be a benefit to him.

I went to my new boss, and she told me that this trip sounded fine, but it wasn't at zero yet. How would I get the students there without paying a penny? Talk about cheap! I wasn't even allowed to use the university vans because they use gas. At this point, the trip would cost around $20 total. I was about to offer her the money out of my pocket just to shut her up.

But I know how the mind of a drone works. If it's written on a piece of paper it might as well be written in blood - she would have turned down the money. I went back to my office and hopped on the Internet. I found a free medical shuttle between our campus and an offsite medical center a few hundred yards from that bottling plant. I found free transportation between the two locations.

Looking back I realize that she gave me tasks she considered impossible, but I don't know how to operate without winning...

Thirteen days later I was fired. Someone found my old dating blog and connected it to me. Honestly, I think an ex-girlfriend called and turned me in. I don't know. When I took the job, I read all the paperwork carefully, and there was nothing about telling them if you have an anonymous blog.

I come in one Monday morning to my boss and the head of my division waiting to ambush me. Someone who never deigned to meet me before. They told me that because I had sold ten copies of that book I had violated some rule about not having a second job. The idea that teachers aren't allowed to write books is so ridiculous, but it was the best idea they were able to come up with.

I sat in a room with two women who had spent the weekend cooking up a reason to fire me. I could have taken them to court, and I would have won because their reason was ridiculous. But who has that kind of time or money? When someone wants to fire you, they will think of a reason.

I was amazed that they said something so ridiculous with straight faces. If you've been to college, you know that every professor has a book for sale. But reality didn't matter at that moment because I had no power in that room.

Those two idiots were so smug as they made me hand over my office keys. They had this look of pride in their eyes as they took away my job. I'll never forget it. They were so proud of themselves as they freed me from prison. That is the best day of my entire life.

If they hadn't fired me, I would never have gone out to start my business. Reality overcame my fear. I got a fantastic health insurance package when they fired me. If they had waited two more weeks, that wouldn't have happened. I lucked out in that department. They thought they had destroyed me, but within six months I had replaced my income. Within a year I was making more than my boss and within two I was making more than the division head. If they hadn't fired me, I wouldn't be living on a tropical island, working these hours, with my awesome girlfriend and my wonderful kids.

Getting fired truly freed me.

IX

LET'S TAKE ACTION TODAY

Action is the foundational key to all success.
- Pablo Picasso

64

ACTIONS THAT HELP YOU NO MATTER YOUR DESTINY

There are many paths you can take to make money online. I'm going to teach you several very strong ones, but my list will not be exhaustive. The good thing is that there are a series of core skills that offer a lot of value. Things you can start to learn now that will help you no matter the path you take.

Think of these as the core courses you take at university before you choose a major, except that this material will be useful. I want to give you a baseline of skills so that you start to feel confident enough to take bigger and bigger steps towards that big, beautiful open prison door.

You might be reading this book for a laugh or because you have a friend who might need it. Maybe you have an awesome career and don't need to jump ship. You might be in sales, and your destiny is already in your hands. You eat what you kill, and that's awesome.

I still want you to get some personal value from this book. There are a few things that you can learn that at some point in your career will be useful. These are foundational skills that everyone will need in the future.

65

FIRST ACTION STEPS

The first step you should take today is to set up an Internet property. Buy a domain and set up a blog. Learning this process is imperative and doing it yourself will give you a feel for what you can and cannot do. You will get a feel for what skills you have and what you won't be able to learn without a lot of effort.

I explain the process in great detail at:

---

http://servenomaster.com/book/

Just scroll to the bright blue banner that says "Start Your Own Blog Today."

I have step-by-step instructions with a lot of pictures. It's much easier to follow along when you can copy and paste, rather than trying to hold this book up against your computer monitor to follow the steps. I don't want to leave you hanging, so I'll give you the basics right here.

You start by picking a name for your website and buy it. Then you want to pay for hosting - the computer your website will live on.

There are thousands of great options, but I use Namecheap to buy domains and ASmallOrange to host them. Next, you point your domain name from Namecheap to ASmallOrange, which takes about 3 minutes. Then you log into your new account at ASmallOrange and click on the "Install Wordpress" button.

If this sounds too complicated, remember that I have a step-by-step explanation with screenshots and images on my website to make it super easy for you. It will take less than fifteen minutes to do all of this.

Just going through this basic process will provide you with an Internet property to develop. You get a feel for what it's like to write a blog post that the world can instantly see. You will see the moving parts of a website and what all of that means. Starting with a blog is great because it gives you that first feel of how the Internet operates. That's how I started and accidentally built my first fan base (and lost that job)!

I run contests all the time, and one of them is a thirty-day blog challenge. Everyone builds a blog at the same time, so you get a sense of solidarity and community. There are always cool prizes for people who finish the challenge. The dates for the next contest are always available on my blog.

66

WEBSITES

The ability to build and develop websites is extremely valuable in the online world. There are plenty of ways to make money online without ever touching a website, but this gives you a significant level of control over your destiny. If you are running a business through a Facebook page, and they decide to cancel your page, you're out of business.

I like to remove as many vulnerabilities from my life as possible. If you can set up your own property (and there's a reason I use that phrase), you have a skill that people will pay you for. If you look on UpWork or Fiverr, you will see little gigs to set up blogs all the time. Being able to do this yourself saves you from hiring someone else and gives you a basic skill that you can sell.

There are other great platforms if you want to get into e-commerce, but most of the websites out there are built on the Word-press platform. It's robust, constantly updating and best of all - it's free!

This is a cool skill because it's simple to do and delivers real value. Once you know how to do it, you'll be surprised how many people around you mention that they are struggling to get a website up. It's easier than you'd expect and a great way to offer value as you build your network.

67

GRAPHICS

Setting up a website isn't everything. The Internet has changed a lot in the last few decades. Before Windows came out in the early 1990s, computers were entirely text driven. There were a few graphics programs, but to start one you had to use the Disk Operating System, which was pure text. If you didn't know the right code words you couldn't do anything.

Now, people expect websites to be sexy and beautiful. I can't tell you how valuable the ability to do basic Photoshop tasks is. Whether you are designing banner ads, simple book covers or Facebook banners, the skill of graphics comes up all the time. You don't need to become a graphic master unless you're artistic, and you want to leverage that talent. What you want is the ability to do basic tasks. Move stuff around, remove backgrounds, and create basic images. These skills are great for two reasons.

The first is that you won't need to hire people to do them for you. Some tasks that take me less than ten minutes cost $20 to pay someone else to do. The problem is that you spend money hiring someone to do something like that, and it takes them a few days to do it. You're never going to be anyone's top priority at that price. You go right to the bottom of the queue. The only way to get fast results is to hire someone full time, and that's not a direction you want to go in for now.

The ability to maintain momentum when you are working on something is crucial. There is nothing quite so frustrating as working on your Facebook page and being frozen waiting for a graphics person to finish a banner you need to use. Your time is super valuable, and we want to focus on efficiency right out the gate. These skills are really about something you can dabble with quickly and learn today.

If you don't have Photoshop, there are tons of great alternatives. I don't use the current iteration of the software. Nothing I'm doing requires the latest technology. A few years ago, they shifted from letting you own the software to renting it. I'm not interested in paying a monthly fee for the rest of my life, so I just stick with version 6. It's part of my plan to control costs. If I am going to pay an extra ten, twenty or thirty bucks a month, then I need to make that much more money to cover that cost.

There are some great alternatives that you can check out on my book page. Dabble with each of them and see what direction you want to go in.

68

SOFTWARE

As you begin to build your business online, every idea you have on the potential of software will change forever. Maybe you only use a few pieces of software daily – stuff like Word, GarageBand, and Skype. There's much more software out there, and people are willing to pay massive amounts for some tools.

For people that get into foreign exchange and money markets, there's software that costs tens of thousands of dollars. It's very easy to get into deep debt just buying such powerful software. Some software programs have simply amazing sales pages that convince you there is a magic button you can press to make a ton more money.

Here, I just want to share with you a few basic tools that I use every single day. These tools are the foundation of my business, and I'll explain why. I cover a lot more tools that I use at ServeNoMaster.com/book.

The first tool is more about techniques. I don't think in straight lines very much. I tend to think in circles. And it turns out that I'm not alone.

Some genius invented this idea called mind mapping. It's building outlines in a circular format. For some reason, it works perfectly for my brain. I have been using mind maps for quite a few years now. All of my video products and bestsellers, including this one, started out in a mind map. I love how easy it is to move things around and change the order. That's very valuable for me.

There are a lot of expensive mind mapping tools out there. I have received emails about mind mapping products that cost over five hundred dollars. I'm the first person to invest money in my business if there will be a positive return on that investment. I'm rather obsessive about efficiency. Before I make a purchase, I ask myself a simple question, "Will this tool make me more money?"

The tool needs to either increase my productivity or accelerate some other part of my process. I have used two mind mapping tools in my life. I use one on my iPad that cost 99 cents when I bought it. It's called iThoughtsHD. I think it's ten bucks now, so I'm not giving that a firm recommendation.

I recently shifted to mind mapping on my computer, and it's a lot faster. I now use Xmind. This tool is fast, very efficient and doesn't cost a penny. It's a great place to start your creative processes. I have used mind maps to create things that have generated more than $10m in sales. And my total lifetime investment in mind maps is less than a dollar.

The most important tool in my arsenal, hands down, is Scrivener. It is so much more than a word processor. I grew up on WordPerfect. Then somehow that software disappeared, and I used Word. I used Word for probably twenty years. I am no power user by any means. I can only do very basic tasks in Word. The problem is that it's built around the mindset of a typewriter. The way it approaches writing is frozen in the 1800s. I make most of my living from my writing. I write from 2-5,000 words an hour. People come to me all the time when they need content, and they need it FAST. I take writing very seriously, and when someone told me about Scrivener, I was extremely skeptical. Like a fool, I thought that all writing programs were created equal. You get a blank white page, and you start putting in words. I couldn't have been more wrong.

Scrivener is like a mind mapping word processor. It's kind of amazing. It comes with a simple tutorial that takes about an hour to work through. At that point, you know everything you need.

It lets you chop up your book into little sections. I have each module of this book as a folder and then tiny subsections. It makes it very easy for me to jump around. I can work on this little section and jump to the beginning and write something there. I simply love that ability. Before, I was scrolling up and down looking for different sections. I spent a lot of time trying to go back and find sections to make sure they all tied together. It's also as easy as drag and drop to move sections in your book around. I do that a lot too. It's very hard to know in advance how each chapter will look, so the ability to move things around without the awkwardness of cut and paste is brilliant.

This software wipes writer's block away - permanently. Most people dream of writing a book, but the thought of sitting in front of a blank page staring at that flashing cursor while trying to write an entire page is terrifying! With Scrivener, you chop the project into tiny chunks and focus on one at a time. When I'm trying to hit a target word count, I can create a small word count for each section. The more you break a project down into pieces, the easier it becomes.

Now you're not writing War and Peace anymore. You're just writing one 500-word section at a time. This helps your productivity. Scrivener isn't free software, but it does cost much less than Word. It costs forty bucks most of the time, but if you keep your eyes peeled for a sale (usually synced up with National Novel Writing Month), you can often find it for half price.

I know it might seem like I'm nickel and diming here. I'm just focused on cost control. That's one of the fundamental principles of my business – or any business that wants to go the distance. If you're laser fastidious in the small things, it's much easier to maintain that focus with the large things.

The third piece of software that I use a lot is something you might be able to wait on. I record a LOT of training videos. You get to watch me doing something on my computer, and you can follow along. Or I use beautiful graphics and do a voiceover. To do all of this I use a piece of software called Screenflow 5. Each new iteration costs around a hundred dollars, depending on sales and promotions. I have been with them since version 3. This software is available only on Mac. The PC equivalent is called Camtasia. I think the PC software is superior for certain tasks, so don't let this software determine what computer you buy next.

The software simply records what I'm showing on the screen at the same time as it records my audio. If you want to do anything with video, then this tool might become quite important to you. I waited almost eighteen months before I upgraded from version 4. I'm paranoid about upgrades. I don't want to be a tester for a piece of software that I use for work.

I've probably sold hundreds of videos that I made using Screenflow. There are two reasons I finally upgraded, and both have to do with saving me time. With the newest version converting my finished product to a video is faster. The software is smarter and a task that took twenty minutes in version 4 now takes twelve minutes. That alone is reason enough to upgrade.

The other great ability is batch exporting. I know that sounds boring and technical. Let me put it this way. Before, I had to record a video, edit it and then click the "Export" button. Then it would take the software twenty minutes or more to convert that into a video that I can upload to YouTube. I would make each video and then have this awkward downtime where I couldn't do any work while it was "exporting" my video. With this new batch ability, I can record and edit my videos all day. Then at the end of the day, I tell it to convert a whole list of videos in one go. I go to lunch or dinner and come back, and they are all converted. Batch exporting increased my efficiency by another forty percent at least.

It used to take two to three days to finish projects I can now complete in a single day.

Whenever you are looking at a piece of software, pay attention to cost and how it will help you. I only switch to new versions of stuff with a real reason. I only upgraded my Screenflow when I read an article about that batch export feature. I knew that would improve my workflow, so I pulled the trigger.

There are a lot of other tools that I use, and I talk about them more on my site, but these are the three tools that I use nearly every day in my business. They are my staples. I can't imagine running my business without them, so I wanted to share them with you here.

You should at least grab Xmind today because it is free. Every single person I convert to Scrivener tells me how it changed their life. It's a massive boost to time and efficiency. You might not be able to afford Screenflow or Camtasia right now, but that's ok. You can try out a program called CamStudio for free. I haven't personally used it, but a lot of people I know say great things about it, so it's a great place to start. It allows you to get a feel for the process and make some videos.

X

WHY DO SO MANY PEOPLE FAIL ONLINE?

Only those who dare to fail greatly can ever achieve greatly.
- Robert F. Kennedy

69

ALL BUSINESSES FAIL

According to recent news reports, 8 out of 10 entrepreneurs who start businesses fail within the first 18 months. That's a whopping 80% failure rate. If you're looking to beat those odds, you've chosen the right person to pair up with – I've beaten those odds time and again. But what separates me from all the people who fail like that? What makes me so unique?

There is a trend that you may have noticed in this book. When it comes to controlling costs, I'm as serious as a heart attack, and every software purchase, every training course, every person I hire, I treat as a serious financial decision.

How do I do that? I always try and wait until I'm going to use something before I spend the money. Right now I'm thinking about a course that I want to buy that will teach me a new skill I need. I know 100% that I will use, implement and make money from this training. But I haven't spent the money yet. I won't be able to start that project for a few weeks, and I don't believe in spending "someday money."

I watch a lot of those television shows about businesses that run into trouble and need outside investment. You almost always find that they spent some money poorly, and that has come back to haunt them. They hire too much staff, move into an expensive office or spend too much money on unproven inventory.

I am very good at making money. At this point in my life, generating income is like breathing. Controlling the money going out, however, is something I had to learn. I have to be very active about controlling my spending. The first time I met my accountant, she nearly had a panic attack. She asked me how much money I make and at the time, I had no idea. She asked me what I did when I ran out of money, and I told her that I just make more.

It turns out that that is a rather naive approach to finance. When you're a rainmaker, it's easy to fall into the path of spending whenever you feel like it. But that road eventually leads into trouble. I have a friend I spoke to just an hour ago. He's much more financially successful than me. He runs a great business with one weakness - he's always had only one source of customers. After five years of making millions, that source just dried up. He has to close up that entire business. Fortunately, he has two alternative revenue streams, and he's about to make a new one grow. But all of the people working for him in the dying business are in trouble.

His business had a single point of failure, and it eventually caught up with him. It stinks because he's a great guy and mentored me, but I wasn't entirely surprised. Rainy days are going to come; controlling costs and opening diverse revenue streams are how you prepare for them.

I see some businesses that are making millions of dollars in sales and yet their profits are in the thousands. They are so inefficient that it's shocking to me. When I bring in money in that volume, I want at least 40% of it to be profit. Depending on the nature of the project, the profit could be as high as 80%. That's the way we want to approach money.

I would never go into any business with substantial costs up front. That's just not my approach to life. Some people do that and succeed. But the ones who try that method and fail end up with tens of thousands of dollars gone from their life.

Don't assume that you will make the same money next month that you did this month. I see that a lot. It's what happens to most musicians and athletes. The average career in the NFL is three years. Yet the players all spend money like it's going to last for forty years. They buy awesome cars and mansions and jewelry. At twenty-seven the run is over, and they collapse financially. I'm not hating on athletes; I feel really bad that they get such bad financial advice.

If the average player took his three-year salary and figured out a way to live off it for forty years, then he would be living well for a long time. Players wouldn't live like kings in their twenties, but they also wouldn't end up living like paupers in their thirties.

Musicians are even worse. They build up huge entourages. They blow big money on the album. They buy amazing houses. They make all these financial decisions because they believe the second album will do as good as the first. They think that because a few bands have been killing it for sixty years, they can do the same thing. How many bands can you name from even five years ago that are still making the same money today? Most second albums stink. And of the bands who pull that one off, most of them tank on the third album. It's just the nature of the beast. I'm always diversifying and working on different types of projects to protect myself from a stinker.

Control your costs now so that when the rainy day comes, you don't drown.

70

MOST PEOPLE WON'T EVEN FINISH THIS BOOK

The majority of the population are cows. I bet you thought I was going to say sheep, but that's not quite accurate. If you take a cow and feed it and give it a place to live, it doesn't care if there are fences around it. Cows willingly walk into slaughterhouses because they have a complete slave mindset. I don't mind cows. They're animals, so I don't begrudge them that behavior.

But as people, we should do better.

The ability to read and finish books has been steadily declining for decades. In 1978 there was a Gallup poll on how much people read. Only 42% of people had read 11 or more books in the past year. But by 2014, that number had dropped to 28%.

According to one statistic I read, 57% of all books that people pick up are never finished. That means the majority of you won't even finish this book! Those statistics are even worse for non-fiction books like this one.

The fact that you've made it this far into the book is impressive, and you are already in the minority. I think that the inability to finish projects, such as reading a book, is quite common these days. Entrepreneurs surround me, and the ones who succeed are most often the ones who don't give up. If you finish this book, you have an excellent chance of grabbing the freedom you crave. But if you don't even finish reading the information you paid for, your odds plummet down to zero. How can you do something when you don't read the manual?

71

SHINY OBJECT SYNDROME

This inability to finish a task or training is often combined with this syndrome. My puppy has this problem. He will enjoy playing with one of his toys but if my daughter grabs one of the other ones and makes it squeak he will run after her for that toy. If that wasn't funny enough, the same thing happens with her. Nothing makes her want a toy like someone else playing with it – even if it's the dog!

We always desire that which we do not have. The grass always seems to be just a little greener.

These problems are all tied together. I love when someone goes on a show to ask for money to start a new, unproven direction for their company. They have been killing it online, and now they want to move into retail stores. They had a great food truck, and now they want to sell frozen food. They always have the same reason for the new venture - they WANT to. They are motived purely by desire. They never have hard numbers or any proof that it will work. Making money online is nothing like making money in retail. The numbers are different, and the process is so much more complicated.

That is why I have told you over and over that I don't sell physical products. I won't touch anything that you put on a shelf. Not because it's terrible, but because it's outside my wheelhouse. I would have to start at step one if I wanted to learn that. Why would I want to rewind my life six years and have to start over again?

Shiny Object Syndrome affects online entrepreneurs every single day. You can ask anyone trying to make it in online marketing how many ideas they have tried in the past year. Those who are struggling try something new every month or even every week. Do you think you can build a successful, self-sustaining business in thirty days? That's pure insanity. You can make a quick buck sometimes, but something that lasts takes much longer.

Chasing the next great book or the next great idea will keep you from success. If you know ten percent about making money fifty different ways, you will make nothing. That is what that knowledge is worth. I like new projects as much as you, but you must approach them linearly.

Let me give you a final example.

By the time you read this book, my podcast will be live. But today, while I'm writing this chapter, I haven't even started on it. I've spent the past year only working on Amazon and Kindle projects. That has been my primary focus. Now that the business is rolling along, and I have that business mastered, I want to open up a new arena. I love the nature of podcasting, so I've wanted to start one for a while.

If I had tried to learn both Amazon and podcasting at the same time at best, I could expect middling results, but most likely I would have two failures.

Stick to one path until it works. Don't step into this all-too-common trap. Distraction is the death of a small business.

72

CONTROLLING RISKS

There is no such thing as a risk-free business. Every project can die. I write a lot of books and make lots of income from that. But if some new super disease came out and took away everyone's ability to read, or if Amazon radically changed their rules, I would be toast. It's not very likely to happen, but the risk exists. That is one of the reasons I'm making more and more video products, and I always put out an audiobook version. I am protecting myself from even the most unlikely risks.

When you start a new business, you are filled with optimism. Every time someone points out a risk point, you tell them that it won't happen to you. That somehow you are different, and that particular snare won't catch you.

When people don't believe in the risks, they are more likely to spend money now because they expect to make it back next week. This cycle can work for a while until something happens and a planned check doesn't arrive.

The biggest risks in business are that nobody will show up and that nobody will want to buy your stuff. I meet people all the time who think their ideas will sell like hotcakes. You see these people on television all the time pitching their ideas. They invested their life savings in buying ten thousand units of their idea, but they have only sold four of them to friends and family. That's a terrible statistic. They are so blinded by how much they like their idea that they ignore the feedback and think their critics are just being mean.

They let hope blind them to risk.

I hope by now you are noticing how these mistakes are all interrelated. One often leads to another until the business collapses. The best way to control risks is to approach them analytically. "What will I do if this danger occurs?" This question is how you stay prepared. I see people all the time who make amazing stores. They invest in the retail game, but when no customers show up, they have no idea what to do.

They think having great products at a fair price is enough.

If they started out thinking that customers might not show up, they would have developed a backup plan in advance. I have released many successful books on Amazon, but history does not predict the future. That's why I launched my podcast at the same time. My podcast provides tons of amazing content for free and generates traffic in a different way. I'm also running a contest on my website giving away thousands of dollars in prizes. This amazing contest is a third way to bring in traffic. The more reasons you can create for people to come to your website or store, the better your chances of overcoming risk. That's why I'm giving away thousands of dollars in prizes this month on my website.

I can't help you eliminate every single risk from the universe, but I can help you to minimize most of them. When you control your costs and stay focused, the less it hurts if the whole thing comes crashing down.

73

WHY I WILL NEVER OPEN A STORE

A few years ago, one of my relatives told me her dream of opening a fashion boutique, and she came to me for advice. I was happy to help because I'm always fascinated by breaking into new markets. I spent a few late nights and developed a plan for her to become a social media trend spotter and blogger. My plan would have her at six-figures within eighteen months. Her response was, "Great, so then I can use that money to open my boutique?"

Her response blew my mind, so I performed some research and found an article all about the cost of opening this type of brick and mortar business. This lady opened a consignment shop in Texas, and it took her thirty thousand dollars just to open the doors. Most people think that's the total startup costs. Those are people who go out of business in less than two weeks. She will have to pay for electricity, salary for her staff, and that lease every single month. So we have upfront costs but also continuing costs that she has to pay even before the store makes any profit.

My relative wanted to open up that boutique in New York City, not a consignment shop in the middle of nowhere Texas. So you can expect each of those costs to be at LEAST triple. Don't forget the clothes in a boutique cost a lot of money. You have to buy all of that stuff up front.

So let's say she pulled it off. She spends around $100k to get her dream shop off the ground. The shelves are stocked, and the clothes look awesome. She gets the amazing team that a store needs for success. Is all of that enough to win?

First of all, you have a ton of complicated sales taxes. Every time she sells something part of that has to be tracked because that money belongs to the government. The cash in the register at the end of the day doesn't all belong to the store. Second, she needs at least a few months of savings to keep the store running. How will she pay the rent on her apartment and her lease and the salaries for everyone? She has to pay those people whether the sales come in or not. It takes time for even a successful store to get off the ground.

The other risk is the one that scares me the most. What if she stocks up on something that people don't want? What if she buys the wrong size in something? Something that cost a few hundred bucks is now worth toilet water. Any business where you hold stock is full of massive risk. According to Fortune magazine, she should be looking for a 3.2% profit margin. That's the best-case scenario, and that number alone is enough to send me running for the hills.

The last and scariest thing is the idea of signing a commercial lease. People sign up for three or five-year contracts. If their business fails, they still have to pay that money. Now they're in a legal nightmare and might have to declare bankruptcy. I don't like a business that requires debt to get started and has the risk of litigation if it fails.

If I spend $100 and get back $103, I'm not going to be a happy customer.

My relative wanted to take a massively profitable business that I would help her build and pour that money into a project that would at best earn her 3% back?

If that's your dream, then nothing I can say will help you. I'm not here to help make your bad idea dreams come true. I'm here to help you figure out a path to escape the job you hate and make enough money to do what you want with your life.

Please don't take smart money and dump it into a dumb idea.

74

THE DIP

It's the worst possible time to quit – but for a few deep psychological reasons, people do it all the time. The first ninety-percent of a project is done, but that last little bit proves to be too much. So people quit - right before the project was about to turn a profit.

It sounds absurd, but it's entirely natural. You're always going to hit moments where you are frustrated, and it feels like things aren't going the way you want. You will have moments where you are tempted to seek outside investment or just walk away from it all and try something else.

I can't promise that building a business is all roses and sunshine. It's just not. It's competitive! If you step into the boxing ring, you are going to get punched. If you understand that ahead of time, you can adapt and conquer. If you run into those days where you feel burdened, frustrated, annoyed and overwhelmed – KEEP FIGHTING! The people who quit too early are the ones stuck in cubicle farms.

There have been plenty of times when I have thought about giving up working for myself. I've even sent out resumes before when I just felt overwhelmed trying to do it on my own. Fortunately, nobody wants to hire me, so I have no choice but to endure. I haven't considered working for someone else for at least four years, so don't worry, it's not like I was blasting out resumes yesterday! We just all have those days where we want to pass on the responsibility to someone else, a boss or a guru or a master that will take care of us and show us the way.

But the terrible and life-affirming truth is that there's nobody that can take care of you like you can take care of yourself.

You must have faith in what you're doing. Look at other people that are succeeding where you want to succeed. Be able to envision it for yourself. Listen to their advice and drown yourself in stories from people like me. Eventually, you will break through the dip to the other side. Some people find amazing success right out the gate, and some have to spend months slogging before they hit their pot of gold. The important thing is to keep fighting until you get what you deserve.

There will be moments when you want to quit, but never give up. You're not fighting for me – you're fighting for yourself and the people you love.

75

BURNING THE BOATS

In 1519, a Spanish explorer named Hernán Cortés arrived on the shores of what is now called Mexico. He had six hundred men without armor, sixteen horses and eleven boats. That's not much of an army. But he was determined to conquer the Aztecs and take every nugget of gold he could find. Outnumbered, he made a single choice that changed history. He burned his boats. His men had two choices - win or die. Quit was no longer an option.

Let's sidestep the dissertation on imperialism and focus on what matters. This concept is still strong today. In Navy SEAL training, when you want to quit, all you have to do is stand up and ring a bell. When a sailor walks over and rings the bell, it's over. But something interesting happens at that moment. At that moment, the instructor walks over and offers a second chance. Some people take that chance, but not one single person who rang the bell has ever completed the training. I know some Navy SEALs. Those guys are tough on a level that I can't even describe. Having a drink in a bar with a buddy who can kill you faster than you can sneeze is pretty crazy.

The guys in training, the ones who succeed? They start out with two options - win or die. The guys who entertain the option of quitting never finish. Once someone rings that bell, the possibility of quitting is real for them. Some things are so hard that even knowing quitting is an option makes it inevitable.

I'm not saying you need to light your boat on fire or hang a bell in your garage. I'm not demanding that you quit your job and call your old boss something so horrible that going back to work is impossible. When I got into this game, there was no boat behind me. I was fired. With a hard kick in the pants. I had to succeed or go hungry. Many people find success when they have no other options. Right now you can keep your job and keep that revenue stream, but there comes a time when you have to leave that career behind so that your new project can explode.

Eventually, you have to light up those boats if you want to be free.

It's scary leaving your job and knowing that those paychecks are gone forever. But there's an advantage too. It puts you in a place where you have no choice but to succeed. That level of motivation will separate you from the masses.

XI

SKILLS

You know, like nunchuck skills, bow hunting skills, computer hacking skills. Girls only like guys who have great skills.

- Napoleon Dynamite

76

SKILLS HAVE VALUE

This is one of the rubber meets the road elements that will determine how many options you have for building your business. The more skills you have, the more you understand the work your hired talent is doing, the more you can customize things, the more you can get individual tasks done faster and cheaper – as long as you're not the spoke at the middle of your whole business.

Certain abilities can make you money faster. We already talked about the services you can sell to other people. But here, I want to focus on some skills that are especially valuable in the online world. When you finally burn those boats, I want you to be able to make money fast when you need it.

In this section, we'll dive into specific skills that you can use and market online. Some of these might seem quite obvious while others may be things you've never thought about before. Earlier, we went over some baseline skills that will help you get into the game. These skills are the next level. If you have a natural ability in one of these areas you can specialize and leverage it to great success.

Many of the skills that we let drift away after high school are quite valuable these days. Take some time to figure out which skill fits you best or simply the one you could see yourself enjoying. If you hate writing, trying to become a master writer is going to be awful, no matter what course you read that told you it was easy or that you should. There's no reason to focus on something outside your natural skill set.

77

WRITING

Writing happens to be my core competency. It's the thing I'm best at. I can write fast, and I can write very well. On average, I write over 2,000 words an hour. A lot of that number depends on if I'm going back and forth from a mind map. For this book, I'm writing closer to around 5,000 words per hour. As a comparison, most famous writers averaged 250-350 per day. While that is great if you can write books that millions of people want to read, writing at that speed won't keep your family fed unless you are one of the top writers of all time.

The problem with being a writer is that everyone on Earth thinks they can do it just as well as you can, and even if you are a great writer, you still have to find an audience. That's tricky work, and even with all my success, I know that not every book I put out there will be a hit. Sometimes the audience just doesn't connect with a message or something else happens in the marketplace that sinks my book's chances. At the end of the day, business is a democracy, and your audience gets to vote.

You don't have to be the best writer in the world. I'm certainly not. I'm very good at two aspects of writing. I'm one of the best researchers in the world, and I write fast. I can study a subject and learn enough to do it or teach it in a few days. I know how to assemble that knowledge from tons of different sources into a fantastic book without plagiarizing in under a week. When the big boys need something done amazingly quickly, I'm the one they call – and they pay a premium because they know I can do it right.

Sometimes I get a flat fee, and sometimes I get a royalty. In both cases, the ability to write generates income far in excess of the time it takes me. You can leverage the ability to write efficiently into many revenue streams. There is always work for native English speakers who can write. In this field, you start out around 2-4 cents per word. If you can write 1,000 words per hour, you will make from 20-40 dollars in that hour. As you get faster, you make more money. If I were in perfect form and wrote out 5,000 words in an hour at that four cents a word price, I would make $200 an hour. That's ten times more than you make starting out. Writing is a linear marketable skill; as you improve, you can quickly make more money.

Eventually, you will take over more control of what you write, creating stuff that interests you, building a reputation, and going from a flat fee to a percentage of the action. You can start putting books on Amazon. And if you want, you can follow my system to learn exactly how to do that.

I teach new writers all the time how to write fast, find a big audience, and make a living on Amazon. Writing is valuable in a host of different ways. Writing articles, blog posts, PDFs, training manuals, content for slides and so much more. All of these are jobs that need writers all the time.

There is loads of content on my site to help you make money writing very quickly. You can easily make a few hundred extra bucks this month just writing articles for an hour or two a day. This is the fastest way to make a little cash online and the only requirement is that you speak English.

78

SPEAKING

Is your voice pleasing to others? If you are a great speaker, then you want to focus on this area, because you can make a top-flight living online without writing a single word. The first category of speaking skill is purely based on sound. If you can read in a way that just sounds great, there is so much voiceover work out there; it's insane. You can make a living doing voiceovers for small videos and even longer presentations. You can find jobs on the sites I list at servenomaster.com/book as well as some blog posts walking through getting into the business. With a little research, you can find dozens of places to put your voice and generate inquiries. I hire people all the time to read my audiobooks for me. There's a good chance you are listening to some other guy's voice reading this to you right now. Sure I sound ok, but reading an entire book without making any mistakes? That's hard!

When you are in the audiobook game, you can get paid part of every sale or a flat fee just like a writer. When you voice an audiobook through Amazon, you get 50% of every sale that comes in. That means you and the author both have skin in the game and are both motivated to get as many people onto that book as possible. It's a great symbiosis.

If your talent is more inclined towards thinking on your feet and being entertaining, starting a podcast could be an excellent idea. If you need to follow someone, I break the whole process down on my website. I have a blog post series breaking down my entire process from idea to execution. You don't have to be alone creating a podcast; you can record interviews with other interesting people with a fan base, and suddenly you have one of your own. Their followers will listen to your interview and become your newest fans!

You can also present webinars professionally. Someone else makes the product, and all you do is present the product's story and explain the benefits live on a group phone call. You can use your affability to generate sales and connect with a whole new batch of customers. A webinar is basically a dry run for a live presentation, so your voice can easily be your ticket to the big stage. Think you can get booked to do a live seminar if you sell $50,000 of a product online? Absolutely, and it's much easier than it sounds!

You can also do what I do. Record videos of your voice with something on the screen. That's how I make the majority of my products, and I do it for other people as well. When you get really good, you also get really fast. You can make money quickly and easily. Eventually, you can make a training course teaching people how to follow in your footsteps. That's what I did when I made my video creation training course. I show you the exact process that gets me paid a thousand bucks for a single day of work.

As it is with most skills in this book, once you succeed at doing it, you can teach it. You can train other speakers and coaches and presenters to improve their talent and achieve higher levels of success with their presentations. My course only teaches how to make amazing videos; if you put together a training about improving language or sounding amazing, I would love to promote it on my website!

The sky is really the limit when you begin to grow and nourish your speaking talent.

79

COPYWRITING

Out of all the skills, we're going to talk about in this chapter, copywriting is probably the most valuable skill. A good writer can get a flat fee of $25,000 for a writing project that takes a month to complete. Many of the top writers show up at a company and simply get a percentage of the growth they generate. You can earn fantastic residuals.

When you can write words that make people want to buy, the sky is the limit; you can dominate your field and live any lifestyle you want. You can accelerate this skill when you combine it with networking. That is like throwing gas right onto your money fire. You can have the best product in the world, but if the sales letter stinks nobody will ever see that product. Copywriting is an incredible skill that you can develop rather quickly. Will you become one of the top copywriters in the world in less than six months? No, but you'll become a top gun, guaranteed.

Here's how to learn copywriting for free and become a master fast.

If you want to get good at copywriting, just research and find a list of the top 100 ads by a great copywriter from history. Every night, for the next six months, copy them by hand for 30-60 minutes. That exercise is pretty tough, especially if you haven't been writing that much since high school. Your hand will cramp, and your eyes will get sore, but you will learn SO MUCH just copying other people's work, it'll blow your mind. I have an explanation of that entire strategy along with links on my website as well as a podcast episode that covers how to make money during the learning process.

Copying by hand activates the part of your brain that learns through experience. Most of the great copywriters have used this exercise to get where they are. It takes time and a little hard work, but the payoff is worth it.

The ability to write words that sell is universal. When you saw the Amazon page with this book, that entire page is copywriting. Every bit of the book cover, the title, and the description are all carefully designed to get you interested and buying. Every single page of Amazon is that way, and copywriters generate every television commercial and sales letter you run into in the wild. Copywriting is a skill that you can use forever; as you get better, you can sell it, leverage it, or simply use it to sell your own products.

The ability to write good copy will separate you from the masses. If there is only time for you to pick one skill from this entire book, then copywriting is what I highly recommend. You can quickly take control of your destiny and every month raise your prices. I know people that started out charging $97 to write a short sales letter who are charging more than $10,000 less than a year later. You really can work your way up. As your talent improves and you deliver quality results, you can take more and more control of the projects you work on and the prices you charge.

Eventually, you can create your own courses and sell them using your amazing copywriting skills. Remember, our end goal is always passive income that earns money while you sleep, and having multiple income streams is always a winner.

80

GRAPHICS

I have some basic graphic abilities, but when I want to make something that's amazing, I have to bring in specialists, Photoshop wizards that know what they're doing. I made a mockup of the cover of this book myself. I then sent my idea to three different designers to see what they could do. One of them took my idea across the finish line and created the fantastic cover that you can see before you.

Having a broad range of skills is important - my basic skills allow me to show someone what I want. Then their superior ability takes it to the next level. I hire designers for book covers, banners, flyers and a thousand other tasks. There's always work for someone with graphics talent. You can start doing work for other people and just honing your skill. As you progress, you'll get faster, and your income increases with your productivity. Then you can start filtering your clientele and raising your prices.

The next step is to start making graphics products. See what we're doing with all these skills? Learn, and then get paid to share and teach. I buy bundles of graphics all the time. Whenever I need a particular type of arrow or a different simple image, I pull it from one of these resources. The ability to make graphics packs can lead to big business.

You can get into the book cover game as well. You make a ton of book covers, and you'll figure out the types of designs that do well and move away from the stinkers. You can then create a pack of book cover templates that people can edit on Photoshop at home. You make those templates once and sell a package for $97 all day long after that. It's a great way for a graphic designer to earn residual income. I have purchased several of these templates, and I used one to create the back cover of the paperback version of this very book!

Nearly every marketer I know has a pool of graphics that they use all the time to look professional at the drop of a hat. And we're greedy, always looking for something new – it doesn't have to be epic quality, just good and new.

The great thing about graphics is that you get two shots at every customer. The first time they see your offer, they might buy it in case they need those images at some point in the future. They are stocking the cupboard.

All those people who don't buy on the first pass will come back later when they realize they need that specific image. They need that fancy red arrow, and they come back to your website to buy it. The price might have gone up, but they still pay, because people need resources. In the long run, it's cheaper than hiring someone, and it also helps you expand your pool of potential clients every time you make a sale.

81

VIDEO

Right now, the world's #2 search engine isn't Bing or Yahoo – it's YouTube! As the Internet speeds up, more and more people are switching from text to video. Like I told you earlier, literacy rates are plummeting. People want their information mixed with entertainment and video is the way to achieve that. People want to stream video pretty much all the time. Speaking their language is just smart business.

No matter your passion, you can start up a YouTube channel as you hone your video skills. You can start a political channel and put up a video once a week talking about your favorite news stories. You can set up an account on Patreon, where people fund you for each video you produce. Get sponsored by ordinary people at $1 a video and you can quickly replace your income as you build up that fan base.

It's a pretty cool way to structure your business and requires no advertising on your channel. You can also just make videos and run YouTube ads on your channel. It's similar to Google ads, probably because Google owns YouTube. They just put commercials in front of your videos sometimes, and you get a small piece of the action. You can also drive fans to your main website where you sell DVDS, shirts or just about anything else.

There's a lot of money here, but you've got to realize that you MUST create stuff that is emotionally satisfying and consistent. You can't be boring – you need strong ideas and opinions. When you have a strong opinion growing your channel is a piece of cake.

The tremendous opportunity right now is in making videos for children. The top videos I watch have about a million views. The ones my daughter watches are creeping towards a billion. That's where the big money is. It's a whole new ball game. You can make videos with cartoons and old nursery rhymes and children's songs that are no longer in copyright. Children will watch a video they love hundreds of times and each time your view count ticks up. Those big numbers mean big advertising dollars.

My daughter's favorite videos right now are regular people who dress up in superhero costumes and walk around their house. They don't do any talking and just mime different stories. I don't get it, but when I see the views these videos get, I realize that these people are geniuses. They bought a costume for fifty bucks, played around in their house with their friends and now they are the most popular people on YouTube.

If your talent runs toward the video production end of the spectrum, you can turn a spare room in your house into a studio. Setup a green screen and let other people come over to record at your place. As you get dialed in on how lighting works and the best way to remove green backgrounds you can create training courses for people. The best investment I made early on was in a course that taught me how to make professional quality lights from parts at the hardware store. I learned about lighting color and temperatures. It was so valuable to me, and I know other people love courses like that too.

You can do a lot online with video, and it's a growing medium. You can make live action videos, cartoons or just do like I do and record your computer screen. The ability to create content that looks great is very valuable.

In between, there are people with film editing skills. If you can edit well, splice together video, and sync up voices, there are always people looking for that talent on the sites for freelancers. Getting great with video is a cool skill that allows you to do more than just sitting at a keyboard all day.

82

NETWORKING

I've already covered the networking skill in great detail, but I just want to drop a little reminder. This skill can and will turbocharge your business, and believe it or not; you can get referrals all day long from an active network.

You can even turn networking itself into a business. You go to conferences (or even network online) and keep building up your Rolodex of contacts. When you connect two people, you get a piece of the action. This is a real job that is called being a JV recruiter. There are other names for it, but it's a serious business. Many people will gladly offer you a taste of the action for a great introduction.

Relationships are everything in this game, and the ability to form connections with people quickly will make them want to spend time with you, work with you and make money with you.

Some people get into online business because they think it means they never have to communicate with another human being again. It's possible to live in isolation like that, but if you want to make big bucks, then networking is a powerful skill to develop. Many people who work online are socially awkward, so if you can get out of your shell and provide the social lubricant, they'll love having you around.

83

SALES

I have a guy working for me that has one skill – and that's sales. He gets a percentage of all the business he brings in. I'm in a time zone 13 hours ahead of most of America, and it is impossible for me to connect with people on the phone during most times. If you are a strong salesperson, then start looking for opportunities right now!

There are companies always looking for sales consultants. You come in, help them streamline their process and improve their numbers. Then you take a fat check and waltz on out the door. So how do you get a foot into this game? You start out freelancing, helping people write and refine their phone sales scripts. As you build up a reputation and get more testimonials, you can take on bigger projects with bigger paychecks.

From there, as always, you can turn your skills into products - teaching a growing crowd of people how to improve their sales skills. You can become a master of the sales world, just by teaching basic principles to your customers.

Whether you want to work for other people or yourself, the ability to sell is invaluable. When you are on the phone with potential clients, the art of sales is critical. Getting someone to hire you and pay what you are asking for is all part of the craft. There are tons of courses on sales, and a lot of what I shared about favors and building relationships will help you to get started. You can learn even more about persuasion by reading the blog posts on my site.

XII

ARBITRAGE

Risk comes from not knowing what you're doing.
- Warren Buffett

84

BUY LOW SELL HIGH

Arbitrage isn't the easiest thing in the world to master, but it is easy to learn the basics. You buy something from one person and sell it to someone else for a higher price. Most of our economy is built on this model, and if you own a computer, I can guarantee there was some arbitrage along the way.

The same factories in China make almost every computer. Then they slap on different logos so American companies can resell them to people like us at a massively inflated price. Rather than complain about this practice, let's get in on the game.

Whatever skill you decide to develop, arbitrage is an excellent way to grow your business. Instead of writing books yourself, you build up a stable of ten ghostwriters and pay them four cents a word while you get paid six cents a word. I know that seems like an absurdly small amount, but over time that will be a huge amount of money. You've also just turned yourself into management. POOF! Your days as a grunt are over!

Earlier in this book, you read about people passing up my six figure ideas? Odds are you read those passages and thought, "Wow, those guys were dumb to pass up a genius idea!"

Okay. Your turn.

This is an easy business model that you can develop in less than a month. Start an arbitrage business by advertising on college campuses. Those kids are used to writing all day long, and they'll be more than happy to make a little extra change by putting in some extra time. As your staff graduates, flakes out, moves on, whatever, you can keep expanding by hiring new freshmen. As people who work for you get better and raise their prices, they can go out on their own while you bring on new people to train up.

Is this the only form of arbitrage? Absolutely not! Just think of where people are buying and where you can get it done well for less.

85

IT'S NOT JUST ABOUT THE STOCK MARKET

Another form of arbitrage is like a super powered version of the stock market. On the stock market, you only get to place one bet at a time. The only way to scale is to place larger bets, and you have very little impact on what actually happens. You purchasing a stock won't raise the price unless you buy huge volume. With pure online arbitrage, you can increase your scale – and do it quickly.

The most popular way this works is with the CPA market, where people pay you each time you get them an email address from a new person. What you do is buy traffic from a source. There are tons of people selling traffic, everywhere from ads on Facebook to direct mailings. You can pay someone to send an email you write to their customer list. So you send that traffic to a CPA page. Let's say you're following in my footsteps and doing gift cards, like I did years ago. You get $1.08 for every single email you get submitted. Each time a person fills out the form, this is your reward.

When you start running traffic to the offer, you keep tweaking. Eventually, you get it to point where you spend $1.03 for each email submit. So if you spend $1.03 a day, you will make 5 cents a day. This seems like small potatoes until you scale up and spend $10,000 a day for $500 profit! This is the real arbitrage game. To get into this one, you want to start out with a little spending money, ideally around $5000 in your war chest. With a budget of around $100 a day, you can learn to master this game in 3-6 months. It takes a lot of the basic skills we covered earlier to create ads that convert and get as many people as you need to go through your arbitrage funnel.

This is a great business if you're technically minded and like looking at stats. As you get better numbers, your days flip from red to black, and you can start scaling. This is a fun game that has all the excitement of the stock market, but unlike Wall Street, you have the ability to impact and control your results.

86

GLOBAL MARKET

People have been dabbling more and more with something called geographic arbitrage for the past few years, where you hire someone in a foreign country to do your work for you. You can hire a full-time programmer in India for a few thousand dollars a month and then resell that work for ten thousand dollars a month. You have to know what you are doing to ensure that the work you resell is up to snuff. I've dabbled in this game in the past and sometimes the people you hire will turn in crap. If you don't catch it during your quality assurance process, it can get past you and all the way to the client, and rest assured; one bad outsourcer will CRUSH your business if you don't stay on top of things.

You should only resell stuff that you understand. You can apply this principle to almost any industry right now. Whatever your current day job is, there is a good chance you can hire a foreigner to do all the work for you for a fraction of your salary, especially if you work on a computer. Companies are sending jobs offshore all the time; you might as well get in on the game.

In this business, you become the manager of a team. You have to keep track of your workers and make sure they deliver quality work on time. You will find that you do well with some countries and poorly with others. That's just figuring out your strengths and weaknesses. It's something interesting in the new global market and allows you to turn negatives in our economy into advantages.

The more you explore online, the more you will get a feel for this concept. I would start by providing a service that you understand, and then expanding your offerings by hiring people internationally.

Stay in the middle of the flow, and you ensure that any product goes through you. Your clients don't care who does the work; they just want the work done well and on time.

To get more advanced with this technique, you can take advantage of expat communities around the world. Where I live, there are tons of Westerners who just want to chill out and live the surfer lifestyle. There are people like this in locations all over the world. They take jobs in local hotels, cafes, and restaurants. They're tour guides and surf instructors and English teachers. So they are living here making a much lower wage than they would back in their home countries. They just want to make enough to support their lifestyle.

I hire people around here all the time. I have an awesome girl on my team who is doing bigger and bigger projects. She works hard, and I keep training her on more advanced skills, sometimes in person, and sometimes over video. We see each other in person once a week, when she comes to pick up her salary. She works her own hours, and I don't track her time at all. I give her a timeline, and as long as she delivers on schedule, I don't care if she works eight hours a day or two. I apply the same principals from my life to the people who work for me. She gets to work in between the best surfing times and has complete control over her destiny. Before working for me, she was working in a cafe with a schedule and making less money for more hours.

This is a more advanced arbitrage move. You get Western workers at something approaching international prices. She's been earning my trust for months now, and I'm hoping to let her run an entire revenue stream soon. I just love working with people that I don't have to babysit.

I also like hiring college students. They have access to academic pricing on software, they don't demand super high wages, they're eager to learn, and best of all they have access to all those overpriced academic journals. I use a lot of cutting edge science in many of my products. So I want to read and quote journal articles from this year. Some of those magazines charge ten to twenty thousand dollars a year for a subscription. That's pure insanity. A college student gets them for free because the university pays that exorbitant price.

Hiring a virtual assistant from another country can cut down your time in the office massively. You can get a full-time assistant who speaks English for under $500 a month all day long. A good one will manage your schedule and organize things for you like a champion. They can do research and set up all your meetings. Just having someone to manage your personal affairs and remind you it's time to pick up the dry cleaning before a black tie affair can be priceless. Don't assume that offshoring staff is only for the big corporations.

87

THE POWER OF THE DOLLAR

The dollar is the strongest currency in the history of the world right now. I'm not a currency trader, but I do track how it competes with other currencies. I can't give you exact numbers because they change all the time, but in the past ten years, the dollar has gotten stronger against the Euro, the Canadian dollar and the Australian dollar. You can hire someone for even less in another country because of that exchange rate. I pay people in local currency all the time. It allows me to pay them a real wage and the strong dollar means it costs me even less. A good exchange rate can save me 25%.

Putting all the technical details aside, pay attention to the power of your currency. Knowing if your money is strong or weak right now should affect your hiring decisions. You don't want to hire people in China because their currency is tied to the dollar. You'll never find an edge there. But many other countries provide great opportunities. When a currency is weak against the dollar, you want to hire people from that country.

Most people ignore this little step, but it can cut down your business costs very nicely over the long-term. And it's like I've been saying throughout this book – rich people get rich by controlling what they spend. There are quite a few countries that use dollars in the stores, like Panama and Cambodia. When the dollar is really weak, you hire people in these countries and avoid dealing with exchange rates.

The key to working internationally is understanding the exchange rate and pouncing when the time's just right.

88

KNOWLEDGE IS THE MOST VALUABLE RESOURCE

There is nothing more valuable in our society right now than knowledge, and people will pay a premium for it. Right now I'm about to pay for knowledge on two topics. Today I'm going to buy something about training a Golden Retriever and something on teaching an infant to swim. I'm not just a producer of knowledge; I'm also a consumer.

The knowledge business is so strong because most universities are a garbage fire. At your average college, maybe five percent of what they teach has any value outside their halls.

They don't teach you how to manage a credit card bill, fix a broken washing machine, splice a wire, negotiate a discount, get bumped up to first class or anything else that would improve the quality of your life. The education system totally sucks, and it won't get better in my lifetime. They're entrenched in their ways, and that means it's a great time to slide under them and teach stuff of value.

If the education system in America improved, it would probably knock down my business. But thanks to all those unions, there will never be meaningful reform, and I'll be making money for a long time to come.

The great thing about the online world is that you can learn something, make it work, and then train people to do the same thing. I learned how to master Amazon by emptying my wallet for dozens of courses. I think I own nearly every course on the market. Then I filtered out the garbage that no longer works and added in tons of my personal techniques. My system uses the foundations from other places, but my experience allowed me to improve that system over and over. This approach to knowledge, learning and then doing, and then teaching again, means that you're always up to date.

Believe me; you have knowledge within you right now that people will pay desperately for. It's all about finding the right approach.

Just now, I stopped writing to find those two resources. I found a woman who has a great DVD on teaching infants to swim. Unfortunately, she hasn't updated her website or product in years. She offers no instantly downloadable alternative. Why would I want to pay extra for her to ship me a disk that can get damaged, especially since it's an international delivery? I wanted to buy her knowledge, but that one little mistake lost the sale. If a competitor entered the market with the same knowledge in the medium I prefer and offered instant delivery, they could capture that sale.

The only reason you are reading this book is that I have knowledge within me that you desire. You have knowledge within you that I desire too. No matter what your profession or hobbies, there are things that you only learn when you get deep.

Most people have no idea what the different codes on plane tickets mean. If you work at the airport dealing with shouting customers all day long, you could leave that job behind just by teaching those same people how to interpret the secret codes on their tickets. So many people would pay to learn how to better navigate the nightmare that air travel has become. And the kind of people who would pay for that knowledge would pay a LOT because they're busy. There are tons of somethings that you think are nothing – and figuring out one of them could change your life forever.

XIII

FINDING A MARKET

What new technology does is create new opportunities to do a job that customers want done.

- Tim O'Reilly

89

WHERE ARE ALL MY CUSTOMERS?

So many new companies are altars to the ego of the founder. It's a big mistake, and I see this in big and small businesses all the time. They put their store in a neighborhood they like to hang out in, stick low-rent stuff in "classy" (read: expensive) areas, and stick a singles bar in a neighborhood where everyone is married. If the main reason you do something is that it feels like a good idea to you or reinforces your self-image, you need to step way back and reassess.

Trust me; there's nothing worse than having a beautiful store in the wrong neighborhood. You want to find out if there is a market before you start anything else. You could put out fantastic training and techniques for getting pagers cheaply, but nobody would care because it's not 1992 anymore. You want to be sure that there are people who like what you want to talk about before you walk too far down the path.

One of the first people I tried to help out had a music store. He was a friend of a relative, so I met up with him to help him find customers. He had great gear at great prices with one of the coolest websites I've ever seen. He paid thousands of dollars for that website. Unfortunately, it was coded in Flash, which is now essentially a dead programming language. Go to a flash site on your iPhone and nothing appears because iPhones can't even read that language. Neither can Google. So Google was sending him no traffic.

One little mistake kept his market from finding him. You want to find your market where they are. Figure out what's working, and don't try to outsmart your customers.

90

INTEREST

Here's how I start my research process:

The first thing I do is fire up Google to see if people care about the topic. Before I started my blog, I began searching around for terms that apply to my site, such as: quit my job, escape the 9-5, digital nomad, and a bunch more. I wanted to see if other people were performing similar searches. Some powerful tools show you how often different searches are performed every month. That's a good baseline to see if people even care about the term you're targeting.

If your idea is only getting a thousand searches a month worldwide, then people just aren't thinking about it yet. That book you're working on about teaching your dog to smoke might be an innovative idea, but you don't want to jump the gun. When you perform these searches, you want to check out the different sites that appear. First of all, you're going to get information, second, you're going to get a sense of the emotional appeal. What's being sold? How are they selling it?

I also love to find a good forum on a topic. The questions people ask in a forum can be very telling, and again, you're getting people's real language, their true emotion. You want your website or product to answer the most popular questions.

In dating, it blows my mind, but a large percentage of the questions on the forums I check are about long-distance dating. Men and women frequently write about being in multi-year relationships with people that they have never even seen a picture of, let alone met. I thought that everyone has a digital camera or a friend with a smartphone by now, but the frequency of that question showed me a need in the market, and it led me to write a book about long-distance dating.

You will be surprised by what you find. Your ideas as someone who knows the topic won't always match the questions that people ask the most. Whenever I talk to someone running a small brick and mortar business or something physical, I ask them about the most common questions that customers ask them, because that's the main thing that should be on their website. This is where the knowledge of your market can be invaluable.

If you search and scour the Internet, but nobody is talking about your topic, you might have an idea that won't go anywhere. It sometimes happens no matter how much prep you put in, but it's way better to try and find out before you sink any money into a bad idea.

91

COMPETITION

There are around twenty excellent websites that are all about what I'm teaching in this book. There are blogs about quitting your job and living the full-time traveler lifestyle. Some are about becoming a nomad, and some are about moving somewhere new and staying there. Instead of freaking out that other people stole my idea, this gets me excited.

You don't want to be the first one with an idea. If nobody is talking about it online, your product might just fix a problem that nobody has. The fact that there is enough traffic to sustain twenty other people talking about my topic is great news. There's already an audience connecting with the concept.

Those guys are your competition. They're also your friends, so spend some time studying them and seeing what you like most. Personally, I have no interest in re-inventing the wheel. I look at all the sites similar to my idea and pick out the things that I like. Maybe I like the colors on one site and the organization of another. I look for elements that I think work.

There's always room for other people in the same industry. Because geography does not limit my customer base, I always see other people in the same space as a good thing.

I was doing a search this morning, and I looked at more than thirty websites for editors. Almost all of them were just terrible. Images in the wrong places on the screen, broken code, no way to make contact even if you DID want to hire them by some miracle. They also had a broad range of pricing structures without any justification for why some had a higher price point. Most of them didn't even have examples of their previous work or a walkthrough of their process.

The structure of these sites threw me off.

There is a big opening in that market for a skilled editor who has a website that isn't garbage. The large quantity of sites tells me that it's an active and growing market. The bad quality of those sites shows me my opportunity. If I have a better site, I can start to siphon off some of their business.

The more you understand the strengths and weaknesses of your market, the faster you can build a strategy.

92

DO PEOPLE BUY BOOKS ABOUT IT?

Maybe you have a magnificent idea. You want to help people quit tobacco and save some lives. That is a great idea! So you write a book about quitting snuff. The only problem is that nobody has taken tobacco that way since the Middle Ages. It baffles me that people don't check Amazon before writing an entire book.

I like to restrict my searches to just Kindle books because the numbers are much more accurate. I need to see at least five books on that topic that are in the top thirty thousand Kindle books, or I move on. That number is my litmus test for a subject. Books ranked below that are making pennies.

A perfect example is teaching your baby to swim. When I taught my daughter how to swim, she was two years old. I wanted to get a book on the topic for some ideas. She hated the water and would scream like crazy any time she got near it. One of my neighbors even came over to yell at me because of all of the noise. But I couldn't let that stop me from trying.

When I was eighteen, a fellow college student drowned right in front of me, and it's a memory that haunts me to this day. To make matters worse, I live on an island where there are pools everywhere. Teaching my child to swim isn't a luxury; it's about safety and protecting her life.

Things have changed since then, she's a very strong swimmer and totally comfortable in the water. In fact, she's the best swimmer of all the kids her age, and when she was in a kayak that flipped over last year, she was completely fine.

When I was researching techniques on teaching her to swim, I started with Amazon. I discovered books that I could tell were produced by other marketers. They just had a look that I can recognize. They all had a mixed bag of reviews. When I looked at their rankings I realized that sales were abysmal - people don't want to teach their kids to swim from a book. It's a much more popular search term on Google and YouTube. I learned that people wanted videos, not a book.

This year I began teaching my six-week-old son to swim. I did some research, and most people think that's the earliest you should start. Again I turned to Amazon to find a good guide. There is only one book there worth reading, and even that one was filled with too much Eastern philosophy. I don't want to teach my kid the oneness of all things or show him how to float in the space between raindrops. The little dude just needs to learn how to swim! That's it!

What I learned as a customer is that there is a deficiency in quality in this space. I might put a book out about teaching my kids to swim because I see opportunity. I already have books about raising my children, so a book about swimming would fit in that brand. It would be a follow-up book. Someone buys one of the more popular books and then buys the swim book later. My research showed me that the market is not popular, but that if I do it right, there is a little bit of opportunity there.

One of the reasons that I prefer to research on Amazon is that people are there looking to buy. People search for stuff on Google, Bing and Yahoo all the time, and they're in research mode. They are looking for free information. That's fine. But converting those people to customers is quite hard.

Every single person on Amazon is already in buy mode. Nobody is there to kick the tires. The information you get is a little more streamlined. You are moving beyond pure interest, and into the realm of people wanting to pay for information.

93

RESEARCH STRATEGY

Some topics are only popular in video, and some are only popular in books. The results you get from each of your different research strategies will be different. That's why you want to examine multiple places. Some topics do well for me on the Internet, but the numbers on Amazon are abysmal.

When I first started selling services online, I found the majority of my customers just by posting ads on Craigslist. There's less traffic, but people only look on that site when they're ready to buy. I got a lot of traffic to my site through search engines, but the conversion rates were terrible – most of those visitors were in "lookie loo" mode.

Audiences exist in different places, and sometimes an idea fades away. Topics that trended last year may have faded away by now. This is the nature of the world, and it's why you want to stay on top of your market as you build your business.

If you understand the topics people in your audience care about, the questions they ask, and the products they buy, you'll start out ahead of everyone else trying to build a business online.

Way too many people skip the research phase and go right into a passion project. I'm all about passion, and that's a great place to start, but we want to focus on a passion that intersects with a real revenue stream for you.

XIV

CHARGE A LOT

The more expensive the better' is kind of the American way, and if you spent $600 for a sweatshirt, then that makes it better.

- Macklemore

94

GET PAID TO LEARN

Here's how it works for most people - when you first start out, you have no knowledge and a limited budget. You build a website and create a product. You write blog posts and then try to get visitors to your website. You put in all of that effort and at the end if everything is perfect, you might start to make some money because these projects only pay out at the point of success. You're doing a lot of work for free in the meantime, and one little mistake can cause the machine to break.

When I was starting out, I wanted to learn how to rank websites on Google. So I found some clients who would pay me to rank their websites. I took that money and purchased the resources I needed. You can do the same thing. The great thing about this model is that you get paid up front. Instead of starting out in the red, you start out in the black. People are happy to pay you to learn something on their behalf.

If you want to find out how to rank books on Amazon, you can find an author and offer to handle all their marketing for the price of my Amazon course. You get the money up front, access to the training, and you even get a guinea pig to practice on. The great thing is that my system works; you will deliver the desired results to that client. It's a wonderful feeling.

This method is how you learn as a street fighter. You have to work your way to the top. The danger of starting a project with a lot of capital is that you start to throw it around too quickly. When people start projects with tens or even hundreds of thousands of dollars, it's easy to spend some of that money poorly. You overpay for courses and workers as you rush to that end result.

I met a guy at a conference once who was wearing a power tie like you wouldn't believe. I asked him how much to get a landing page put together. The market value of a tier 1 landing page right now, if you pay for the best of everything from the copywriter to the graphics is under $5,000. That's way more than I would ever pay, but I'm talking about if you hire the most expensive people and pay their top rates. I don't know of any possible way I could spend more than that. Normally, something like this should be under $500. But this guy looked me right in the eye and told me he pays $25,000 for landing pages all the time.

He's paying about fifty times more than he needs to be to get a quality product. And my first thought was not to tell him that he's getting ripped off. Why would I want to hurt his feelings when obviously he's finding ways to get a positive return on his investment? No, my first thought was that I would love to be his vendor. I could take that 25k and hire a team for 2-3k to do a crazy overpriced job and make a 20k profit every single time.

The other move is to become his consultant and offer to cut his costs down by around 80%. I could double his business value in a few days and still take a generous amount home.

This stuff is very common for people with big budgets. They don't know what anything costs, and they end up paying more than everyone else all day long.

Where I live, there are two prices for everything; one for locals and one for foreigners. Most tourists don't ever catch on to the system, and they happily pay the inflated price in ignorance. There is nothing wrong with that. If they pay a reasonable price and walk away happy, nothing bad has happened.

The real secret is to avoid being that person yourself so that you can control your war chest. Controlling costs is crucial. It's why I like to get paid to learn.

A few great things happen when you are getting paid to learn. You have to finish the fancy course you just purchased because you aren't playing with your money. It lights a real fire under your butt, and you'll feel a stronger sense of obligation to learn, implement and succeed. You also get a great testimonial from that first client. Getting paid up front helps this game to seem a little more real. Instead of chasing a magic rainbow, you now have very real cash in your pocket.

95

MY FIRST PAYCHECK

When I got started, I needed to make money fast. I had just been fired from my job, and now I had rent, a car payment and other bills chasing me. The ships were burning, and I needed to earn if I wanted to stay alive. I put up a barely passable website. The background was black, and the writing was dark blue. You had to squint to see what was going on, and reading the text was nearly impossible.

I made like ten thousand mistakes. People tell me that all the time now. But I did one thing right - I immediately started posting ads on Craigslist.

I posted my very first ad on Saturday and had my first client by Thursday. She handed me a check for $200, and I was in the game! It was such an amazing feeling. I have never worked harder for someone in my life. I shot videos of her operation. I jazzed up her website. I fixed tons of tech problems in her funnel. For her search terms, she had her website, two videos and several social media profiles all on the first page of Google by the time I finished. It took a ton of work and over time I realized how to manage time and expectations better.

I used to provide coaching in this same industry. I no longer do client facing work, so I was teaching people how to replicate my business model. The one thing I learned is that people have an incredible capacity for excuses. Guys would tell me that they can't start posting ads until their website is perfect. They can't let clients call them because they don't have an 800 number. They want to change the color of this and tweak that.

There's a reason I stopped coaching people like that. I tracked each of these guys for a year. They never succeeded. They refused to implement my training, and it broke my heart. You don't have to be perfect to get into this business. When your stuff is perfect and your ducks in a row you can raise your prices. But if you don't take clients you won't make any money.

I simply can't understand that mindset, even though that is how most people in our society think. You should focus on making money rather than excuses. They always told me that they didn't want to damage their brand. If someone sees your website, thinks it's garbage and doesn't call you - that is the same result as if they never saw you in the first place. No call means no possibility of a sale. Who cares about the reason?

You don't need to worry about your reputation this early in the game. So many small businesses talk about brand and reputation all the time. That stuff doesn't matter until you are moving millions of dollars around. You can change to an entirely new brand very quickly if you need to. Anytime I hear someone with a new business talking about protecting their brand or the value of their brand; I know they are about to make a poor decision.

When someone is online looking to hire someone, they are ready to take action. Let's imagine that I have a local small business and I want my website at the top of the search results so I can get more clients. I hop on the old Internet and search wherever I feel comfortable. Could be Bing, could be Google and it might even be Craigslist.

I go to the first website, and it looks horrible, so I move on until I find a website that matches my expectations. I call that number and hire them. I don't remember the names of the first six places. Why would I? Has their brand been negatively impacted? Of course not.

Your brand is only damaged if you take someone's money and fail to deliver. That is what brand is really about. Don't worry about having the perfect logo and the perfect website. Brand protection is not important. I would rather make a bunch of money.

You can take the same money-first approach to your first product. Put it up for sale and only after you have sales, start making it. There are a lot of products that are delivered as live training calls or webinars. Those people waited until there was a market willing to pay them before they invested the time and energy in actually making it, and that's a smart, efficient way to do business.

This is the next generation beyond simple research and a great way to ensure that you make money from day one.

96

NEGOTIATING

This might be the most important thing you learn in this chapter, so listen closely. The first time you step into a room with a potential client you have to negotiate. People like to get a good deal. If you let them squeeze down your price, they will. When you absolutely need that paycheck, and they can sense it, you better believe they will grind you down to dust. Nobody pays extra money out of goodwill. That's an imaginary thing.

"I can pay this guy extra money to make him feel good or I can get my kid braces."

What do you think he's going to choose?

The first mindset of negotiations is that whoever cares less is going to win. It's crazy, but it's true. There are tons of stories about great salesmen who will let a silence last for thirty minutes or an hour just to get the sale. People who have created iron personalities. They are playing to win the game. That's the right mindset when you go into a negotiation.

You start off with the razzle-dazzle. Show them what you have done for past clients and demonstrate your expertise. If you don't have any past clients – make them up! I made three websites when I got started. I made websites for three businesses that didn't exist, and then I got them to the top of the search results. They provided proof that my system worked. You can do the same thing with any other service. You should do demo work as fast as you can so that you have an actual portfolio.

Show your potential client all the money you are going to make them. Focus on how your work will benefit them financially. The more you can create a memorable character and play the role, the easier this becomes.

When I first got into the business, I would talk like I'm an underground tech ninja hacker who was fighting for the good guys. "The Internet is the Wild West, and you have two choices if you want to stay alive. You can pick up a gun, or your can hire a gunfighter like me. I don't like to lose. I'm not in the game to make your company grow. I want to crush your competition into the ground. That's how hard I'm gonna fight for you."

Can you feel how exciting that is? Who doesn't want someone with that mindset on their team? You can follow it up with a little taste of fear. "I'm the best gunfighter in this town, and I love my work. If things don't work out between us, that's totally fine. Once I'm hired, I only work with one client per industry. You seem like a great dentist, and if I'm on your team, then I'm your gunfighter. But if we part ways, and another dentist approaches me then I'm on his team. And I will do everything in my power to put you out of business.

There are no hard feelings, but I am a mercenary. I work for the client that hires me. My job is to get him more customers, and I notice a bunch of customers in the front of your building in the waiting room that would look amazing in his office. But honestly, I like the cut of your jib and I'd much rather empty out his office so you can buy out his practice at pennies on the dollar."

Can you see how there are now two reasons to hire me? I can help you and then I won't destroy you. You don't want to go too far down the fear path. Just explain that they are purchasing your loyalty as well as your expertise. That adds a lot of value. Once you've explained your value and what happens if they don't hire you, it's time to talk about money.

97

ALWAYS DOUBLE YOUR NUMBER

I have a simple model for my prices, and it shocks people who hear it for the first time. Each new client pays double what the last one did. Eventually, you find out the top price the market will bear. I started out getting $200 a month from that first client. I had asked for $500, but I was willing to take whatever I could get. The next client paid $500 a month, then $1000 and then $2000.

This is a simple model, but it's great because it leaves you a LOT of wiggle room. It's important to set your price far above your costs at this point in the negotiation. OR you can go the fixed price route, where you charge everyone the same rate and lock in at that. If negotiations terrify you, that is the other option, but you will make less money.

Once you have figured out your fixed price, you can skip the next section. But while you are figuring out the price, you want to keep doubling it until you hit the ceiling. I honestly thought that no one would pay more than $500 for my services when I started. I just kept saying higher numbers, because I wanted to see what would happen.

There are all these studies about how men are better negotiators than women. I've negotiated with a lot of women and noticed that it's really different. If you are a woman or even a man that falls into this area, let me help you. Many women I negotiate with start out at their final price. They start out at the lowest number they will accept, and then their feelings get hurt if they don't like my counter. When I'm hiring a woman for something new, and I have no idea what the market rate is, I ask her to name her price. Tell me how much you want per month. I am not sure why, but the women I have negotiated with always ask me to go first. Some men do as well. The thing that is unique is what happens next. When people pressure me to go first, and I'm the one paying I ALWAYS lowball, we're talking $100 bucks a month or something else like that. This is simply the inverse of when I'm the recipient. When I say this to a man, he laughs and says the real number he wants. When I say it to a woman, she gets personally offended and walks away from the deal altogether.

When someone lowballs you, don't take it personally! It's not a sign of some deep disrespect; they're just feeling you out. And the way you respond is instructive. Why would I want to work with someone whose feelings get hurt by a guess? I was asked to make a guess at the salary she wanted. Why wouldn't I guess a number that benefits me? I worked with a guy a few years ago who wanted ten grand a month and a huge percentage of my business. We parted ways, and he's doing great now. I have no ill will. When a deal is not right, you should be able to walk away without being upset.

If you attach feelings to a business deal, you will always make a poor decision. This applies to men and women. I don't negotiate when I'm angry or sad. If someone lowballs me, I know it is not a personal attack. It's just business, and if you can't separate those two feelings, you're going to really struggle. The more you are willing to say ridiculous numbers the better you will do. I have cut prices down by 80% and gotten paid more than 400% more than my asking rate just by throwing crazy numbers out there and waiting.

I was once paid four thousand dollars to upload twenty videos to YouTube for someone. I did it all in one day and just took the rest of the month off. I named a crazy price, but to them it seemed reasonable. We both walked away happy with our results.

I'm not a tier one negotiator or dealmaker by any means. I just follow a simple formula. It has been consistently successful for me for a very long time. If you are afraid of hurting the other person's feelings by asking for too much or offering too little, it will hurt your bottom line. Over time, those little things add up.

I've had people say really horrible things to me during negotiations, but it's water off my back. I can see it as the attempt at a chess move that it is. And thus I ignore it.

98

LET THEM TALK YOU DOWN

The reason I like to inflate my price is that every client on earth wants to go back to the partners or the spouse and brag about winning the negotiation. If you walk in with no room to move, they are stuck. They might pay your price, but there's no room for them to feel like a winner.

I remember my craziest negotiation. I was at a car dealership, and I razzled them, and I dazzled them – slideshow presentation, lots of quotes, high energy. They were so excited that the whole team was chomping at the bit. At the time, my top client was paying me $1,000 a month.

So I told them my price was $10,000 a month. And then I froze. And if I said another word or even twitched I would reveal how crazy that number was to me. Because I started off there, they assumed other people were paying me that. It's imperative not to speak after you say the price. Let the other dude go first. The first person to speak after the moment of silence usually loses.

Some people get nervous and start negotiating against themselves. That is a classic mistake. Let the silence speak on your behalf.

Those guys were shocked but I walked out of that room with a check for $2,000, and they were high-fiving like you wouldn't believe.

They got their gunfighter at an 80% discount! They got to feel like amazing winners who got a great deal. I got a check that doubled my last one.

Allowing people to talk you down makes them feel really good. The great thing about it is that some people just accept your initial offer. Now if you feel antsy about all of this, you can look at what your competitors charge and be 10% less. Then you can have the mindset of "the price is the price." You act like a big store. Do you walk into the mall and ask for 10% off of a toaster? Of course not. That would be ridiculous. That is the mindset if you have zero interest in the negotiation game. Just pretend that you work for someone else. Your boss set the price, and you're just telling the customer. You don't have the power to change the price. That mindset can keep you strong when people are trying to knock you too low.

99

BE READY TO WALK AWAY

Walking away is one of the most vital skills you have to develop – just saying NO can add so much to your wallet and give you so much peace of mind. I can't tell you that I've walked away every time I should have. I've walked into bad deals and taken gigs I shouldn't have. I learned from my mistakes the hard way, and I'm just hoping that you don't need to. If you walk into a room, and you aren't willing to walk away, your client will crush you. You are utterly powerless, and that's a horrible place to be.

Sometimes you've got to demonstrate your resolve. When I was first taking on clients, sometimes I'd take a deal because I had a bill chasing me. It's a terrible place to be because you wind up with clients that don't treat you properly. I had one client who went to the same high school as me like ten years before me. He started giving me nicknames like I was a freshman and treating me like an employee. He thought that for $1000 a month I was a full-time employee. I fired him. Working with him in the first place was a mistake, and I learned my lesson.

If you aren't willing to walk away, at least fake it. You need to deal from strength or you'll get rolled over and over again and end up working for slave wages. You think you're desperate and miserable now – wait until you've got a schedule full of bad clients that barely pay you anything and heap on condescension and abuse by the truck-load. I also know some people that go too far in the other direction. They demand a fee that nobody will pay, and they go for months or even years without work out of pride. You have to do a balancing act in your mind, and there isn't a perfect solution.

Sometimes it's better to walk. If you take a low paying job, then you don't have as much time to find a better client. You don't want to establish that you have a low price in the market because this can curse you for a long time.

Five years ago I sold full-length courses for $7. It's pretty hard to jump from there to charging a thousand bucks or even five hundred. People think of you as the seven-dollar guy. I had to stop selling courses for several years to allow that perception to reset.

Controlling perception for future income is just as important as getting paid today.

100

CHEAP CLIENTS ARE A NIGHTMARE

When I started out, my prices were way too low. I lost money by the truckload because I didn't know how to measure the value of a client. One secret I learned is that you need to know the value of a customer to your client. My first client was a masseuse. A new customer for her was worth $40 a month at best. She is in a high volume, low price market. That means that I need to generate at LEAST 13 new clients a month to justify a price of $500 a month. Otherwise, she's taking a loss.

But if you work with a dentist, each new client is worth thousands of dollars. Two new clients a year and they are in the black! Target clients who your work can help the most. It took me a while to learn that not all businesses make great clients.

The other thing you want to avoid is people who can barely afford you. The people who are spending their last five hundred bucks to hire you because they are desperate. That puts an enormous amount of stress on the relationship. There is an inverse relationship between how much people pay you and how often they call you. I worked with a massive land developer once. He called me once a month at most. He was my highest paying client, and I was getting him awesome results. One new client for him was worth millions of dollars. Talking to me literally wasn't worth his time.

When people really can't afford you, they will constantly call to check on their investment. They're scared and nervous, and they will infect you with that feeling. I once had a client who wanted to start a website that would be the "Facebook for Sugar Daddies." I thought this idea was terrible. It seems that if you are paying your girlfriend, that is the kind of thing you want to keep quiet, not post all over social media. They had this picture of an older man with a fistful of money with a finger in front of his mouth. He was making the "shhh" gesture. They wanted it on the home page and every day they would call me asking for me to make the picture bigger so you could see the money better.

On the very first call, I was hesitant about taking on the client. I am not a web design guy, so I knew I would have to outsource. I got some bids from teams I knew and doubled that price for my bid with the client. He agreed, and we got to work. Over the next month, he called me constantly. I ended up making less than a dollar an hour if you count that phone time. Finally, I delivered the completed project. He told me he was happy and wanted no more changes. So I paid my team and thought it was over. Two days later he was on the phone demanding a new round of changes. I had to hire a new team and ended up taking a loss on the whole project. I LOST money.

The lesson here is to avoid clients who seem needy and can't really afford your service. It's better to wait a week or two and get someone who can pay you a better fee and will be low maintenance. People with real money don't have time to micro-manage. They are too busy running their companies.

XV

THE ART OF THE EMAIL

I'd rather send out a mass email than hang posters all over the place.
- Todd Barry

101

EMAIL IS AN ASSET

The greatest asset in the online market is the ability to reach a customer multiple times. When someone visits my blog or reads my book, I have one chance to get them to take action. If I try to get someone to leave a comment, buy something, fill out a form, read another article AND give me an email address - none of it will happen. People can only handle binary decisions quickly; they want a yes or no option. When you add more options, the decision-making becomes more complicated.

Your first goal is to capture the email address. It allows you to create a relationship. You can send an email every day to strengthen the bond and begin to guide them down the path you want. The more touches you get with a person, the more valuable they are as a customer. This is how traditional companies view mailing lists. They want to send a postcard, but these days it is all about email.

With a large list of fans and followers, you can make money every single time you hit send. It's amazing the first time you send an email and watch the money start to roll in. It seems almost impossible until it happens to you.

When you're sending emails as a business, you have to approach it like a business. There are two ways of sending emails. The first is called a broadcast. It's the type of email you are most familiar with. You crank out an email and blast it to your entire list at once. This is great when there is a sale you want to tell everyone about or the launch of a book.

The other type of email is called an Autoresponder. Software controls this type of email. It sends messages based on the actions of someone on your list. For example, you can set it up to send an email to someone as soon as they sign up. I have my software deliver your free gift from the front of this book immediately. If I tried to handle that process manually, I'd be tearing my hair out, checking my email all the time, and I wouldn't have time to do anything else! If you want to see it in action, just click this link right now.

ServeNoMaster.com/quit

My software makes sure that you get an email with your gift instantly. I don't even have to be awake. You can program your software to send an email the next day as well. When a new fan meets you, they get a series of emails that warm them up. They learn about you and get to understand what you are all about. Over time you can mix in offers for products you have made or are recommending.

This is how you can make money automatically as you build up your mailing list, and it's one of the main tools you'll be using to build passive income going forward.

102

RELATIONSHIP AND RESPECT

The most important thing about emailing people, especially if you're using automation, is to treat your prospects the way you want to be treated. Trust me, if you stuff someone's inbox with ten messages a day, they're gonna hate your guts.

When you have someone's email address, you're establishing a level of trust. Break that trust and the relationship will never recover. So you should take your time and write emails that you would enjoy receiving. Don't copy and paste other people's stuff. Don't send stuff you don't believe in. And stay in compliance with the law – trust me, you don't want to be in jail telling people you were an email spammer on the outside... because those guys hate spam too!

People need to be able to leave your list by clicking a link that is at the bottom of every email you send. That's also the right thing to do. Keeping people on a list when they try to leave is just bad mojo.

Want a business that lasts? Build a tribe. You want an army of fans who like you, trust you and implement the advice you give them. That's my goal for our relationship. Believe me; I'm not here to sell you more stuff. You already bought this book and that means a lot to me. What I want is for you to succeed. I want you to find a path to your destiny. To escape the stress of having one boss control your finances. I don't need to make more money - I'm doing fine.

I want to be a part of your life for a while. So that when you finally quit your job, you email me. When you move to an island, you post a picture on my blog. That's the stuff that gets me excited, and it can grow my business more than a thousand people opening a few emails.

I send all my emails from my real email address. If you reply to one of my emails, you get me. You will discover that the people who email you most are the ones you want to invest the most time in. They are the ones who are serious about following your path. If someone is initially skeptical but takes the time to email you, they are looking to be converted. Once you convince them that your message can help them, they will become a fanatic. They'll support you and tell everyone they know about what you do.

103

AUTOMATION

There are two main pieces of software that I use for email automation. I explain all the differences in detail at ServeNoMaster.com/book

They both have great free trials, so you can get a feel for how they work before making a financial commitment. Honestly, they are both excellent. It comes down to your personal preferences as far as design and implementation. I use both companies for many projects, and they are the gold standard. Sign up for both free trials and play around inside.

Practice writing an email and see which editor you prefer. Then stick with the one that makes you happier. Don't use the fact that I'm giving you two options as an excuse for inaction.

You want to have this software in place before you start getting visitors to your new blog because your first fans will often be the most ardent followers. You don't want to miss out on the chance to start a great relationship.

There are only a few small investments you have to make to start building your online business, and an email provider is the most important. At the bottom of my book page, I show you the steps to follow after you have set up your blog. In Step Two, I walk you through the process of setting up your first email form on your blog. This is where people can let you know that they want to be a part of your tribe.

Once you have your software set up, it can do amazing things. You can change the messages someone receives based on which links they click in your emails or which products they buy. I often think of receiving my emails as being a part of a "choose your own adventure" book. The actions you take affect the story. Email should be interactive. It's a two-way conversation, and writing your half of that conversation can be a lot of fun.

104

THE BASIC SEQUENCE

When you write emails, there are a couple of steps you can take to improve the relationship. When somebody opens those emails for the first time, they're excited about what you can do for them – and they're paying as much attention as they ever will. You need to take advantage. That's why your first emails are all about starting the relationship on the right foot. Your ultimate goal is to train your readers to take action when you ask them to. People want to do stuff when they know you and like you; you want to tell stories about your personal life because that's how people come to feel a connection to you. Generic emails with nothing personal in them are cold and stale.

In every email, you want to plant hints about what you will talk about tomorrow. Start a story, but don't finish it. This is a technique that many books and television shows use called a cliffhanger. Tell stories that last more than one email and continue to build the suspense over a few days. There should always be a reason in today's email why they should open tomorrow's. We want them to feel connected across all the emails we send.

Be honest about what is going on in your life. People want to get to know you. The more you reveal your life, the easier it is for them to feel a real connection. The stories I tell in my emails are always about my real experiences. Just like all the stories in this book are about things that have happened in my life or are happening right now. In emails from a few years ago, I never wrote about having kids. That's because I didn't have any yet. Your stories and emails can be frozen in time. The realness doesn't change just because your situation does. It's the energy and truth that you put in at the moment of writing that matters so much.

In each email, you should have a link to something you want them to see. Sometimes it can be an amazing post on your blog, and sometimes it is something great you saw on social media. You want them to get used to clicking the links you send. If you are focused on providing high-quality content, then they will be happy they clicked. I use the same process in this book.

I created a bonus page at ServeNoMaster.com/book. The reason I made that page was for your convenience. It has links to longer stories, training, and the actual software I mention in this book. If you take the time to visit that page, you will discover that it has a ton more value to add on to this book. It has step-by-step explanations with lots of pictures explaining each process. I know many people are visual learners, and they'll discover how amazing that page is.

I didn't put that page together to make a buck. It's there to give a ton more value to my readers and reward people who sit down at their computer to do something instead of passively watching life pass them by. It's a way to pick up where this book finishes.

That page is the first step towards us developing a relationship. If you get used to visiting my blog, then we have a real chance to move forward together. Maybe you'll start reading my blog posts and continue to get inspiration. When you leave a comment, it'll lead me back to your blog.

That allows me to see what you're doing and to leave a comment. I can see the great things you are doing and tell my other followers all about it. We're building a relationship organically!

As you continue to grow your email business, you will run into all sorts of stuff you want to sell. Maybe your new book is coming out.

So you tell them about your new book and include a link. Because they are used to clicking your links, they will take that action. Now the action you have taught them has helped you to sell another book.

All this happens quickly and smoothly when you focus on value. Never promote a product you don't believe in. Never send an email you didn't write. Never lie to your subscribers. When you break that trust, you can never get it back again. And don't get discouraged if your stuff doesn't sing on the page. You can get better at writing emails and storytelling - I have some great resources on my blog to help you get better and better!

XVI

CONTROLLING TIME

How did it get so late so soon? Its night before its afternoon. December is here before its June. My goodness how the time has flewn. How did it get so late so soon?

- Dr. Seuss

105

WORKING ALONE

We were raised and trained in a world of oversight. For most people, the thought of total self-reliance is terrifying. The last time we did anything without a boss was homework back in school. If you're anything like me, you struggled with your final thesis or dissertation. Time management is challenging. They don't teach it in college, but they sure expect you to figure it out by the time you graduate.

Just sitting down at your computer is difficult. For most people, the home computer is a source of entertainment, not a productivity tool. We watch movies on our laptops, play games, check email and connect with people on social media. It can be very hard to decide suddenly that it's work time. It took me a very long time to create a firm mental division.

There are certain tools out there that force you to focus. But those don't work for me. How does closing all my other apps help me when my mind map is in another app? Now I can't see my notes. I also make quick idea changes on the fly and need to do research in the moment. I like to check for the latest statistics before I share them. I quickly just checked the most current statistical data on how many people finish the books they buy. The last time I looked at that statistic was a few years ago. Without a quick reference, I could have put an outdated number into this book.

Additionally, I write my blog posts online. I need an Internet connection to make it happen. Yes, some cool tools let you write blog posts offline and then sync, but that doesn't match my workflow. As I'm writing a blog post, I like to insert links and images. I like to handle all of those steps at once. Dividing the process into writing and then adding the images later doesn't work with my mentality.

Creating a place in your home that is a work location is crucial. If you sit on your bed playing games and then sit there to do work, your mind will struggle to know when it's work time. Plus, the people around you will disturb you all the time. People don't want to bother you when you're doing work, but if you're just looking at Facebook, they'll interrupt all day long.

Here's a little story – and this just happened half an hour ago. I'm working in the living room instead of the office today so that I can keep my eye on the kids. My girlfriend just knocked on the wall and called me into the other room. No explanation, she just said it was "a five-star emergency." So I look at the kids. Neither of them is on fire, so that's one star down in my opinion. I look at myself. I don't smell like smoke, so we're down to three. But I get up and see what's going on, and discover that the dog chewed up his collar.

I asked her if this was more important than my work, or if she would have come to the office to tell me about this, she said no. And of course, it isn't. Now, is my girlfriend sabotaging me to be a jerk? No. It is just psychology. People disturb us more when it is convenient. Creating a barrier that reminds them we are serious helps a lot.

There are an unbelievable amount of distractions in the world. Coming home from work just to start another job is hard. You need to start by looking for a rhythm that works for you. Some people wait until their kids go to bed and work in the garage. Other people I know prefer to get up for work two hours early. They put in time on their new project, and then they cruise into their paying job. People that can do that one often tell me about a productivity spike. These people are massively more efficient working at dawn.

When I first started working for myself, I was a total night owl. I was pounding cans of energy drinks until daybreak, typing like a madman. That's only something that works great if you are young and have no responsibilities. Now that I have a family going on, that red bull and pizza game is no longer an option. I get up before six in the morning now. On office days, I work out, chill with my family then walk over to my office nook between seven and eight. I work until three or five, depending on what I have going on. I like to finish while it's still bright out. When I go downstairs, I teach my son to swim and then I take my daughter out into the ocean for some father-daughter time. Separating work and family means those days are productive for me.

When I'm in the nook, I am in total work mode. I stick to one task at a time. I don't check email in between writing sentences. That would destroy my productivity. Having a single location that is my work spot helps me. I know that when I'm here, I work. When I'm not in this room, I don't do any work. I don't even use the Internet anywhere else in the house. I don't need it for anything, and it only offers me the temptation to "get just one more thing done" while I should be enjoying my family.

It's important to keep your family from creeping into your work, but it's just as important to keep your work from creeping into your family time. One of my great regrets as a child was how much my father worked. He put in a lot of late nights at the office, and I missed him. He made it to every game I had in any sport I tried, but even on vacation he always brought a big stack of work. I never understood his experience as a child. He was trying to provide for us, but now as the father myself, I don't just want to be with my kids, I want to be present in body and mind. And that's a big difference.

Think about a location and time that matches your work needs. That way, your body knows it's time to work when you sit down in that chair. You don't have to leave the house, but it might help. You can just start with having a chair that you only use for work. That's the first step. It helps a lot.

Everyone works with a different rhythm. I've tried a lot of office configurations. For a while, I had a little office that was near my house. I would lock myself away and get in the zone on projects. It was efficient, but I started drifting away from my family. I love my work so I can easily work twelve hours straight without noticing it. Working from the house means I see my kids a lot more. My daughter likes to sit near me and play with her educational tablet while I work. It's her version of working next to daddy.

You want to find a balance between efficiency and enjoyment. I am more efficient all by myself, but that's not the life I want to lead. My balcony spot is fantastic, but there are some downsides. I live in the tropics, so the sun is directly in my eyes in the early morning. I can't work out there before 10 AM because the glare is so intense that I can't see the computer screen. Later in the day, it's so hot that I need the fan on full blast. That means I can't record any audio; it will sound like I'm reporting live from a traffic helicopter.

Just inside the balcony, I have a setup with my recording equipment and my sound panels, so the audio is crisp. That's where I work when it's too hot, too bright, or I simply need the quiet of great sound. This is where I record every episode of my podcast. When I'm recording, my kids know to play downstairs and not disturb me, but otherwise having them visit throughout the day is a great joy.

You do not need to replicate my office setup. I have tried probably thirty configurations in the past. I kept trying until I found one with the right balance of productivity and joy.

Each of my work locations has different benefits and disadvantages, so don't look at your situation and decide to do nothing just because something's in the way.

106

ARE YOU FOCUSED?

This is a tough question, but the answer is "probably not". Most people try to focus on tons of different goals at once. People told me to quit smoking, build my business and lose weight all at the same time. Those are all great goals, but doing them in series led to my great success. All the people who try to do everything at once talk a big game, but in the end, they fail at everything. Our brains are designed to focus on one task at a time until mastered.

Right now you're probably thinking about ten things at once. You are thinking about starting your gig, but you are probably also thinking that a raise at work could be nice. You are thinking about your family, your body, and your spiritual happiness. Those are all great things to pursue. But you need to have a level of focus if you want to achieve success. There is a direct correlation between my level of focus and my income. Distraction always kicks my bank account in the butt.

And everybody thinks they're the exception to that rule. People brag about their ability to multitask all the time. But what does it matter that you can do five things well, but nothing great? I seek greatness in my life, and I want to associate with great people. That's where the real profit lies.

I'm going to talk a lot about habits in the next section. Defining a clear goal is the first step to habit success. I tried to break that down for you early on in this book when we talked about your financial goals. But let's be honest with each other for a second. Did you write down those numbers? If not, you can probably only estimate them now. I doubt you can tell me exactly what all three numbers were. If you don't write things down and bring them into the real world, then they don't exist. It's the physical that is the key to success. We live in a digital world, sure, but our brains aren't designed that way.

You might not be a fan, but I think that vision boards are great when done correctly. Most people cover a vision board with pictures of models or expensive cars. That's not a vision board. That's a vice board. It's a visual representation of your greed, your lust, your gluttony, and any other deadly sins you're into. That type of focus will never get you anywhere.

Instead, you want a board with specific goals on it. I want to make this much money in six months. Instead of six months, you can put a specific date on the board. That's what I'm talking about. Your goals should be written down, and then they should be in front of you. The pictures on the board should be symbols of freedom rather than consumerist trophies.

You should have pictures of your kids with their smiling faces. The sooner you succeed, the sooner you can spend more time with them. If you are single, you can have a map on the wall with the countries you want to visit marked on it. You can have pictures of a tropical island if that represents freedom to you. Freedom is a value worth pursuing, but stuff is something easy to settle for. Your brain isn't going to focus on getting you a bigger TV; but are you going to compromise on your spiritual freedom? If you're reading this, chances are you won't.

That is what makes this type of vision board so powerful.

107

TO INTERNET OR NOT...

The greatest productivity killer of all time is the Internet. It can do a lot of good, but distraction is just a click away. Within a single second, I can be watching a movie, reading a blog, checking out the news, or looking at photos of my friends. That temptation can be overwhelming. It takes a LONG time to train yourself to resist those distractions. You might find that you are more productive without the Internet on. You can accomplish many tasks without an Internet connection. I don't need to be online to write most of this book. I don't give myself the temptation. I unplug the router until I need to look up something specific.

I only have the Internet on to hop back and forth with the book page on my website. I want to be sure that the chapters and sections sync up nicely. I'm also listening to some streaming background music. But I could just as easily play a CD on the stereo. The Internet mostly poisons my work, and I kept the Internet off for about ninety-percent of writing this book.

The best solution for you may be to simply have times of the day when the Internet is on and other times when it is off. This comes down to your personality and the way you learn. Creating a hard and fast rule won't work for everyone. I only switched my Internet usage when the company changed their billing plan recently. They no longer offer an unlimited data option, so I have to pay for each fifteen-minute block I use. I thought it was a kick in the pants, but then my work improved. I'm writing almost twice as fast. Now I treat the Internet like a diminishing resource. I want to use it fast and efficiently and then unplug so those pennies don't keep bleeding out of my wallet.

There is not a perfect answer here. Simply asking the question will cause you to look at your behavior. The best question is, "Does having the Internet on right now increase or decrease my productivity?" It's funny because for most of the book I had the Internet off, but it's on right now.

Someone is messaging me on Skype right now, trying to get on board as an intern. I keep forgetting to check the messages because this book is my top priority. I have to manually train myself to only focus on this book. I keep checking my word count because that is the only goal I want to think about. As long as I'm focused on that single, super tight goal, I can block out distractions and work well even with the Internet turned on.

If you need to be online, try leaving off Skype and all your social media and anything else that sends out beeps, alerts, and push notifications. One little beep and twenty minutes can disappear. You always want to drive yourself toward maximum efficiency. If you can get three hours of work done in just two hours, then you've gotten a piece of your life back.

You don't want to be the person who spends twice as long working just because you're easily distracted. There is an overwhelming temptation to click away and do something fun. The more time you can work without the Internet on at all, the better.

108

THE 80/20 RULE

Not all distractions are entertainment based. Have you ever been driving and you notice a fly stuck to your windshield in the corner? All you can think about is getting rid of that little fly. It causes total distraction.

The same kind of thing can happen with a business project. Here's a good example. For some reason, the Goodreads logo on my social media links for one of my pen names looks too big to me. My computer swears that the circles are all the same size but that one looks bigger. It's freaking me out – and it would take hours to figure it out. It's a tempting path to go down.

In business, we seek perfection. But you'll notice in a few months that most of what you worked on didn't matter. Twenty percent of your effort will generate eighty percent of your income. It's hard to know which twenty percent at the time. Eventually, you will get better at noticing what the most efficient uses of your time are. At work, you have a boss or manager who is in charge of noticing when you're inefficient. I know that most of them don't do that very well, but at least there's oversight.

In the real world, all the ideas have to come from you – and a lot of those ideas are going to lead you into brick walls. Sometimes, you spend time trying to chase or recover time you already lost. There isn't a magic formula to predict when an idea is a bad one. It takes time and experience to figure that out. You can reach out to me for some guidance if you feel like you're hitting a wall. Just reply to any of my emails; I'll be the one who replies. I don't have an assistant who manages my email or anything. I like to keep my finger on the pulse.

The secret to success is to notice when you are doing things that don't make you money and then adapt. A lot of guys that try and replicate one of my local consulting businesses spend all their time making the perfect website. That's great. Too bad they all end up going out of business. They dedicate all their time to looking great when clients show up rather than trying to find clients. When I got my first client, my website was pure garbage. But it didn't matter. I made the sale. The sooner you see money in your pocket, the happier you are going to be entering this lifestyle.

You always want to look at a task and think about your bottom line. Will doing this task make me money? How much will it affect my bottom line? How long until I feel that effect?

I have two main types of projects that I invest time in. I take a lot of ghostwriting and contract jobs. I get paid fast for a few days work. If I take two ghostwriting jobs a month, which take me four to six days to complete, I can take the rest of the month off. Those two projects will cover all of my family's expenses for the month. I also work on projects, which are long-term revenue earners. Ghostwriting a book can earn me a few thousand dollars now or a few hundred bucks a month over the next few years. There is the balance between short and long-term income. Each task I work on throughout the day factors in that balance.

As you work for yourself, you will begin to sense which type of project you are working on. Many times we "work" our twenty just to fund our passion, which takes up the other eighty percent of the time. Be careful that you don't let the passion for your project suck away all the benefits of the twenty percent that is paying your bills.

109

THE DANGERS OF RABBIT HOLES

Distraction is a pain, but it becomes a cancer when it becomes your primary focus. You start off looking at that fly in the corner of the windshield, and it just gets more and more annoying. Pretty soon you are leaning outside your window to try and reach that monster. You aren't paying any attention to the road, and you flip your car. And what do you say when the cops show up? "Don't blame me! It was the fly!"

I have seen people spend days working on something that won't make them any money.

This has even happened to me. I already told you some stories about my friends screwing up, so I know it's my turn. A few years ago, I wanted to get into the royalty free photo business. I had a ton of photos and a few photographers working for me. I invested lots of time and money into that idea. My friends warned me that it was a bad idea; one had tried it already and failed. But I was stubborn - I kept telling myself that I was different, and my angle would work. Of course, that rabbit hole led to nowhere except broken hearts and broken dreams.

If you watch those television shows where people beg investors for money, you get to see rabbits sometimes. These people have spent years designing their product. They are in massive debt. But they have never sold a single unit. They haven't even tried to sell anything. They wanted the product to be perfect. They focused on an aspect of the business that doesn't generate any income.

Sometimes, I'll be sitting in my office scanning one of the local classified ads. Suddenly, someone posts a link in there to an interesting blog post. I don't notice it, but I burn up an hour doing nothing. If my work is done for the day, I need to shut down and go spend time with my kids. That's a much better use of my time. Part of that is that I like my kids. I never thought I would be a kids guy, but hanging out with mine is pretty fun. Who knew?

I tried getting to the point where I read zero news a day. That's my goal but for now, I only spend twenty minutes a day on the news. That's my limit. I mostly just need to scan the headlines to get a feel for what's going on. The thing about the news is that it doesn't matter. The only two things in the newspaper today that will affect you are the weather and the movie listings. The movie listings will tell you when the new Star Wars is out, and the weather tells you if you need to take an umbrella there. The rest of the "information" there won't affect what you do today.

So you want to set up a system that causes you to check on your efficiency. Some people use time-based systems such as Pomodoro. They pre-allocate their entire day into twenty-minute blocks. I'm a hard creative type, so to me, that feels too restrictive. I have a friend down the street living on the same island in my old apartment who swears by that method. I don't dislike it; I just don't use it. I tried, but it doesn't feel right to me. I recommend trying to find the right tool that fits the way your mind works. Unlike the education industry, I realize that people think, learn and work in different ways. It's the beautiful rainbow of our minds.

My writing method is to allocate a word count per day. That unit of measurement works better for me than a time block. It's hard to stop writing when I have a rhythm going just because an alarm is going off. Once I hit my daily goal for writing, I can start to wind down. Writing this book I have my baseline goal and my stretch goal, which is twice as many words. Some days I am just on fire, and I hit my stretch goal. A little flexibility works for me because most of my work is creative in nature.

You want to be sure that you invest your time wisely. I've done my best to set up a system for you that will protect you from chasing rabbits for too long. Just check with yourself at the end of every day, and ask if you wasted any time.

110

EFFORT VERSUS PERFECTION

There are two driving forces as we work on projects. The first is effort. How much time, energy and thought do you put into a project? There comes a point where more effort doesn't lead to very much more payoff. Let's say you build your website and it's ninety percent of where it needs to be. If you keep it that way, you will generate $1000 a month. If you put in another week, you can get your website up to 100%, and you will bump that monthly income to a whopping $1,001. Does it seem like all that extra effort is worth it?

We attach a psychological value to that extra percent, and we fail to make these calculations all the time. We don't notice when we hit that moment of diminishing returns, the time where more effort stops paying off. I'm not claiming to be better than anyone else here. This is something that I struggled with for a very long time. I don't want to say something is done until I get that last percentage point. It took me a lot of work to learn that some effort is simply wasted. There are things that I'll spend hours on that no client ever notices. It's work that made me feel good (at least once I was finished) but didn't affect my bottom line.

This is one of the killers for writers. I know writers who agonize and keep telling me that their book isn't done. They leave a book on the shelf for years because it's not quite perfect yet. If you stand on a street corner in Los Angeles and throw a rock, you will hit someone with a script. When you ask them if it's completed, they all say no. For some reason, starting scripts is very popular but finishing them hasn't quite caught on yet. They have a load of excuses, but it usually boils down to seeking perfection. People are afraid to let something out into the world unless it's perfect.

I can't stand grammar mistakes – they make me break out in hives. I'm terrified that I'll make a mistake in this book and get two dozen snarky reviews pointing them out and calling me a hack. Which sounds unreasonable, but sometimes people do that on projects of mine. Some reviewers are just mean for no reason. Maybe it's an attractive gimmick, or they like venting.

I just spoke to my friend about doing a punch up on this book. I wanted him to hop in and add a little jazz, a little eloquence. He would be focused on increasing your enjoyment rather than the educational aspect. He told me that he normally handles about a thousand words a week. I don't want to delay the release of my book for two years!

Finding the perfect balance between effort and perfection is hard. You don't want to put garbage out into the wild, but you also don't want to go broke because you're scared to press send.

111

CLEAR GOALS PROVIDE FOCUS

In the next section, I'm going to show you how to create goals that make winning and getting to those goals easier. There are tons of steps and systems people teach in goal creation, but I've narrowed it down to two things.

First, you have to start out with a very clear and specific goal in mind. Many people set the goal of "losing weight." That is way too vague. If you cut back on Burger King and lose 1 pound, have you hit your goal? You must have an exact target weight. That's one of the reasons I have been so successful with weight loss this year. I finally made it a priority goal, and I know my target weight.

Most people start losing weight and get around halfway to their goal. They exercise a little and stick to their diet for a couple of weeks and lost that initial water weight. They never wrote a goal down, so they just decide they meant to lose ten pounds, not twenty. This is the opposite of mission creep. Instead of going too far, people quit too soon. Before you can start building a habit strategy, you need specific goals.

My process for moving to this island started very loosely. I began traveling around the world and trying out different countries. I was planning on hopping to a new country every one to three months. I was single and making a killing online, so it was time to have a great adventure. After a half dozen countries or so, I met my girlfriend. It was random because I was only supposed to be in the country for a week. That was three years ago. I liked her so much that I decided to stay here and even have a couple of kids. But I can't live in a big city again. I needed this slice of paradise.

After a lot of research, we came here for a month-long vacation. It was a bit of a disaster - the Internet crashed all the time, and the power would sometimes go out for a few days at a time. Great scenery! Great people! Unfortunately, it's impossible to run an Internet company without Internet access. We spent the next year and a half trying other beaches and islands. Just trying to find the right fit. At the same time, I changed my business model. My old structure required me to be online every day to send out emails and communicate with people in real time. A single day with no Internet hurt my income.

That is a very serious obstacle. For that reason, I pivoted my primary business considerably. I moved into the Amazon game because books sell whether I'm online or not. I moved into a direction where losing the Internet for a few days wouldn't hurt me. This island became my clear goal, and I began to tackle each infrastructure challenge individually. There were two possible solutions to the Internet problem. The first was to spend around one hundred and twenty-five thousand dollars setting up a satellite dish. The Internet would have been slow, but I would have had control of my connection. I decided to shift my business model to adapt to my goal instead. I'm glad I made that decision because in the time it took me to transition my business the island improved. That satellite dish would be totally obsolete now!

Once I knew the exact island I wanted to live on, I could take actions to bring me closer to that specific goal. Wanting to live on a tropical island is cool, but it probably won't happen without a better goal. You need to pick a specific island that you want to move to. That will change your focus dramatically. Suddenly you have more information to work with. You can research the visa situation for that country. You can study the currency for that island and the cost of living there. You can look at real flight options. A concrete and specific goal turns ideas into reality.

I figured out how much rent I would need to live at the level I desire here. You can survive on this island very cheaply if you don't mind sleeping in a hammock, with mosquitos using you as an all-night buffet. I don't like mosquitoes. I didn't want to survive. I wanted to live!

I did some research and established a very clear budget. There were some surprises, of course. The day after we moved here, my girlfriend became pregnant with our second child. Sometimes you have to adapt your goals.

That is the reason I told you to set specific financial goals and write them down. Having a real goal in front of you makes you much more likely to hit it, without getting sunk by the desire to "adjust" later on!

XVII

THE HABIT OF SUCCESS

We are what we repeatedly do. Excellence, then, is not an act, but a habit.
- Aristotle

112

SOME FAILURE IS GOOD

I've read a lot of books that pump you up for the dream lifestyle - quitting your job, starting your career, living life on your terms. They're exciting to read; they make it seem like you're going to go right in there and start winning your first time out.

You go out all excited... with no preparation for failure. And why on earth would you be prepared for that? Who would read a book about coping with failure, preparing for failure, or recovering from failure? So that first failure destroys you emotionally. Either you feel like the system failed you, leaving you more bitter and cynical – or you feel like you failed the system. That leaves you feeling like you're lazy, weak, stupid, and unlucky. It's hard for me to decide which is worse!

Those optimistic books that feel like pep rallies are wonderful for selling books and getting five-star reviews, but the price is that you don't help people.

There are two types of failure, and it's really important to know the difference. There is random failure, and there is systematic failure. Random failure is where you have problems with different parts of your project. Maybe you try and write a book, but nobody likes it. The second book you just can't get any traffic. The third book you have problems finding people to leave reviews. If you are starting a blog, the first issue is that something goes wrong setting up the blog, then you have an issue in the code, and Google won't list your site, then there is a problem with images, and they all look weird.

Both of those series of events are devastating. It seems like the world has turned against you and you have no hope of success. But that is only because you have been misinformed. Those are both the random type of failure, and that is the good kind. With random failure, you run into different failures all the time. You're learning and growing in the correct way.

Random failures are how we master any skill or process. With my very first product launch, there was a glitch in the membership signup process for my members' area. When someone would buy the course, they would get logged into the members area. But when they came back they couldn't log in the second time. It's a super weird problem that you would never think to test for. When I had people test my technology beforehand, everything went smoothly. They made a demo purchase and went into the member's area.

When the product went live; people started having problems a day or two later. I woke up one day with two thousand customers, and nearly all of them sent in support emails. Have you ever woken up to thousands of people cursing you out over email? It was a total nightmare. I eventually found the mistake – one little box that was checked the wrong way. I'd upset ALL of my customers with that one little mistake.

I could feel like a total failure at that moment and decide that this business is not for me. Or I could move forward and make sure that mistake never repeats.

Throughout my career, I have made a lot of mistakes and even had some pretty big failures. Some of my ideas were total stinkers. The key is to realize that random failure is good. When each failure is something new and totally different, you know you are on the right track. The real problem is systemic failure.

Systemic failure is when you keep making the same mistakes over and over again. Most people are so busy getting distracted by small random failures that they don't notice the systemic failures in their lives. Having a single income stream and thus a single point of vulnerability is a systemic failure. Anything hits that one stream, and your life is changed radically. We spend our lives ignoring systemic failures because random failures are more exciting. If you misspell every blog post you write, that's a systemic failure. If your website crashes every day, that's a systemic failure. If you write three books and all get terrible reviews on Amazon, that's a systemic failure.

The key to systemic failure is that you can avoid or correct those mistakes and move on.

113

MOTIVATION

At this stage of the book, you're probably super pumped. And you should be! These kinds of stories excite and inspire people. The thought of starting your own business and firing your boss is exciting. It happens to me too. The first chapter of a book or the first video in a training course is the most exciting. We keep grabbing new books and courses just to get that initial feeling of euphoria and excitement.

Motivational energy is a finite resource. You only have so much of it, and when that initial excitement wears off, you can lose interest in the book or project.

Your desired goal is to Serve No Master. You want to take control of your financial destiny. Your motivational energy comes from envisioning this prospect and being excited about it. By now I know that you're not quite as excited as you were when you read that first chapter.

If you want to recapture that feeling and have it power you wherever you go in business, you need a motivational strategy, and it needs to be a little less expensive than gobbling up every course you come across, looking for a fresh hit.

Everything that you see in this section is designed to help you build that strategy. Different strategies work for different people, but taking action early is a universal constant. That's why I started this book by asking you to think about and write down your goals. That's much stronger than only thinking of them.

Having a written down goal lets your mind understand why it is investing energy. Most people vastly overestimate how much emotional energy they have.

They decide they want all the information first and take it in like a murder mystery or a movie. They treat it as entertainment and at the end they'll do the little tasks if they like it. That's a nice plan, but let's be honest. How often are you doing that? You've gone from reading something for the first time to flipping around pages, scrolling through your Kindle, trying to find that one task you think you saw back in Chapter Four.

By the time you get to the end of the book, the hype has diminished, reality has set in, and you've got to grind. Now you're facing a choice; you can do all this grinding when your emotional energy is already low, or you can grab a new book, find a new story, get excited again!

Most people choose the latter. I have seen people who have fifty books about meeting women or finding the right guy or starting your own business or how to ask for a raise. They have an entire bookshelf of self-help, but they do very little helping themselves! They think that the more books they have, the smarter they'll be.

Are you one of those people? Most people who didn't write down three financial goals at the start of this book are going to fail – because this gap is a crushing psychological roadblock.

If you're one of those people, stop and ask yourself how serious you are about actually reaching your goals. How many books have you read that told you to write your goals down? How many times did you do it? Is today going to be different or not?

Reading motivational books and never writing down your goals is a systemic failure. You are making that same mistake over and over again. Go back to that section and take a physical action. Get yourself in that habit. Try something different.

All the reading in the world doesn't help you to implement.

For example, this woman just can't meet the right guy. She buys a book on the topic and tries the method on the next guy she meets. He's not up to snuff, so she decides the book doesn't work, and then she's off to empty her purse on a new one. She hit that first random failure and then quit. But now she's got a real problem. She's introduced a systematic failure into her life.

She buys a book, implements incorrectly, and then goes to buy a new one. That repeating mistake is going to be fatal!

Many people don't even get that far. They buy the books but never read them, or they only read the first chapter and move on. They don't even notice that they're failing their one life because they're on this treadmill of excitement, powered by buying a new book every few days!

Obviously, this problem doesn't apply only to women. I have heard some amazing stories about guys in the dating world. I met one guy who'd spent three years trying to learn how to talk to women. He spent three years reading books, watching training courses and hanging out on forums. He was full of excitement, talking about every technique he'd studied. He threw out so many acronyms and insider terms; it was like he was in a cult! He knew all these insider terms but didn't have any personal stories to share. I asked him how many women he'd dated in the past three years. Zero. I asked him how many women he'd even TALKED to in the last three years. Another zero. He broke my heart. All that "knowledge" and he never once had a conversation with a woman. He never even tried to implement it. He should have just spent those three years watching movies.

Knowledge without action is garbage.

Unfortunately, people do this all the time. Having a motivational strategy is the key to success. Taking real actions in the real world that match your desires is how you create a motivational strategy. There is a reason that I have mentioned ServeNoMaster.com/book so many times. If I can get you to look at that page, you will be sitting in front of a computer. I'm using every tactic I can think of to get you in front of your computer. Once you are sitting there, it's a little easier to get you to open a new tab, sign up for something, start a website, and get your journey going!

I'm not smarter than you. I'm not quicker on my feet. I'm not lucky. Those are not the reasons I'm writing this book, and you're reading it. The reason I succeed where other people fail is that I approach every task I take on with a street fighter mentality. I look for a way to fight to the top, and I don't quit. If I can inspire you to do that, and then teach you how to build those habits, you'll be able to get anything you want from this life.

114

MICRO STEPS

The first step in creating a habit for success is figuring out what you need, and then breaking it down into usable chunks. Remember a few chapters ago where I talked about the software tool I used called Scrivener? I'm using it to write this book right now. It breaks the process of writing a book down into tiny steps. I write one section at a time. Each time I finish one of these little units, I get a feeling of euphoria and success. Instead of having to write the entire book to feel good, I get a little jolt every twenty minutes or so.

With any new project or habit, you want to start with an outcome goal. That's your objective. It can be losing twenty pounds or making ten thousand dollars a month online. That is your outcome goal, your final destination. Then cut that goal into tiny process goals. The smaller you can make the pieces, the better.

Our brains aren't very good at focusing on long-term goals, so you need to set targets you can hit quickly. I rarely think about my big weight loss goal. I have a process goal. I try to work out every day. Whether I kayak, surf, stand up paddle, run or ride my exercise bike, I want to sweat every single day, because that will at least maintain my weight. I also try to eat healthy every day. When I hit my two daily goals, my weight decreases. I've been trying to drop my weight for about nine months now. If I approached only the outcome goal, I would have failed and quit by now.

Addiction programs don't start you off talking about getting your "five years sober" chip on day one. They tell you to take things one day at a time. You might not be able to imagine yourself sober, or loving, or productive forever. But can you stay sober, be a better parent, build your business for just one day?

Maybe on day one, you are going to pick a website name and get your first blog set up. That's your first goal. You can break it down into smaller steps. Pick a name. Buy the name. Buy hosting. Connect the name to hosting. Install Wordpress. Choose a look that you like. Write the first blog post. You get to feel a sense of accomplishment seven times instead of just once. I break down each of those tiny steps for you on my blog so that it all feels manageable.

This micro-step process connects to your brain in a powerful way. A significant cause of failure is negative emotions. Most people try something, fail on the first try, and feel worthless. This can happen as early as step one. You think of a great website name, and when you go to buy it, you find out someone already owns it. Suddenly, you feel like every good name is taken already!

When I was thinking of the name Serve No Master, I had a different original concept. I just wanted to start a new blog about traveling and having a cool life. I tried out like a dozen names. I don't remember all of them, but one was called Blogger Without Borders. It's a decent name for that old idea, but it certainly wouldn't make sense for this book! That name was already taken. I hate when I check out a name I want, and someone is not using it. It happens.

When people see ServeNoMaster.com, they're impressed. It's easy to remember and clearly explains my mission. What they don't know is that it was my thirtieth idea. It turns out that failing to get that Bloggers Without Borders domain was a good thing. I failed my way to a MUCH better name.

When you are building your first website, you might not realize that a dozen little screw-ups happen every step of the way. It happens all the time. The problem is that you think of it as a failure. Please focus right now because this is super important. When you do this, you are attaching a negative emotion to the act of trying.

I have to say it again:

When you focus on the failure, you attach a negative emotion to the act of trying.

That process will destroy you. You train your brain that when you try things, it leads to feeling bad. You can train your brain to stop trying. I see people do this all the time. The secret of my success is my micro steps. I attach positive emotions to each tiny step. This allows me to feel good even when I fail. I've had projects crash and burn in spectacular fashion. But along the way, I experienced hundreds of feelings of success before that moment of failure.

Break down each goal into process goals. Then break those down into tiny steps. I have a process for ghostwriting a book for a client. I wrote it out for a friend once because he wanted to see. It has nine phases and sixty-one process goals. Think about that for a moment. Most people think of writing a book as a one step process. Either you wrote it, or you didn't. As someone who has written over a hundred books, I see it differently. I may have written over one hundred books, but I have accomplished thousands of goals.

The process itself needs to be enjoyable, or trying to hit that faraway goal will feel like a slog through the mud. Training yourself to enjoy each tiny step in the process will teach your brain to enjoy trying.

115

MEASURE SUCCESS

All this stuff has a purpose. Most of us aren't naturally designed to be great entrepreneurs. We need to learn step-by-step and rewire ourselves for success. That's why setting up proper feedback is just as important as tracking our success. With weight loss, you can simply get on the scale every day, but you can't remember what you weighed three days ago or eleven days ago. Every time I take my measurements, I enter them into a tracking website. It gives me line graphs so that I can see my progress. I do the same thing tracking my books on Amazon. I want to see trends, not just today's numbers.

Whatever method you choose to pursue, it needs to have a tracking element. You can use a task manager or a notebook. You can even start a blog about your process of writing a blog. Each day, you write about the goals and what you achieved. You will find that shockingly rewarding. After the first few months, you'll have some money coming in online, but you will feel like you haven't accomplished enough. In those moments, you can read your first blog posts and see how much you have accomplished.

Whatever method you choose to use, checking off boxes and being able to see the accomplished goals behind you are crucial. You need to see that you have made progress. You might think your brain can remember those feelings of accomplishment, but it simply can't. Our brains are terrible at long-term thinking.

I track big and small goals all the time. For this book, I have a total word count goal of one hundred thousand words. That's how long I want this book to be when I finish it. That's a huge goal. That's like planning to climb Everest. I have broken it down in two different ways. I have a book goal of one hundred thousand words and a daily goal of ten thousand words. With Scrivener, I click an icon, and it shows me where I am with each goal. The daily goal resets at midnight so I am always current. Sometimes looking at how much I have written today feels good. Sometimes I like to watch that little bar graph march closer and closer to my overall goal. Both give me feedback, track my progress and give me good feelings.

I have also chopped this book into dozens of tiny sections inside each module. As I finish a little section, I get a sense of accomplishment. I have multiple tracking methods to ensure that I am always feeling good. You want to find a measuring system that works for you.

We all require different types of feedback. Some people learn visually, and some people learn by listening. That's why this book comes in audiobook format too.

There is no picture-perfect way to track your progress that works for everyone. Try out different methods and see what works the best for you. Which way of tracking makes you feel the best and most successfully motivates you? That's the answer you want to find.

116

POWER OF PROCESS

There are some micro steps that we only have to complete once. You only have to buy your domain name a single time. That's a one-time micro goal. But there are other steps we're going to need to do over and over again – every day, every week, every month. Those goals aren't as hard as they might seem because the brain likes repetition.

I told you my morning process for starting my day and moving to my office nook. If I got over there at different times every day, it would no longer be a process. Coming here at the same time has created a pattern that my brain likes and my increase in efficiency is the proof.

When you are running a blog, there are tasks that you have to repeat over and over. Turning them into repetitive goals that you do in the same order creates a process. You have to write your blog posts, and you've got to put them out consistently, or your whole site will die on the vine. It's something you don't want to screw up.

You can write a post every day. That is one process, and it works for some people. You can write fifty posts at the start of each month. Or you can write five posts for the week every Monday. That process works well for other people. On my blog, I have over a hundred posts that I haven't published yet. I think of an interesting idea, and I save it in draft mode along with an image inside my blog. When I want to write the idea is ready for me. That's part of my process.

Another part of your process will be finding images for your posts. You might decide to look for images while you are writing each post like I do. Or you write five blog posts on Sunday and then Monday you get images for all of them. Find the process that works best for you.

You'll also need to check comments and do housecleaning once in a while. You need to update the software and make sure everything continues to run smoothly. Wordpress is going to help with that, as a lot of the updates now are automatic, but you still can't be totally asleep at the wheel. You also need to check your email.

Instead of leaving your email open to beep at you as an email comes in, you should set a specific window where you check email. That way a surprise email doesn't destroy your workday, and you aren't hitting refresh on the thing like a zombie.

The more you break down your days and weeks into small goals and tasks, the easier it will be to maintain the crucial momentum it takes to succeed.

117

ROUTINE

Let's talk about routine. It's the structure around your work time. When you're planning a routine, you want to take into account as many factors as possible. Let's imagine that you want to learn guitar. To establish a routine, you start by asking some crucial questions.

- What time will you practice each day?
- When will you have lessons?
- What is your budget and plan for buying your first instrument?
- Electric or acoustic?
- Where will you take lessons?
- Where will you practice?

You might already have these questions bubbling in your head, but if not, now's the time. Start by figuring out how much time you can realistically invest in this project. If you've got a family and a full-time job, a lot of your day is already allocated. If you're out of work, then you can put in fourteen hours a day or more. Those kinds of hours can be both a blessing and a curse. You have so much time that you start to be inefficient. Just like someone who starts a business with a ton of cash and makes poor spending decisions, you can easily chase a rabbit for six hours and still get something done with the rest of your time. If you don't track your time properly, you will look at your total accomplishment for the day rather than your efficiency.

You might not even have a computer at home, especially if you're younger. You can get games, movies, and everything else through a tablet or smartphone. If that's the case, you need to plan a budget for a computer that will get the job done without breaking the bank. There are tons of computer setups out there that will let you get basic tasks done without breaking the bank. Running Photoshop and rendering your videos will probably be the most intense things a work computer does, and you can do both of those well with a $600 system. Plus, that computer is now a business expense! Can you say tax return?

Establish your budget for training and software now and stick to that number. Most of you will decide to go into this with a plan and stick to it. If you're going to join any masterminds or local groups for people trying to make it online, put that into your schedule. Plan it out in advance.

Are you going to work before or after your main job? Will you eat dinner before you start or after? These little steps seem tiny now, but having a clear routine will make an enormous difference over time. When you go into an office, there is a lot of routine and structure in place designed to maximize your success. Lunch is at a fixed time. Breaks are at a fixed time. Do you leave the office after an hour for lunch? Of course not. You don't eat lunch randomly at the office, and you should have the same mindset at home.

If you can't work in your house, you need a good remote location. There are offices that you can rent by the hour. These shared spaces are pretty cool. First of all, you know you are paying by the hour so you will be super efficient. Secondly, they come with high-speed Internet and other amenities. You can have a little office if you need to make phone calls. Depending on your personality, that isolation might not work for you at all. You may need to be in a coffee shop instead. That way you are in a social environment. That's fine too. Just make a plan and then implement. Choose a location where you can work efficiently. If you need to speak out loud on phone calls or webinars, a coffee shop will be very limiting.

The more you plan out your routine now, the quicker you will hit your stride. Having a stable routine will help you stay on track as you work your way to the top.

118

FAILURE IS COMING

There's so much conflicting advice out there about when to give up; it can feel like a tidal wave of clichés sweeping us away from good decisions. Never give up. Don't throw good money after bad. Don't quit right before your breakthrough. Don't beat yourself up over mistakes. Don't get scammed.

Knowing when to move on is hard.

I have had a lot of projects fail online for different reasons. Seasons change, and people move on. The Internet is always changing. A few years ago, MySpace was the king; now it is a virtual ghost town. I haven't logged in for a decade. The same thing could happen to the current social media king. That's why companies now constantly buy other companies. They are diversifying. The most valuable thing about Yahoo right now is the stock they own in Alibaba. It's worth more than the rest of the company combined. Diversification protects you from the hard times.

You want to open new revenue streams to prepare for the rainy days. The more revenue streams you develop, the more secure your family's future.

The biggest mistake you can walk into is assuming that there is no more failure in your future. Look how many great people failed their way to the top. Ronald Reagan lost the election for president in 1976. Nobody remembers that failure anymore because he won in 1980. Wins will always be remembered far longer than losses. Most great people failed their way to the top.

I want you to prepare for those failures that are coming your way. Have a plan for dealing with them. The real danger is if one failure knocks you off the rails. You mess up an interview or something small, but then you are so upset that you don't work for the next week. That's when a failure turns into a cascade, and THAT can ruin you. Knowing that failure is coming will prevent you from overreacting when things get tough.

Whenever you hit a failure, focus on adapting and overcoming, not kicking yourself while you're down.

119

SCAFFOLDING

I'm a pretty talented guy, and I know how to crowd out distractions when I have to. But there are limits. I can't record a video at a coffee shop. I can't do anything at all from a nightclub – not even send an email!

Distractions don't just come from environments; they come from people too. I can find a place to work in my house, but could you imagine trying to accomplish the same thing with a friend stopping by every five minutes to ask for a favor or the phone constantly ringing?

If I'm in a noisy place, if I'm surrounded by distractions, if the people around me want to sabotage me – that's going to crush my potential for success just as sure as anything. All of these things - the emotional surroundings, the physical surrounding, our routine, the people – all of that is scaffolding.

We want to be sure we surround ourselves with people on the same path. Then you can share ideas and commiserate. That is one of the reasons why I created my forum. It's a place where other people are waiting to meet with you and chat about the struggles and successes of making it online. It's also worthwhile to find people near you who are on the same page. Finding other people who are trying to build their businesses in your community gives you people that you can talk face-to-face with. I found a lot of value in these groups when I was just starting out.

You'll often find that other people have great solutions to your problems. They are on the same page, so they have a great perspective. If you spend all your time with people who aren't interested in freedom, they will constantly distract you from your path. They'll start doing things that seem "nice" on the surface, but they'll get more and more aggressive. Just ask someone trying to lose weight. You want to work, and they want to go to a bar. You want to network, but they want to play PlayStation.

That's the danger of lacking a supportive group around you. Please take the time to work on your scaffolding. Find people that motivate you and follow them. If you like what I'm talking about, then following my blog might help to keep you inspired. If I'm not the right fit, find someone who is. There are tons of great mentors out there. Just following someone else's journey can help you to stay motivated.

We are building an online business, but doing that in isolation can be brutal. That is why the beginning of this book was about networking and connecting at live events. That's where you will find the best people to inspire and motivate you.

120

TEMPTATION

Right now, I'm trying to lose a ton of weight and get super fit. My current temptation is garbage food. If there are snacks in the house, they are going to end up in my mouth.

There are limits to temptation. I might want to get a snack, but am I going to drive halfway across town to get a bag of potato chips? No way, too much effort. My family doesn't keep anything greasy or salty or sugary in the house. Just last night I was rifling through the cupboards like a curious bear; I was a little ashamed of myself. But guess what? There weren't any snacks around.

That forces me into Plan B – get a glass of water and admit that I'm not hungry.

I'm acutely aware of how much temptation I can resist and where my failure point is. You need to learn what you're failure point is. If you are in the grind on some work and get a text from a friend, will that throw you out of your rhythm? Will you suddenly want to go meet up with your friends? Then you need to turn off your phone while you are working. Email is a similar and very distracting temptation. The Internet as a whole is a pipe to unlimited temptation. Everyone has a different limit.

There are plenty of people who can be in a room with a bag of cookies, and nothing bad will happen. If I'm there, those cookies better have an up-to-date will, because they won't be there in the morning.

The main reason I can have my phone near me when I'm working is that nobody texts or calls me. I only use my phone to connect with my family and send baby pictures to relatives. Your phone can be a real nightmare, though. If you let apps send you alerts, then you can expect a barrage of annoying beeps and vibrations. This game has some free imaginary points, you've got a new voicemail, a new show is out on Netflix. Your phone can turn into that needy ex that you thought you broke up with.

Some people go to the gym and spend two or three hours on a forty-minute workout. Why? They spend more time talking than they do sweating! The need to be social kills their effectiveness.

When I pick a gym, I like going somewhere dirty, with as few amenities as possible. The kind of place that scares all the women away. I'm there to complete a task, and I don't need any other distractions.

Your workspace isn't just about feeling good. It's about focusing on what you need to get done. I love where I work right now; it's like a temple of achievement. I can get into the office mindset, but every time I look past the computer monitor, I can see the blue ocean or my daughter swimming in the pool.

It's a constant reminder that I have a great life and that my work is paying off. The harder I work, the more fun my family gets to have.

I know a lot of people love having an impressive office with fun couches that people like to visit. That doesn't work for me. I'm here to put in my hours and then enjoy my free time anywhere else. This is a place of work and nothing more. Rather than mixing chilling and working for six hours, I get that job done in four. That gives me two extra hours surfing or hanging with my family. That's a great result.

XVIII

TALENT

Nothing in this world can take the place of persistence. Talent will not: nothing is more common than unsuccessful men with talent. Genius will not; unrewarded genius is almost a proverb. Education will not: the world is full of educated derelicts. Persistence and determination alone are omnipotent.

- Calvin Coolidge

121

BORN FUNNY

A comedian walks onto the stage, and he's just killing it. Everyone in the crowd is screaming with laughter, and you're bent over, face turning red. You start thinking about how hilarious this guy is. Maybe you start wishing you were born funny so you could make people laugh in the same way. Wouldn't it be great to make people laugh around the office? Or even around the house?

I used to teach people how to be funny by going to small events and giving presentations on humor. I did a lot of research to figure out why some people are funny, and some people are simply death to a good joke. It boils down to a single moment in childhood.

Children don't create jokes; they repeat them. As a child, you repeat a joke you heard from an older sibling or on television. Every kid has a moment when they tell a joke that just bombs. It's an older kid joke that they don't understand, or they just tell it wrong. One of the other kids turns to them and says, "You're not funny." That single statement changes the course of your destiny. You go home and realize that you just aren't funny. That statement changes your life, and you no longer believe that you are funny.

I'm great at telling jokes, and it's how I made friends when I was younger. It's a very valuable skill, but that's an important distinction. It's a skill, not a talent. There isn't a stand-up comedian out there who has never bombed.

They master the craft by putting in sweat equity. They start out writing jokes at home and practicing on their friends. They hit open mic nights all over town. It's a real struggle to turn the ability to make your friends laugh into something that strangers will pay to see.

Most people had that moment in childhood where they decided that being funny is for other people, and they just let go of the desire to try and tell jokes. They stop putting effort into learning this skill because they mistakenly believe it is a talent. I have told hundreds of thousands of jokes in my life. Along the way, I've told an uncountable number of bombs. I have offended hundreds and possibly thousands of people. To master the art of humor you have to master the art of calibration. You have to say something that is unexpected enough to be funny but not so far as to be offensive. It's a fine art that you only learn through experience.

Whether you are funny or not comes down to how much time you invested in telling jokes and learning comedic timing. Many people spent that time in high school running track or learning an instrument. We can't be everything to everyone. But humor is a skill. You can learn it, no matter how old you are when you start.

122

BORN THIS WAY

People have a tendency to think that I was born already successful at online marketing. They see where I am right now and assume that there was no struggle to the top. That I just walked into this life. I wish that were true, but it's not. My struggles are what shaped me into the man I am today. I hit some painful roadblocks along the way.

Shortly after being fired from my university position I lost my apartment. I had to move into my mom's basement right before my 30th birthday. I was living my ultimate nightmare. I had tried and failed, and now I was back living with mommy like a child. It was horrible. But it was a necessary sacrifice. I determined to do whatever I had to. I was not going to "celebrate" my 30th birthday down in that basement. So I fought my way out.

When I started succeeding just a little bit, it was still really hard. I moved in with a friend. I moved into his studio apartment and slept on the couch about a meter from his dirty feet. He snored so loud every night that I was always tired. It was brutal, but it was a step forward; at least there was a window. After a year of that, we upgraded to a two-bedroom apartment. For eighteen months I struggled to break free, and my reward was a bedroom of my own - something that most people take for granted.

Most people ignore that sacrifice, and that's a problem. If you blame my success on luck, then your only hope of escaping the tyranny of your boss is for luck to intervene in your life as well. You were born with all the skills you need!

I wasn't born a great writer. I didn't even learn how to write well in university. I taught myself by blogging for a long time. I put in a lot of slog. I am a very fast writer now, but developing and honing my craft took effort. I just keep working harder to get faster and faster.

The effort you put into your business, into your life, has real value. There is nothing that I use to make money that I was born with. My skills in networking and making friends are entirely artificial. At seventeen, I was alone and suffering. Unlike most kids in that situation I simply took action.

I found someone who was popular and likable. And I studied him like you wouldn't believe. Everything from his hair to his clothing got absorbed into my personality. I studied how he started and ended conversations. I paid attention to how he treated people. I watched how people reacted to different things he said. I was a nerdy apprentice for a very long time.

When you make a decision to change and accomplish something, all that's left is staying the course. I put in the effort. I created and built a remarkable life all by following one guy. And he has no idea. I just watched and replicated someone who was doing it right. Honestly, he just taught me how to be a better person. Now those lessons are ingrained in my personality, but they were learned.

People used to tell me that you were either popular or not. That's just a lie the popular kids tell to maintain their power. You can become anything you want once you realize that it's just about putting in the effort. I didn't want to be lonely anymore, so I learned how to be the kind of person that other people wanted to be around. I shared those crucial skills with you earlier in the networking section so that you don't have to travel the same difficult road as me.

Don't get caught up in the thought that some people are born knowing how to make money, and some aren't because that is a lie too. That little thought is a real business killer. As soon as that thought enters your brain, quitting becomes a larger and larger option for you. Don't let a single falsehood destroy your destiny.

123

THE UNCONTROLLABLE 3RD PARTY

When a guy wins the Olympics, many people watch and talk about luck. They say that he was born a natural athlete. He comes from athletic parents. He has good genes. He's lucky. We look for any cause of his success other than his effort. Do you know how much training goes into making the Olympic team? It's brutal, it's lonely, it's painful, and they don't get paid squat. We look at that moment of glory and fail to give him proper credit; it's a real shame.

A common dream for guys these days is to play video games professionally. They think it's all fun and games and getting paid to hang out with your friends. I watched a documentary about one of the first pro-gaming champions. This guy put in hours doing the most boring drills you could ever imagine. He spent eight hours a day minimum, seven days a week training. For him, it wasn't a game. He took his job seriously and applied military training methods. Anyone who claimed he had natural ability or blamed his fast-twitch muscle fibers was just looking for an excuse to ignore the sixty-plus hours of training a week in this champion's training regimen.

I recently found out that one of my neighbors on the island is a former professional video game player. He played for his nation at several international competitions. He leveraged that into building a massive video game site in Europe. I have a fantastic podcast interview where he shares that journey, so if you want to be a professional or if your kids want to get into that business, you don't want to miss that episode.

I have tried to be as open as possible about my journey so that you won't make the mistake of thinking that my success is anyone's fault but my own. Every mistake I've made is my own. I get credit for the failures and also the successes. That's the way it should be. If you look at someone successful and blame it on luck, God, fate, Mother Nature, Gaia, or the universe you are doing yourself a disservice. You are taking all of your power in the universe and flushing it down the toilet.

Blaming someone else's success on an uncontrollable third party is a way of ducking responsibility for your life. Luck made him rich, luck made you poor, and nothing is your fault.

But look at what you're trading to quiet the voice in your head urging you to be more. If it's not your fault that you are poor, then you are powerless over your destiny. Those are the words of the willing slave who refuses to be responsible for his freedom. Admitting that the bad job you hate is your fault is the first step to real power. If your bad results are because of your actions, then you have the ability to change them. Good actions on your part can give you good results.

Don't pass the buck because it's easy. There are a lot of people wealthier than me. I don't blame their success on their wealthy parents. That's silly. A lot of people inherit great sums of money and burn it all to the ground very quickly. Having rich parents does not ensure that someone will be good at business or make smart decisions.

You have the power to change your destiny, no matter where you are right now. You have the knowledge now to rip off those shackles. You can break free and grab your destiny by the horns. You are the one who decides if you will succeed or fail. At the end of the day, only you get to decide if you will serve no master.

124

GRAB YOUR DESTINY

Take control of your life right now. There are only two things in this universe that you currently have power over - how you feel and what you do. You might be feeling a little depressed because I said your lack of success is your fault. Why are you giving me power over your emotions? I don't know you. I'm not judging you as a human being. I'm making a statement that applies to every person on our planet. How can you take a statement that applies to over seven billion people personally?

Take control of your emotions and stop giving other people authority over them. I get hate mail sometimes. People email me to tell me I'm fat for some reason. I don't have a course teaching weight loss, so it's weird, but doesn't hurt my feelings. I see someone who was so affected by my teachings that they took the time to email me. The negativity is irrelevant. These people see my success as a critique of their life, and they choose to lash out. Why would I give a stranger control over my emotions? That only leads down the path to madness.

I also used to receive a very large amount of hate mail for being a vegan. People used to talk about how vegans are cowards and weak. It was some pretty heavy stuff, especially because I'm not even a vegetarian. People who try to hurt you online are often shockingly misinformed. Why would I let the same people who hate on my "veganism" hurt my feelings when they call me fat? What people say doesn't matter. It's how you react to their actions that matters.

I have handed you a great deal of knowledge in this book. You paid just a few bucks for it. I paid for the same knowledge in blood, sweat, and struggle over the course of years. What a discount you got! You have the ability now to grow and develop into something amazing. You are the only one who decides from this day forward if your life changes.

You should never again let someone else determine how you feel. That's the first step on the path to success. As you follow the lessons of this book and begin to build your online empire, you will get to the point where nobody else can ever tell you what to do again. That is true freedom.

You have complete and total power over your destiny. Before, you were trapped and had no idea how to escape. I have provided you with a plan. Now it's your job to go forth and do great things. You have the knowledge and the ability to be free.

125

SERVE NO MASTER

Freedom in life isn't something we are given or born with. The circumstances of your birth greatly affect the odds. There are horrible countries out there where it's hard to break free, but if you are reading this book, then you don't live in one of them. In our society, it's the institutions that we trusted that made us complacent, that made us afraid, that kept us from exploring.

You can do better; you can break the chains that bind you to an unhappy life. The technology is there, and more importantly, the talent is inside of you. It doesn't come from me; it doesn't even come from this book – but I'm proud to show you the path.

The action is up to you. And if you take those steps, then your success stops being a possibility. It transforms into an inevitability. That is how you achieve your destiny. That is how you can finally -

SERVE. NO. MASTER.

XIX

MINIMALISM

The things you own end up owning you. It's only after you lose everything that you're free to do anything.

- Chuck Palahniuk

126

DOES YOUR STUFF OWN YOU

We are constantly flooded with information about the things we "need" to make us happy. The average adult in America faces over five thousand advertising and brand exposures per day. There's so much noise in everything that we consume that you can't even hear your thoughts.

Most people I know have a series of goals, but it's all external, stuff they saw on TV since they were kids. They want to own a house. They want to have two children. They want two cars. Then there is one more thing they want as a cherry on top - a boat, or a vacation home.

The problem is that people who "own" these things aren't any happier than people who don't. I know people who have a nice house and two expensive cars and put their kids in nice schools. They are paying a brutal mortgage on that nice house, and those expensive cars will take four more years to pay off.

By the time you pay off a car, it's worth about half what you paid for it. By the time you pay off that house after thirty years, it is worth half what you paid as well. While you are making those payments, you can tell everybody you meet that you're a homeowner. Your parents, your Facebook friends, that girl at Starbucks that has better things to do. It sounds great and feels even better. But rest assured you don't own that house. Miss a few mortgage payments and the bank won't bat an eye before putting you out on the street.

Most of these things, we think we want, will make our lives worse. I rent where I live right now. My landlord owns the place, and he works so much harder than I do. If the water boiler bursts, if there's a leak, if the Internet gets knocked out - it's now his problem. When you "own" a house, you spend all your time and money fixing a house that a bank owns. It's a modern form of slavery. Instead of using chains and whips, they use empty promises and debt.

When I told my friends I was hitting the road, they couldn't believe it. They told me how great America is and how traveling full time is insanity. A few months before I decided to become a minimalist, I almost bought a car for a hundred thousand dollars. That would have been the stupidest mistake of my life. A year later the car would be worth like forty percent of that!

I'm not into full blown minimalism. That's where you try to live out of a backpack or in a tiny house made of twelve crates and a little duct tape.

Instead, I like to own very little. The less you own, the more freedom you have. If I had to move off of my island today, we would leave a bunch of stuff behind. But we'd get over it. It wouldn't be the first time we changed islands.

I have no problem if your dream is that white picket fence and 2.5 kids. I just want you to go into that life with your eyes open. It takes thirty years to own that house, and it's going to take a lot of work. Every year the government will charge you land taxes for the right to live in your home. Personally, I think taxing land is the evilest thing that a government can do. It's the main way to remove freedom from your people. You never own your home; you're always renting it from the government.

Many people consider shopping a hobby or even a type of therapy. There is a rush that moment after you buy something great. That feeling only lasts a few weeks at best. Chasing that "purchase high" leads more people into debt every single day. Every time you think about making a purchase, you should have a logical discussion with your partner. If you are single, then just write this down - "Why do I want to buy this? How will this improve my life, save me money or help me achieve my goals?"

Let me give you an example. A few years ago my girlfriend and I decided to buy a PlayStation. Because I live in the middle of nowhere, the price was around $700. That's a lot of money. But we compared playing video games to some of the other ways to relax and entertain ourselves. Going to a bar or something costs way more money over time. I've been playing that machine for three years now, so the overall price of entertainment is under $1 a day. Then you have to factor in the price of each game. A brand new game can cost from $70-$200. But if you wait a year or two you can get the game with all of the bonuses and extra levels for $20-$30. Right now I'm playing a game from three years ago, and I paid about 10% of what other people did. I get the same experience for way less.

Replacing desire with logic allows me to spend more efficiently. Every dollar you don't spend is another dollar you don't have to go out and make. If you spend one hundred dollars less next month, it's the same result as if you made one hundred more.

Thinking about why you want things and how it will affect your life is important. I approach most financial decisions this way, even if it's not a life-altering purchase. It's about the principle, not the price.

When you are buying a new car, sit down and think about why you are buying this particular model. I had a friend when I was in my early twenties. We both worked in the same call center, selling computers. We made almost the same amount of money. He lived on a couch in the hallway of his parents' house and drove an extremely flashy car. He didn't care about how he lived, only about how he appeared to other people. He was willing to sleep on a couch in a hall just to have a more expensive car.

That might seem silly to you, but he was able to explain his purchase decision clearly to me. He knew that his purchase was all about perception, and he was willing to sacrifice his living situation to fund it. I would never make that decision, but at least he had some internal logic.

Many people buy the most expensive car that they can afford. At a certain point, the increase in cost does not correlate with an increase in speed or safety. Then the price of that car turns into a burden. Even after the car is a few years old and you are bored, you still have to keep making payments.

Don't buy your present by selling your future.

127

HOUSE FULL OF ANCHORS

Look around at all the stuff you own in your house. Each object is a teeny-tiny anchor that keeps you trapped there. Have you ever heard someone say, "We can't downsize; where would we put all our stuff?"

When I left America, I couldn't get rid of everything. I sold off a lot of things, including my car, and the leftovers I put into a storage unit. The key for that place should say, "I'm an idiot." There is no worse decision than putting your junk into one of those. I must have paid thousands of dollars to store stuff I'll never see again. A few years ago, I had my bookkeeper open it up and sell off everything. I just let her keep the money from whatever she sold. When you can't see stuff for a while, you stop caring about it.

The fees on a storage unit are always higher than the value of the stuff inside. I have a friend who has a car in storage in America. Now it's on four flat tires, and he doesn't want to fly back just to sell it. He's paid more in storage fees than the car was worth when he first shoved it in there. That storage unit has turned into a neck wound that he can't control. The bleeding will continue for years because he is stuck.

There is a reason there are so many shows about people who buy up storage lockers and sell off the crap inside. They are the ultimate sign that we make moronic decisions based on emotion.

Don't pay real money to keep garbage in a dirty closet. Talk about sending good money after bad! You form an emotional tie to things that don't make your life better, and it can keep you trapped for longer than you ever imagined.

It took me a long time to break those emotional chains, and I poured a lot of money into the toilet along the way. It was a hard lesson, and it still makes me frustrated talking about it. Hopefully sharing my experience with you will keep you from wasting money on storage units.

128

WHAT DO YOU NEED?

I used to spend thousands of dollars on clothes. I had a personal shopper at a high-end department store, and I gave him one order – make me look good. I still have those expensive clothes. I mix them in with stuff that's homemade now and nobody can tell the difference.

I simply buy a pair of shorts that I like. I then purchase a similar fabric from the store right next door, and I take both of those to a local seamstress on my island. She uses the pair of shorts as a template and creates ten more pairs for me that are even more comfortable than the store-bought shorts.

I never considered doing something so radical before in my life. I used to be obsessed with labels. My experience hasn't changed even though my clothes now cost about three percent of what they used to. Yesterday, I was wearing a shirt that cost more than a hundred bucks. Right on top of a pair of my three dollar shorts. Nobody noticed, and nobody cared. Well, I cared a little bit. Because the shorts were more comfortable.

Remember, I'm all about cost control. We talked about business expenses, but now I'm talking about personal expenses. Want to be happy in your personal life? Kill the clutter.

Let's say that you get dialed in with working online. You make $100 an hour. That's a pretty good wage to make chilling by the pool with your laptop. Let's say your cost of living is $10,000 a month. That means you have to work 100 hours every month just to maintain that lifestyle. But what happens if you realize that some of that stuff isn't valuable? You start to focus on the value of freedom and you slash your costs down to $6,000 a month. There is a cost – you'll have less stuff. But you get a full workweek of your life back every single month.

Let's look at the equation from another angle. That last paragraph might have triggered your fear of loss. Would you like to drive the best car on the road and work twelve months a year or drive the second best car and work nine months? What would it be like to get three months of your life back? Is that more valuable to you than the prestige of driving the "best?"

My cost of living is extremely low now. It's about 10% of what it was when I was single and living in America. Now I have a whole family to take care of, and it still costs way less. People think living on a tropical island is crazy expensive. And if you approach the idea like a tourist, it can be.

Tourists in America go to Hawaii, spend the whole trip in overpriced hotels in the tourist district and talk about how expensive it is there. They don't do any research on what people who live there pay for things.

If you stay on packaged tours and stay in the lanes provided by your hotel, you'll only see the most expensive offers. Have you ever looked at the prices in a hotel shop? They charge triple for toothpaste, so why on Earth would you assume that their liquor prices match the average island prices?

Misinformation often causes us to make poor decisions. We just assume something is expensive because it is desirable. On my island, I watch people overpay for surfboards seven days a week. A few minutes of research would save them so much money!

Most of the things that you think help you, actually limit your options. All of this stuff you have to dump or sell before you can move on.

We've been here a while and purchased a scooter and some surfboards. I bought them all used, so my financial investment is small. I could sell the boards within a week. The scooter too. But if I have to give it away, that's no big deal. I'm not going to let a few small purchases trap me. Because I'm a minimalist, I thought about those things when I bought them.

I plan on living here for a very long time, so I'm willing to set down some roots and make life easier. But I went into those purchases realizing that if I need to move for some reason, I still need to deal with them. You can own stuff, but I want you to at least have your eyes open. We have things we haven't looked at in ages, but we keep them "just in case." That hoarding mindset is a huge drain. It's fine to be prepared, but notice when your decisions are emotional rather than logical.

XX

THE ADVANTAGES OF TRAVEL

Travel is fatal to prejudice, bigotry, and narrow-mindedness, and many of our people need it sorely on these accounts. Broad, wholesome, charitable views of men and things cannot be acquired by vegetating in one little corner of the earth all one's lifetime.

- Mark Twain

129

THE FOURTH CHAIN

People move to the United States seeking a better life. That's why your ancestors moved there.

I left for the same reason.

The government of the United States is a bloated train wreck. If it were a corporation, the CEO would have been thrown in jail decades ago. If you don't believe me, go and renew your driver's license in person. The last time I did that, the lady made me go home and get five letters and all these other documents. It took weeks of trips, phone calls, and headaches. They even demand that you have a utility bill to prove your identity. The government depends on private companies to confirm your identity.

I finally got all that garbage together and brought it in. She looks at the computer and goes "Oh, you're already in here!" All of that hassle because she was too lazy to enter my name in the computer the first time.

If you deal with the government on a day-to-day basis, you know that's not just an anecdote – if anything, I'm taking it too easy on them.

As long as you live in the United States, you're running with weights attached to your shoes. If you buy a house and pay it off, you still don't get to own it. Every year you have to come up with enough money to pay the taxes or the government will steal your home. If they want to put a road through your house, they can do it; it happened to my neighbors when I was a kid. The government paid them for the land, but the government also decided what it was worth. Don't expect to get the full price when they want to turn your front yard into an off ramp.

Whenever I talk about this subject, there is always someone who thinks this means I don't love my country. There is a lot that is great about America. But I'm also a pragmatist. I pay attention to the value that I get for my money. In the past three years, I have had only one interaction with the federal government. A few months ago I needed a replacement social security card. And the embassy completely screwed me.

There are dozens of shipping companies in this country, and naturally, the embassy decided to use the only one that doesn't deliver to my island. To send my passport back, they mailed it to another island. They refused to use any other service, even when I offered to pay extra.

These islands aren't across the street from each other; it's not like going downtown. There is one ferry there in the morning and one back in the afternoon. An entire day of my life wasted sitting on a boat, all because the embassy has no incentive to care about my experience. They know I can't fire them, and they act like it.

Fortunately, I'm pretty sly, so I called the first shipping company and paid a girl who works there to take it to another delivery company and mail it to me. It cost me about ten bucks extra but saved more than six hours of my life.

Let's imagine the nightmare scenario – I'm grabbed off the street by terrorists and they start splashing my face online. They are going to execute me live on the Internet if my government doesn't meet their demands.

Do you think the government will send the Navy SEALs for me, or pay a ransom? No way. The government is a one-way street. They want every penny they can squeeze out of me, but unless I'm politically connected, they would never even consider rescuing me. My only hope is for my family to hire mercenaries to save me. Otherwise, I'll be just another horrible video on Liveleak.

Our government was originally built on a social contract. The people paid the government to protect them collectively. Those days are long gone. There are only two countries in the entire world that tax you even when you don't live there - The United States and Eritrea. That's not good company. When is the last time you heard a good story about Eritrea or heard someone talking about wanting to move there?

If you want to know what Eritrea is most well known for besides having the same tax policy as the United States, it is having the worst human rights record of any nation on the planet. Wonderful company.

I have zero problem paying taxes, as long as I get something in return. I wouldn't even hesitate at a high rate as long as I knew there was any level of beneficence between my government and me. But let's be honest with each other. In America, I'm terrified of an encounter with the police. I know a lot of police officers and lawyers. I know how rigged the court system is.

Where I live now, the police take bribes all the time. But at least they are honest about it. In America, the police can pull you over and "arrest" your money, even if they don't charge you with a crime. Boy, do I wish I were making up that story. Just look up 'civil forfeiture' online and you'll be ready to move countries too.

You get dinged every time you make a move in the West. You work your tail off and want to pass your house on to your kids? The government will charge taxes so high that they have to sell off your house and then take on debt. Instead of being able to leave a gift for your children, you end up leaving them a curse.

There are ways around all of this. You can set up trusts and offshore corporations and bank accounts and pay lawyers to fight for you, but you shouldn't have to fight your people just to keep what you have!

I talked earlier about the three chains holding you back from freedom – if there's a 4th chain, the United States government is it. Governments have power, and you shouldn't assume that the one you were born under is automatically the best one for you.

130

HIT THE ROAD JACK

Leaving the country allows you to break the fourth chain. Whether you leave for a week or the rest of your life, there are a host of benefits to seeing the rest of the world. You don't realize just how insular America is until you visit another country. Can you name the president, king, queen or prime minister of even a single foreign country? Do you even know if Canada has a prime minister or a president? (I bet you are going to pull out your phone to find out right now)

Americans are one of the few peoples in the world that speak only a single language. My daughter is three years old, and she already speaks three. Do you think she's going to get job opportunities that your kid doesn't? Will she meet more interesting people? Be more cultured? I think we both know the answer. Expanding your horizons will give you a better perspective; whether that causes you to move abroad permanently or simply teaches you to appreciate the good things about America, it will be worth it.

131

ADVENTURE

The first reason to hop on a plane is an adventure. You get to see amazing things, experience wonderful cultures and meet amazing people. There's something truly wonderful about experiencing truly exceptional things.

I've enjoyed fruit juice over the cliffs of Carthage while smoking a hookah. I've snowboarded on the frozen northern island of Japan. I've seen the world's greatest DJs at festivals in Austria and tiny bars in Thailand. I have done shots in a London nightclub with a footballer on the England national team. I have enjoyed the wonder that is Angkor Wat. I've surfed one of the top ten spots in the world. I have DJed for crowds on three different continents. I nearly died climbing a mountain in Japan.

This is just a tiny sprinkle of the adventures that have filled my life and if you want to hear more of them, feel free to read the adventure section of my blog.

When the clock ticks down, are you going to be worrying about the next season of your favorite TV show? Are you going to wish you spent more time in the office or drove a nicer car? My greatest pleasure is taking the kayak out with my family. We spend the day on the water, getting some exercise and plenty of Vitamin D. Total cost for this excursion? ZERO. We own the boat and fortunately, the water here is free.

So often we talk about other cultures, but we've never been anywhere. America is the only country I've been to that never shows news stories about other nations. It's so weird how we are national narcissists. The world is a beautiful and amazing place.

132

TAXES

The best reason to go abroad is that you save massive amounts of money. You don't have to pay any taxes on the first $125,000 that you make as personal income abroad. In fact, that number is now much higher - check my website for the current figure. Even though the United States is the only country that chases its citizens for taxes, you can still save a huge amount. Make sure your expenses are all business expenses. Get a domestic bookkeeper to handle everything for you, and you'll be okay. You can go more advanced and set up offshore bank accounts and businesses, but even just the basic tax saving is beautiful.

All the money that you make, you get to keep. You don't have the stress of trying to track your withholding and playing the IRS tap-dance game. They change the rules every year, and it's nearly impossible to stay ahead. You can live like a king or queen in most countries with a hundred grand a year in free cash. If you find a place you love, you can change your citizenship and pay no taxes. The super-rich do this all the time, and there's a reason it works for them. Even switching to an EU passport massively changes your tax obligations. As long as you are living abroad most of the year, you don't have to pay any taxes. This is one of the best ways to find freedom and take control of more of your money.

Land in other countries is far cheaper, and many countries will give you citizenship just for buying property there. They see the value of having someone make money in America, but spend it in their country. On the island where I live, I support between forty and fifty people financially. I have direct staff and all the places that I spend money, shopping, and rent, etc. All of that money comes here from America and gets spread around the community. Most of my employees have large families, and they have finances because I'm here to hire them.

Instead of paying taxes for a country that doesn't care about you, why not check out a place that will love you for putting that money into the local economy? Limiting your tax risk is simply smart business. When you work for yourself, you get hit the hardest. If you aren't on your toes, you can end up owing taxes that are greater than your income. You have to spend a lot of time learning the tax game, setting up a corporation, tracking business expenses and keeping receipts. It's a real bear of a task. I did it for a long time, and I hated it.

You pay all those taxes, and you never get any of the benefits. People who put money into the government get the worst return.

133

COST OF LIVING

The cost of living in most countries is shockingly low. The average salary in many countries is $100 a month. Think about what that means for land and rent prices. You can live in a mansion for about ten percent of what it costs in America. Right now, I live in a beautiful villa on the water, nothing but sand and surf as far as the eye can see. For the same price, I could live in a neighborhood in America where I'd have to sleep by the front door with a shotgun in my arms every night. Paradise costs the same price as an inner city nightmare.

You're still making money selling your goods, services, and coaching to Westerners. So you get a western salary in a country where dollars spend like gold. My cell phone bill is around $3 a month. That gives me unlimited texting, which is all that I use. I also get like one or three hours of talk time. I don't know. I never use my phone to call anyone. I use it to send a text to my girlfriend or someone else on the island and then we meet in person. There is no need for long phone calls when you're in a small community.

To get around I have a little scooter. Brand new it cost a little under $1500. It's the most expensive thing I own, and that is a total workhorse. If I'm not using it, one of the girls who works for me is running to the store on it. It covers all of our transportation needs. I can load two giant surfboards on it every day and hit the waves when the tide is high. Petrol is around $20 a month. You can't even drive around in your car for a single day in America spending that little.

Living abroad lets you lower your costs, and that means you don't have to put in as many hours. There is less pressure.

I value freedom above massive income. I just took a break writing this book to go in the kayak with my whole family. We jammed around for a few hours and had a blast. Now I can slip back to the office nook to put in some more time writing. In case you are confused, my office is in the corner of my giant bedroom facing the ocean. It's just physically isolated enough so that I work when I'm over there, but the moment I step away I only think island thoughts.

As soon as you are willing to look at other countries, you will be shocked at what it costs to live there.

The news makes other countries seem scary so that you will never want to leave. They use fear to maintain the fourth chain. If people realized how cheap it was to live abroad, everyone in America would be jumping ship.

134

INTERNET

There are two different high-speed Internet choices on my remote tropical island. They have entirely different approaches to the Internet, so I'll explain how they both work, and you can think about it as you make your escape plan.

With one company, you get better than 20MBs download speeds and upload is sometimes even faster. They have massive data caps on all their plans, so those are unusable. The best choice is to pay for time. I pay around fifty cents an hour and can download as much as I need to. Some of my courses require me to move over one hundred gigabytes of data so that speed is crucial.

I just started using the other provider for my daily use. With them, I pay just under sixty-five cents a gigabyte on my new plan. It works out better for me. I don't have to watch the clock constantly and worry that my Internet will switch off. I use one for daily use and one for moving large files.

For example, if I want to download a video game, I want to pay for time because the file is going to be huge. But if I'm just sending emails, then I want to pay for volume.

It's a little bit of a game and most people only need one service or the other. Even with two services, I still pay less than a third of my Internet bill when I was in America.

135

HEALTH

Many people are trapped in America because they are terrified by the idea of a trip to a foreign hospital.

You can't turn on a TV without some politician bragging about how the US has "the best healthcare in the world." Unfortunately, that is a lie. The United States has one of the worst healthcare systems among industrialized countries. It ranks 37th overall!

If you've ever actually worked with the healthcare system in America; if you struggled to make it through the tangled web of HMO's and mandated insurance plans in Silver, Gold and Bronze, Medicare, Medicaid, the Veteran's Administration and all the rest, then you know that it's not all it's cracked up to be.

The quality of care isn't bad, but it's not very affordable, either.

If you're going to make it in another country, you need to have a mental shift about the way you view your health.

[Since writing the original draft of this book, I went to the hospital in Thailand. You can read about that entire experience on my blog.]

This is a book about taking control of your destiny, and health is certainly a part of that. In the West, we eat like pigs, avoid exercise like the plague, and hope a doctor will swoop in and solve those inevitable problems when they arise.

I'm a lot more proactive out here, and you'll need to do the same thing.

In the past year, I have dropped fifty pounds and the year before that I quit smoking. It helps that the local diet is so much healthier. Remember when we talked about the snacks being out of reach at my house? Well, think about that on a national scale. Even if you're eating out all the time, there's simply not the temptation to eat some of the insane stuff they serve in the USA.

When things do go wrong, and that's life, you can rest assured knowing that you will pay forty percent or less of the cost for the same procedure in America. There is a reason medical tourism is on the rise. Bypass surgery in America is going to set you back seventy-five grand at least. In the Netherlands, you are going to spend 1/6th of that at fifteen thousand dollars. That's a huge difference in price. Suddenly, those insane insurance premiums in America don't make sense. I don't live in a medical tourism destination. But there are three JCI-certified hospitals within a 2-hour flight, and if it's really bad, I can be at a medical tourism destination the same day. If I wake up and need heart surgery, I can be in an underpriced tier-1 facility filled with western-trained doctors by mid-afternoon. I take care of myself, get regular checkups, and try not to worry about that stuff, just like ordinary people who live out in the country in America.

Health is just another fear that they use to control us. We had my latest child locally. The looks of the hospital were abysmal. Compared to Western standards, it was shocking. But a lot of what we think we need in a hospital in America is just overpriced hype. We had zero complications and an easy delivery - at about ten percent of what you pay in America even with good insurance. This place delivers babies all day long without problems. It turns out that a lot of what you pay for in America doesn't make a difference.

I'm not saying there aren't great doctors in America. I just want you to realize that there are great doctors all over the world who charge a great deal less for the same experience. There's not some special magic knowledge that comes from practicing medicine in the United States.

If you are worried about medications, prescriptions here cost pennies on the dollar. Most prices in America are artificially inflated to cover the costs of all those good looking pharmaceutical sales reps that spend all day schmoozing doctors and slipping them money to prescribe you their medicines.

If you do make the move abroad, the most important step is to start taking responsibility for your health. No matter where you live, being healthy can extend your life by thirty years or more. The sooner you take your health seriously, the better.

XXI

TRAVEL SECRETS

The traveler sees what he sees. The tourist sees what he has come to see.
— G.K. Chesterton

136

A TRIP ABROAD

Phone calls with my dad always end awkwardly. I try to keep things positive – I talk about the kids, I talk about kayaking, I talk about the cool people I'm meeting. But inevitably, it ends with him talking about some terrible story he heard on the news.

"I just hear crime is so bad out there."

If you only get your information from the news and the government, you might think that I live in a third-world hellhole. In fact, if you get your information from the news, you probably believe that the US is a war zone too! Maybe there was an excuse for falling for that thirty years ago, but these days the real information is literally at your fingertips.

This fake news is just another way that they use fear to control us.

Get online and research. There are communities of expats all over the world, based in every country so that you can find online discussions easily. And if something important is happening in the country, the odds are pretty good they're talking about it. This is an excellent way to get a feel for exactly how dangerous some amazing countries actually are.

You already know that most other countries are cheap. The only reason people pay exorbitant prices abroad is ignorance. They don't do any research beyond visiting the most popular hotel price aggregators. That's the most simplistic way to use the Internet. There are tons of great books about the art of traveling skillfully. I just want to give you a real taste for how you can get out into the world without breaking the bank.

137

LONGER TRIPS ARE CHEAPER

Most people think that if a one-week trip costs a thousand bucks, a two-week trip will cost two thousand. That couldn't be further from the truth. The most expensive part of most trips is the flight. The more people in your family, the more brutal those flights become. If you stay in high-end hotels and book everything online, you will massively overpay. Poor planning can inflate the cost of your trip.

But if you apply just a little strategy, you can come out way ahead. Even most fancy hotels offer a discount for extended stays. Get off the Internet and pick up the phone! You can save a lot of money on any trip that lasts longer than five days.

Where I live right now, the price is the same for ten days or thirty, because I came in person and negotiated a good long-term price. I do that over the phone all the time, but I happened to already be on the island. Some people book around me constantly. Some of them just pay the online price, but the smart people email and get a massive discount.

You can rent a whole house or apartment long-term quite quickly now. When the flight is the most expensive part, and the hotel cost is the lowest, extending your trip lowers your cost per day. That's the value in taking a longer trip. The price of a house rental doesn't change for one person or four. So the size of your family doesn't affect the price. But plane tickets cost four times as much for an average sized family.

When you are looking at trying out a new place, I recommend booking for a month. You will be in a position to get an actual taste for the country and to also massively cut down on your costs.

When you plan a traditional short vacation, you have to budget in some serious expenses. Food in hotels and airports is always really expensive. We eat in restaurants way more on holiday than we do at home. If you are a little more strategic and rent an apartment or house, cook your own food, and rent a car instead of emptying your wallet for taxis, you can slash your costs and spend that money having fun experiences.

138

CRUISE SECRETS

Twice a year, all the cruise ships in the world move around. Ships in Europe move to the Eastern United States. Ships on the west coast shoot over to Asia. Then six months later they all go back.

See, cruise ships don't do very well in the dead of winter. Nobody wants to relax on the deck of a ship during a snowstorm - too many memories of the Titanic. These cruise ship movements are called repositioning cruises.

A cruise ship might cost hundreds of dollars a night, but a repositioning trip often costs in the range of thirty bucks for the same room. Getting from Florida to London on a cruise ship is cheaper than flying. You get a nice room, you get three or four buffets a day, and you get the luxury of a pool all for the price of a plane ticket. The boat will take a lot longer than the flight, but you get to travel in style.

If you have kids, there are a lot of benefits to the cruise route. You can get one room for far less than four plane tickets, and the entire trip is a vacation.

The ships only move around twice a year, and if you do some research and learn when the movements are you can plan a trip. The great thing about this type of travel is that most people don't have that much free time. When you are a cubicle slave, you get five weeks off a year if you are incredibly lucky. Most people get two.

Let's look at this cruise in another light. You can give your family a home, unlimited entertainment, food and all utilities for a month or more. How much does all of that cost you right now? When you think of the boat as a month of living somewhere rather than just transportation, you can see how cheap the experience is. You can't get an apartment in a bad neighborhood in New York this cheap.

You can take your planning to the next level. There are websites that travel agents use; you can hop on one and place a bid on a cruise. Sometimes they have a fixed bottom price, but you can negotiate to get the cruise lines internal currency. So you get a few hundred bucks to spend on drinks or in the casino.

Factor this in when you're bidding on a cruise. Repositioning cruises never fill up because so few people have the time to go on such a long trip. That means you are always in a strong negotiating position. The people hired to fill up these cruises want those rooms filled, and they're willing to hook you up with great amenities and even bump you up to a nicer room if the ship isn't filled.

139

THE TWENTY DOLLAR TRICK

When I heard about this one, I thought it was ridiculous. For a while, I was going to Las Vegas for conferences once a month, and each one was always in a different hotel. If you've done a little research, you'll discover that rooms in Las Vegas are "loss leaders." Hotels don't expect to make their profit from the room rentals. They make their money from the shops, gambling, shows and food. Once you're in, they know they'll make their money back.

Hotels in Vegas are almost never fully booked. There are just so many rooms in a very small area. When you are checking in, you have to hand the clerk your ID and credit card. The simple trick is to slip a twenty-dollar bill in the middle and say, "Do you have any complimentary upgrades available?"

You are giving a twenty dollar tip and asking them to upgrade your room. The key is not to be ostentatious about it. The last time I did this, I was upgraded from a regular room to a lovely suite. Usually, the clerk will bump you up one level in quality. You know how hotels have like basic rooms, deluxe, mini suite, business suite, etc. They all use different names, but you can pay more for a better room. On that trip, my friend spent $1,000 to upgrade to a suite just like mine for the week.

I paid twenty bucks.

I don't use this technique as much internationally. In other countries, the hotel clerks don't always know how to upgrade your room. But in countries with a lot of Western tourism, you can certainly make this work. It's best in hotels that have computer systems where they can upgrade you with the click of a mouse.

Not every hotel clerk has the power to upgrade you. Sometimes they will get confused, especially if you booked through a third party website. But in Las Vegas, this trick works nearly every time. It's always worth giving a try. It's only twenty bucks after all. The risk is small, but the reward is huge. You are risking twenty dollars, and the possible reward is a bump to a room worth hundreds of dollars more a night.

140

FREQUENT FLYER

There are a lot of ways to get value from your frequent flyer miles. The best move you can make is using the right credit card as a part of your business funnel. Let's say you get into the arbitrage game. You're buying and reselling traffic. If you use a great credit card with miles on your airline, you can rack up miles without actually losing money. With regular purchases, you only get miles on money you are losing forever.

You go to the store and buy a couch. You use your miles credit card and earn a few hundred points. But that money evaporates as soon as you spend it. When you use the same principle with your business, the money keeps recycling. You're spending money, but it keeps coming back. This is powerful if you're in the consulting game. Get a client to pay you to buy something for them. Then use that card again.

There are also great ways to hop between cards to get incredible amounts of air miles. When you do it right, you can get triple the miles on any trips you take. The best strategies for getting great miles are always fluctuating. Keep your eyes peeled and do new research to see which cards have the best miles. For personal finance, I'm not a huge fan of miles on credit cards. The debt you can build up is way more expensive than a few measly miles. If you're not in the black financially, it's a much better decision to use the card with the lowest rate or a cash back offer.

141

CHEAP FLIGHTS

Many of us have a favorite travel website. We stick with the site we love because it's reliable, we like the layout, whatever. We like earning those points that we'll never use. Those points usually expire before you can accumulate enough unless you're in the top ten percent of their customers. The regular people love the chase, but they don't get the benefits.

Those sites often charge a premium, so they can make a profit on top of what the airlines and hotels are charging. It's how they can afford to pay their staff. Just because a site is your favorite, doesn't mean it's the best choice.

Some of the best airlines don't list on those sites because they don't want to give up money to a middleman. I can fly round trip from where I live in Asia to London for about twenty-five hundred bucks in business class. If I use one of the popular travel sites, the same ticket will cost me three to four times as much money.

The first step is to look at all the airlines that fly from your city. The operative word there is 'all', because there are tons you've never paid attention to because they don't have a shiny button on one of those travel websites. Some of those airlines prefer to compete by offering lower airfares. The money that would typically go to a middleman website stays in your pocket instead.

You can also look for a larger airport near you. You may need to book that first flight locally, but there are usually a ton of great options from the larger hub. The great thing about the lifestyle we are building is that your travel dates aren't chiseled in stone. I often look for flights throughout the month. Certain dates have high prices, and certain other dates have low prices. Just to fly from my island to the nearest hub, flights fluctuate from twenty-five dollars a flight up to one hundred and fifty. I often sit next to someone who paid six times more money for the same ticket because they didn't research properly.

Getting great discounts is often more about time than it is about knowledge. That's why this is a great task to delegate to your kids. Put them in charge of looking for great travel deals. Instead of screwing around online with social media, they can help your family cut down costs. This helps pass along solid financial principles, and they can think of it as a game. There are also some great sites that let you set fare alerts when a significant discount opens up.

142

THINKING OUTSIDE THE BOX

Whenever I want to go somewhere new, I start a barrage of online searches. I learn about the culture and the place, but also I compare costs extensively. In some locales, renting a house is the best option. In others, a hotel is the right move.

For each place, the value will be squirreled away in a different place. No perfect method applies to every country. Even one option – say, renting a house – will have a dozen listings for the same property.

The first place I look is a site that is targeted at locals. It's an easy way to avoid those foreigner rates that seem to be present everywhere in this part of the world.

Approaching travel with an open mind can cut your costs down dramatically. People who come to my island without doing any research pay three to four times more than I do for a single night in a hotel. You want to email people and get on the phone with them. They don't want their property empty, so negotiate and take advantage.

You don't have to travel the world and take massive trips like I do. The last time I was in New York, I rented a luxury apartment that was the size of a small house for twenty percent of the cost of a terrible hotel room. Saving money doesn't mean you have to schlub it. Even planning a short vacation, you can benefit from a little bit of strategy.

143

DEALING IN PERSON

Last piece of travel wisdom here, and it's going to save you piles of stress. Only book the first day or two in a new location before you arrive. Sometimes you get to a hotel, and the place is in shambles. The manager quit, the hotel is in a nosedive, and you want to get out of there. But you paid for two weeks in advance, so you're trapped in a bad situation.

Just booking for the first day or two, depending on how far you've traveled, gives you great flexibility. Now you might think that you are going to get hit with higher hotel prices. But it's the opposite. When you go in person, and the hotel has rooms, which they almost always do, you can negotiate to pay a LOT less than the published rate. I see this every single day, all over the world. You have an incredible advantage if you ask for it.

You can always book a room at the standard rate online after you arrive. There is no risk on your part. Just a little adventure with a big chance at an upside. Along this adventure, you'll run into some people that don't understand business and won't negotiate with you. That happens. At some hotels near me, it's cheaper to book online, where the website takes a cut than to pay in person and pay the hotel directly. But that's the exception, not the rule. Those hotels always end up in financial straits and slash the prices eventually.

A few years ago I wanted to rent a unit in a hotel long-term. They told me they weren't interested in that. They told me that if I paid cash for an entire year in advance, they would give me a five percent discount over paying day to day. Five percent! They were so greedy that I walked right out of there.

I drove past this hotel a few months ago. They are now offering long-term rentals at about forty percent of my original offer. And about ninety-percent off the offer they insulted me with. People always eventually realize there is a significant advantage in having the secure income of a long-term rental.

I've lived in several different places on this island. We moved around and negotiated until I got the deal I was looking for. That's why I got such a great deal. You can do well in email, but even better in person. You can walk around the hotel and get a feel for the place before you negotiate. We make a lot of assumptions when booking online, and you can avoid that just by handling a little business in person.

XXII

HAPPY AND FREE

Happiness is the freedom of choice. The freedom to choose where to live, what to do, what to buy, what to sell, from whom, to whom, when and how.

- Eleni Zaude Gabre-Madhin

144

CONFIDENCE

Right now, I'm asking you to take the first step over a chasm. You can't see the bridge below you, so it takes a little faith. I believe in building confidence one step at a time. You might get excited about this book and what I've shared with you, but you'll feel a lot more excitement when you make that first dollar; when fiction becomes reality.

We live in a world where we are truly quite powerless. Most of us don't own our homes. The landlord or the bank can kick you out on a whim. If you can't pay your taxes, you can lose your house or worse. Your job can go up in smoke in a single moment. All of these vital aspects of security are all just an illusion in our society. It's hard to feel confident when you have control over so little.

The path to freedom starts with just one tiny step. When you write that first blog post or record that first video, something amazing happens. You move this book from your mind to your reality. It's very easy to get excited about a book that promises freedom. But that emotional energy will wane over time. When you start taking action, however, you begin a powerful habit. Your body and your mind move into alignment. Now your actions start to match your thoughts.

Often we get excited about an idea and even talk about it with our friends, but we take no action. When we fail to take action, a part of our minds begins to realize that we don't believe our words. Only reality affects reality. Reading this book won't change your life if you take no action. Honestly, I don't care what action you choose to take. You may decide that you hate my style of teaching and grab a book on running Facebook ads. That's fine as long as you go out there and start running those ads. Whatever path you choose won't feel real until you start doing it.

Those little steps that start the process might seem small, but they are crucial if you want to get to the bigger steps. Everything I have shared with you is designed to help you on multiple levels. Writing things down and taking action is how you begin a true habit, but they also help to connect ideas with reality. Until our thoughts affect the real world, they are just dreams without a deadline.

145

DON'T BE ME

You don't need to replicate my lifestyle. Simply replicating my mindset will put you in a position to achieve your personal dreams. You can certainly follow my method and hop over to another country. That's exactly what I've done, and I couldn't be happier. But you are your person. I'm not trying to clone myself here. You can achieve greatness by moving towards your goal. If your dream life is a house with your family, then I support that fully. You have the ability to begin to secure your children's future in a powerful way.

Whatever your goals in life are, it's time to take control of your destiny. You deserve to remove the shackles and have more control over what is going to happen to you today and tomorrow. The world out there might seem scary, but as you take these first steps that fear is going to transition into an incredible sense of power.

You have all the tools and the knowledge that you need to create the life you've always wanted. The education system has spent decades killing that spark, but it's still within you. With a little bit of attention, your life can burn brightly again.

Follow your path, and I can't wait to hear about your amazing success.

XXIII

WORK WITH ME

Unity is strength... when there is teamwork and collaboration, wonderful things can be achieved.

- Mattie Stepanek

146

DO NOT SERVE ME

I'm always looking for amazing people to connect with personally. The best ways to connect with me are to leave awesome reviews of this book on Amazon or even Goodreads. Without those reviews, this book might lose momentum. I want to help many people just like you achieve greatness in their lives.

You can find all my social media profiles on my main site, which I'm sure you know by now is ServeNoMaster.com. I love communicating with people directly. If you want to email me, just grab the awesome free gift from the start of this book. You will get an email from my personal address that you can immediately reply to. You could be talking to me later today!

I'm not looking to turn you into my employee. That's not what this book is about. I don't want you to work for me. But if you have a great idea and want to jam on something together I'm always happy to listen to ideas. Twice a year I take on an intern to help them explode into success. You can reach out to me about mentorship opportunities, but I'm usually booked.

The more you connect with me online, the more we can accomplish together. This book is not a one-way street - it's the start of a conversation. I read all the comments on my blog posts and respond on social media as much as I can. It's your chance to let me know what you thought and what you'd like to know more about. If you thought something was missing from this book, just let me know, and I'll make a new blog post just for you!

We live in a digital age where books are no longer written in stone. We can connect, we can create, and we can grow amazing things. And 'we' is the operative word in that sentence. There are always little situations in business that are unique and apply only to you. Come tackle them as part of a community!

147

PULL THE TRIGGER

I read a lot of books about the military. Books about soldiers and generals fascinate me. I want to analyze them and figure out what separates the great ones from the crowd. Successful politicians don't interest me because I know they are just good at lying. Great soldiers risk their lives as a part of their career, so the selfishness of politics doesn't interfere as much.

The greatest soldiers are action takers. They're the ones who don't see obstacles, just opportunity. I just fought my way through an eight-hundred-page monster about General Patton. That was a tough read, but it was amazing.

When he started barreling through France, the English freaked out. Their general wanted all the credit and did everything in his power to stop Patton. Most English people think their guy was a hero. They haven't read any history books, though. It took this English general over a year to accomplish his goal for the FIRST DAY. He was three hundred and sixty-five days late, but he still wanted the credit for rolling into Berlin.

They tried everything they could to stop Patton. They ordered him to stop advancing. They cut off his supply lines. By the end of the operation, he was leading an army of tanks with no gas. They thought that would stop him. They were dead wrong.

He kept pressing forward, capturing gasoline along the way, and leaving tanks behind when there wasn't enough fuel. At one point his entire division consisted of just three tanks with fuel. He kept tearing through Europe. He was unstoppable. All because he didn't consider quitting to be an option.

That is the mindset that I look for in people I work with and the students that I get excited about. I recently got an email from a sixteen-year-old kid who wanted to learn from me. I emailed him and offered him a shot at being an intern with me. I would give him access to my most premium material and all I wanted in return was for him to make excellent notes that I could include with my courses.

He emailed me back with five problems. He sent a list of obstacles. Why would I help someone for free and have to overcome the obstacles they created? That mindset cost him a great opportunity. And people do it all the time.

Don't look for excuses for inaction. That will destroy you. Look for a way to adapt and overcome no matter the challenge. If you're British, and you read what I just wrote about Patton, you might hate me right now. Read a biography before you tell me I'm wrong. ;)

At least you'll finally be taking some action.

XXIV

BONUS: LET ME PAY FOR YOUR BOOK

The most fun is getting paid to learn things.
- Diane Sawyer

148

GET YOUR MONEY BACK

I know that this book was a small investment for many people. But for some people, a few bucks is a really big deal. For that reason, I have two ways that you can make back five bucks in the next five minutes. You can do it twice and make ten bucks. In full disclosure, when you do either of these I make five bucks too. If that bothers you, then skip over this section.

These are the two fastest ways I know to make money instantly. If I knew a way to make you ten bucks while I made nothing, I'd have that here instead. But I don't know of anything like that right now. If you do, please feel free to email me and I'll change this section of the book.

149

ACORNS

This little program is great, especially if you're younger. When you move money around in your account, it rounds up to the nearest dollar and puts that into an investment account. You can choose how conservative or aggressive you want to be with your account, which makes it perfect for putting money away for the kids. It only takes about five minutes to sign up, and I've had great experiences working with these guys.

ServeNoMaster.com/acorns

Just for signing up using my link, they put five bucks in each of our accounts. You know that I have an active account with them. Otherwise, my link wouldn't even work. That's the fastest way you can earn five bucks that I know about. It's a win for both of us and means that you get to start your business out knowing you've already earned back the cost of this book. You don't have to start out in the red!

I like Acorns because I'm not that great with investing. I honestly am so focused on the skill of just generating money from online businesses that I've never dabbled in the stock market, foreign exchange games or bonds. Acorns lets me manage a small investment account without a lot of complexity. You can pull your money out anytime you want, so it's never stuck.

I like having some money working on my behalf out in the world. It's a little soldier venturing out to do battle and bring home the little soldiers it captures. You may be a whiz at investing. We all have strengths and weaknesses. But if you haven't started investing yet, or you want your kids to start young, then I recommend this software. You don't notice the money going out, but it'll be there when you need it later on.

150

WORLDREMIT

If you don't want to mess around with investing, I have a second way for you to grab a few bucks.

WorldRemit is the program that I use to move money from my American bank accounts around the world. I have tried a lot of different services and this one is my favorite. Where we live is a thirty minute drive from the ATM and it's out of service or out of money half the time.

Before discovering WorldRemit, my wife and I once took a boat three hours each way, just to go to the ATM on a neighboring island and pick up enough money to pay the deposit on an apartment.

Now we can pick up cash at any convenience store in our little village. The best part is that the cost is significantly lower than going to an ATM. When I withdraw cash, I get hit with an international withdrawal fee from my bank and another one from the ATM I am using. It's a real double whammy.

Then they hit me again because all the ATMs around here have a per-transaction limit in addition to my daily withdrawal limit. I almost always have to withdraw money twice in a row, so I end up paying four fees.

On top of that, the exchange rate is never as high as it's supposed to be. With WorldRemit, I can see the rate and any fees before I move money. The World Remit fee is always lower than just one of the ATM fees that I pay during a normal withdrawal.

Lower fees and a killer exchange rate combined with instant transactions make me a big fan of this service. If your traveling abroad, I can't recommend them enough. If you are from a country other than the United States, you may be able to find a better alternative, but for Americans this is the best one I've found.

I've run hundreds of transactions through them and the only problem I ever had was when the power cut out in the middle of the authorization. When the power came back on, I called them and they fixed the problem in a few minutes.

WorldRemit is how I move money around and if you make a transaction for one hundred dollars or more, we EACH get twenty bucks. That's four times better than Acorns, which I absolutely love, but I know not everyone is traveling anytime soon.

ServeNoMaster.com/remit

The beauty of WorldRemit is that I get better conversion rates, I pay lower fees and I can pick up the money way closer to home. It's the trifecta of convenience. This program pays enough to cover the cost if you bought the paperback edition of this book.

Just my way of saying you are AWESOME.

Now you have two different choices for making back the cost of this book today. If you don't like either of them, that's ok. You will still get a whole boatload of value from this book. And if you decided to get the book for free using Kindle Unlimited, I love you. Amazon pays me more for that than for traditional sales. Go figure!

151

WRITE LIKE ME

My current main passion is teaching people how to become amazing authors. So many people have a great idea, but they just don't know how to get it into the world. Whether you are working as a consultant or just want to open a new revenue stream, being able to create a book that can become a bestseller is a very powerful tool in your arsenal.

I have worked with some amazing clients in the past year and put together a training program for my interns. I am going to start sharing that with a very small, select group of people.

I keep the group very small and that allows me to provide maximum value. As a special thank you for reading this book all the way to the end, I have an awesome coupon for you.

I like to reward action takers, and people who make it this far in the book are my elite. When you get to the end this book, you will have a chance to leave a rating at the top of the screen (on Kindle). Just hit five stars for me (if you think I deserve it). If you're reading the paperback version, you have to go to ServeNoMaster.com/review to leave your review.

At the very bottom of ServeNoMaster.com/book you'll see a spot where you can request your secret coupon code. This code will give you fifty percent off my Non-Fiction Writing course.

Just leave those stars and when you log onto your computer, take a screenshot to show me, and I'll email you a coupon code within twenty-four hours.

XXV

THE FUTURE IS LOOKING BRIGHT

Control your own destiny or someone else will.
- Jack Welch

152

MY FUTURE

Sitting on my deck today, and the future couldn't be brighter. The sun is shining, and I'm a dozen meters from crystal clear water. For so long I was afraid to seize my destiny. Walking that tightrope without a net terrified me. I was afraid to take what I wanted because the world told me over and over again that I would fail. That I didn't deserve it.

We've all heard those crippling words, and over time we begin to believe them. I've been told thousands of times that I would never succeed and yet staring over the crystal ocean I can only feel contentment. With two amazing kids and a spot on a tropical island, there isn't much more I could ask for from life.

If I wanted to slow down, I could retire today. In fact, I was just swimming in the ocean and got bored. I came back up here because I wanted to keep writing. I love my work that much. Doing what you enjoy is an entirely new level of freedom.

There will be tumultuous ups and downs as you venture forth on this grand adventure. As you succeed, you will discover new and amazing challenges. These are the things that make life so sweet. Living on the beach is pretty great, but pursuing adventures is even better.

I have accomplished more in my thirty-five years on this planet than many do in a lifetime. But I'm only just getting started. I have the outline for a fantastic science-fiction series rattling around in my head. I just have to sit down and commit the time to start cranking out those books. I have thought about writing a movie or two. I know that I can achieve it.

The greatest thing I have learned through this entire adventure is that I am capable of great things. You are capable of great things too. The only things holding you back have been a lack of faith and a lack of knowledge. You now have the knowledge to succeed. You only need to start to believe in yourself. Within a few years, you could be living a life that puts mine to shame.

I got an email today about a bunch of job openings in my area. I'm not sure why I get these emails, but it's always interesting to see what's out there. I almost clicked on one of the links, and then I just started laughing. How could I ever work for someone else ever again? I have total control of my destiny. At first, it felt like trying to tame a wild horse, and I had no idea where life was taking me. But now the beast is tamed, and my dreams have become reality.

As a child, I dreamed of being a bestselling author. Now that I've written dozens of bestsellers under many pen names I can look back with a smile on my face. I always imagined my greatest books would be adventure stories. I was close. My own life has been my greatest adventure.

For now, I'm settled in my little slice of paradise, but I'm not sure that my adventures are finished. I have a lot more countries I want to see, but first I think I need to add a few more kids to my brood.

When you take control of your destiny, you will go through a period of fear. That old feeling still tries to swing by my house now and again. But there's no room here for fear anymore.

As you get through that barrier, you'll discover what it means to be truly free. Just recently I ran into trouble with my landlord. He tried to yell at me and dominate me like I'm a child. It was a strange experience. Nobody is allowed to yell at me anymore.

He dealt with my family dishonestly and thought that being old and yelling would give him power over me. I walked away and moved into a better house immediately. Nobody has the authority to yell at me. He'd be better off shouting at the wind.

When you take control of your destiny, you achieve real power. Nobody will ever be in a position to yell at you, threaten you or intimidate you ever again. When they try, you can just laugh and walk away.

I'm sitting on the beach, and now he's shouting at an empty house that nobody wants to live in anymore. There is no better feeling than that moment you realize nobody can ever hurt you again. Nobody can fire you, take your house away, or insult you in front of your family.

That's the future that I want to share with you. That's what it truly means to be free. That's what I mean when I say it. I will **Serve No Master**.

153

THE BEGINNING IS THE END

My life these days is close to perfection. I have achieved the majority of my goals at thirty-five, and I'm not even close to slowing down. My new villa is about thirty yards from the waterline. The only thing between me and that big beautiful ocean is a couple of palm trees. I'm writing this book sitting here in paradise. I now make more in a month than I made in a year teaching at one of the top twenty universities in America. I won't say the name, but something tells me you've already figured it out.

Most people my age are working sixty-hour weeks in jobs they hate trying to fight their way through middle management. They work at soulless companies and the master they serve doesn't care about them.

Instead of kissing ass, taking drug tests, and letting other people steal credit for my work, I spend most of my time writing my blog, recording episodes of my podcast and doing awesome things. I surf almost every day with my girlfriend. When we're not surfing, we kayak, stand up paddle, swim and even wakeboard behind our speedboat. I read an entire book every single day.

The best part of every day is teaching my newborn son to swim. He's less than three months old and already he's getting the hang of it.

That's how I spend my days, and I can't wait to see your pictures of paradise.

I could spend pages and pages telling you how awesome my life is and how much money I make. But you already bought this book, so you don't need that. I don't want you to think about how lucky I am.

My story is now finished. It's time for you to start your story. I can't wait for you to write a book in a few years that sells more copies than mine and makes this look like garbage. I want you to stand on my shoulders and shout out against the storm.

Stand up there and shout my anthem again. My creed. Three words that define my entire belief system.

Serve. No. Master.

154

PLANNING FOR THE FUTURE

I have prepared an exhaustive amount of information for you on my website. You don't have to dig into your couch for loose change or spend a single cent from your bank account to use any of it. You can find everything you need to move forward at ServeNoMaster.com/book. I tried to make the link as easy to remember as possible!

There you'll find a shockingly complete set of diagrams, graphics and step-by-step tutorials that take you beyond everything covered in this book. And if there's something you felt was missing, leave a comment or email me. I'll continue to add more content to my website, so you have everything you need to move forward and unleash your destiny.

If you use one of my links to check out a product I use, I do get a commission. You will notice that not everything I recommend does that. I won't recommend the second best choice, even if the first choice won't give me a penny. If you do use my links, I appreciate it.

When you make your blog, you will start to do the same thing. It's wonderful to get paid just to tell people about the things you love. I'm so excited about what the future holds for you. This moment is where hope meets opportunity.

If you could just take one tiny step today. Just one tiny step, then you will be that much closer to your destiny. With this path, you will find work that you enjoy. Something that you crave so much you leave the beach and run up to your desk to work on. That's the future that is in front of you.

Together, we can make amazing things happen. I would love to see pictures of your success and interview you on my new podcast. I want the world to hear about your success and how proud I am of the distance you cover.

155

TAKE ACTION NOW

This is it. We are at the end. My action is complete. I have written and edited and rewritten this book until it's ... maybe not perfect, but the best I can do right now. Hopefully, it's been an amazing journey that enlightened and inspired you. It's a little shorter than my original goal, but just like my son and daughter - I can tell it's ready.

Now the ball is in your hands. You have the ability to change your destiny. Just head to my site today and read a little more. That one action is enough to start the ball rolling. You might have a million excuses, but please don't wait until tomorrow.

If you push back starting until tomorrow, the odds of your success start to plummet. And I don't want that. If I were standing there with you right now, I would drag you to the computer and force you to pick your first website name. But I'm not there, and I can't slap you if you don't do anything. This is about freedom.

You have the choice right now to free yourself.

You also have the choice to walk right back into your cell.

Will you step into the light? Will you start right now?

Are you ready to serve no master?

It's the end of the book. But we're just getting started.

ONE LAST CHANCE

ServeNoMaster.com/quit

Thank you for your purchase of Serve No Master. As an extra bonus, I want to give you FOUR free gifts.

1. QUIT YOUR JOB CHECKLIST

The "Ready to Retire" checklist that lets you know the exact moment you can fire your boss forever. Mark the moment on your calendar when you can start living a life of freedom.

2. AUTHOR AND ENTREPRENEUR ACCELERATOR - LIFETIME MEMBERSHIP

Get lifetime access to the most powerful group you will ever join. As a permanent member of my private accelerator, you will get free content daily as well as support from thousands of others on the same path.

Every day there are new training videos, stories of success and moments of inspiration...all waiting for you.

3. FIVE DAY BUSINESS CHALLENGE - COMPLIMENTARY TICKET

Each month, I run a challenge with interviews from 25 experts at building an online business. Together we will refine your online dreams and help you focus on the best path for YOUR life. At the end of the challenge, you will know the exact steps to take to break the chains to a job you no longer love.

4. GET MY NEXT BOOK FREE

Members of my tribe get complimentary review and beta reader access to my new books, before anyone else in the world knows. Get a chance to read my next book AND affect the final version with your suggestions and opinions.

You get these bonuses as well as a few surprises, when you enter your best email address below.

Accelerate your success and click the link below to get instant access:

ServeNoMaster.com/quit

THE STORY ISN'T OVER

Learn How to Make Your Dreams Come True in the sequel to Serve No Master - Control Your Fate

Turn the page for an amazing exerpt…

CONTROL YOUR FATE - EMPTY BUCKET LISTS

A few years ago, there was a movie called *The Bucket List*, which is a list of things you want to do before you die. I've never actually seen the film, but my mom did and started talking about it. Enough people saw the movie that the phrase "bucket list" entered our culture and our language. Most people understand what you mean when you say "bucket list."

Now here's the thing: most of us have either never actually written a real bucket list, or if we have, we haven't taken action on that list. Most of the things on that list are things that we haven't even tried. We have the idea in our minds, but we haven't gone beyond that phase.

Just like my friend who always dreamed of going to Japan, we never take that action step. And wherever you are right now, I want you to start thinking about creating a real bucket list.

What do you want to achieve in life?

Every year, around the holidays and the end of the year, people write down resolutions. And most resolutions are promises or commitments to stop doing something negative or to start doing something positive. We promise to alter our behavior.

We structure ninety-nine percent of our new year's resolutions like:

- "I'm going to quit smoking;"
- "I'm going to join a gym;"
- "I'm going to lose weight;"
- "I'm going to stop dating losers."

We put all the pressure on ourselves, and we focus on changing our actions. Unfortunately, we totally ignore the way the human mind works and the way we make decisions. As humans, our desires dictate our behavior. You can promise yourself that you're going to do something over and over again, but if you don't want to do it, you're not going to change.

When I quit smoking, I had reached a point where I knew it was going to kill me. I was coughing blood into the sink all the time, I smelled like dog butt, and it was even a struggle to walk up a flight of stairs. Looking in the mirror, I didn't see many years left in front of me. I had quit several times in the years before my final quit, and during those quits, I always told myself, "I've got to stop smoking." But the desire remained. When I removed the desire and shifted from, "I want to smoke cigarettes, but I can't smoke cigarettes," and I changed my mindset to "Cigarettes are disgusting—I don't want them near me," it became easy to quit. I had no temptation.

People have handed me cigarettes since I quit, saying, "Here, just have one, it's no big deal." But I throw it away from me because I think it's disgusting. I've even had several nightmares. In a recurring dream, I have a cigarette, and then I wake up panting and sweating, thinking, "Oh no, I had a cigarette!" And I react the same way I would if I woke up thinking someone had poisoned me.

Before we can change any behavior, we have to change desires. As we start this journey together (and this is how I like to start most of my books and projects), I want to make it clear that this process is cooperative. I want to dial into some dreams in your life.

How can you measure whether or not my system works, or if I'm wasting your time, unless we set a real goal?

I'd like you to start working on a list. Call it what you want—a bucket list or an achievement list—and throughout this book, we will get better and better at setting goals. Right now, we are focused on the big picture. Set goals for what you'd like to achieve this year or things you want to accomplish in your lifetime.

I am a big believer in physical acts. I prefer a notebook in my hands than a file on a computer somewhere. Buy a spiral note book and call it "Control My Fate." You are going to be the author of this book. It can be your command center for all the activities in this book. Working through all the exercises and activities in a single place will make it easy for you to track your progress and see how your life is shifting.

NORTHERN LIGHTS

There are certain things in my life that I have not achieved yet. I've never seen the northern lights, and they are still on my personal list of goals. As of right now, many barriers keep me from seeing the aurora borealis. First, I live on a tropical island on the equator, so it is impossible to see it from here. The second reason is that I'm married with two children. I can't exactly throw my family on a plane or boat right now. There are some logistical challenges. But it's important to see them as challenges to be overcome, not barriers. These are not reasons that my dream will never happen.

I already have a plan in place. We're in the middle of filling out some paperwork with the government here to validate our marriage. In the six months since the wedding, our paperwork hasn't made it to the regional capital, let alone the national one. Currently, only the tiny village where we live recognizes our marriage.

On her national insurance, my wife still has to use her maiden name. This is also causing problems because our children have my name. The insurance doesn't understand why the kids don't have the same last name as her. It's all part of the price of living in paradise.

Once we finish this paperwork process, the next phase of my plan is to start traveling by cruise ship. You can go on a repositioning cruise for pennies on the dollar. When I want to take my family to America, we are going to travel by cruise ship, rather than by plane. I don't like taking young children on planes. Why would I put my kids on a sixteen-hour flight when we could take them by cruise ship over the course of thirty days of raw, awesome adventures for the same price? I'm excited about that.

That is phase one of my northern lights plan. I've already figured out the paperwork I need to complete to obtain passports for my children, and I've figured out the logistics of how we're going to travel. Now, it's just a matter of implementation.

ACTIVITY

I want you to do the same thing. Together, we're going to isolate your bucket list, your dreams, and your desires. If you want to call it a "vision board", and you know I like vision boards, that's fine too. Looking at the big picture is just the beginning of how we're going to set goals.

Your first activity is to sit down right now and stop reading this book—do not skip to the next chapter without doing this activity. When you skip the activities and say, "I'll come back and do them later," we both know you're lying. We both know they're probably not going to happen, and that means your odds of success drop through the floor, and I don't want that to happen.

I want you to succeed.

Please, right now, make a list of ten things you would like to achieve in your life. And they can be anything, whether you want to get married, have another kid, or see the northern lights too, or if you want to go surfing in Hawaii, kiss a shark, swim with dolphins—make a list of ten things, and then you can join me in the next chapter.

FOUND A TYPO?

While every effort goes into ensuring that this book is flawless, it is inevitable that a mistake or two will slip through the cracks.

If you find an error of any kind in this book, please let me know by visiting:

ServeNoMaster.com/typos

I appreciate you taking the time to notify me. This ensures that future readers never have to experience that awful typo. You are making the world a better place.

ABOUT THE AUTHOR

Born in Los Angeles, raised in Nashville, educated in London - Jonathan Green has spent years wandering the globe as his own boss - but it didn't come without a price. Like most people, he struggled through years of working in a vast, unfeeling bureaucracy.

And after the backstabbing and gossip of the university system threw him out of his job, he was "totally devastated" – stranded far away from home without a paycheck coming in. Despite having to hang on to survival with his fingernails, he didn't just survive, he thrived.

In fact, today he says that getting fired with no safety net was the best thing that ever happened to him – despite the stress, it gave him an opportunity to rebuild and redesign his life.

One year after being on the edge of financial ruin, Jonathan had replaced his job, working as a six-figure SEO consultant. But with his rolodex overflowing with local businesses and their demands getting higher and higher, he knew that he had to take his hands off the wheel.

That's one of the big takeaways from his experience. Lifestyle design can't just be about a job replacing income, because often, you're replicating the stress and misery that comes with that lifestyle too!

Thanks to smart planning and personal discipline, he started from scratch again – with a focus on repeatable, passive income that created lifestyle freedom.

He was more successful than he could have possibly expected. He traveled the world, helped friends and family, and moved to an island in the South Pacific.

Now, he's devoted himself to breaking down every hurdle entrepreneurs face at every stage of their development, from developing mental strength and resilience in the depths of depression and anxiety, to developing financial and business literacy, to building a concrete plan to escape the 9-to-5, all the way down to the nitty-gritty details of teaching what you need to build a business of your own.

In a digital world packed with "experts," there are few people with the experience to tell you how things really work, why they work, and what's actually working in the online business world right now.

Jonathan doesn't just have the experience, he has it in a variety of spaces. A best-selling author, a "Ghostwriter to the Gurus" who commands sky-high rates due to his ability to deliver captivating work in a hurry, and a video producer who helps small businesses share their skills with their communities.

He's also the founder of the Serve No Master podcast, a weekly show that's focused on financial independence, networking with the world's most influential people, writing epic stuff online, and traveling the world for cheap.

All together, it makes him one of the most captivating and accomplished people in the lifestyle design world, sharing the best of what he knows with total transparency, as part of a mission to free regular people from the 9-to-5 and live on their own terms.

Learn from his successes and failures and Serve No Master.

Find out more about Jonathan at:
ServeNoMaster.com

BOOKS BY JONATHAN GREEN

Non-Fiction

SERVE NO MASTER SERIES

Serve No Master

Breaking Orbit

20K a Day

Control Your Fate

Breakthrough (coming soon)

HABIT OF SUCCESS SERIES

PROCRASTINATION

Influence and Persuasion

Overcome Depression

Stop Worrying and Anxiety

Love Yourself

Conquer Stress

Law of Attraction

Mindfulness and Meditation Ultimate Guide

Meditation Techniques for Beginners

I'm Not Shy

Coloring Depression Away with Adult Coloring Books

Don't be Quiet

How to Make Anyone Like You

DEVELOP GOOD HABITS WITH S.J. SCOTT

How to Quit Your Smoking Habit

The Weight Loss Habit

SEVEN SECRETS

Seven Networking Secrets for Jobseekers

BIOGRAPHIES

The Fate of my Father

Complex Adult Coloring Books

The Dinosaur Adult Coloring Book

The Dog Adult Coloring Book

The Celtic Adult Coloring Book

The Outer Space Adult Coloring Book

The 2nd Celtic Adult Coloring Book

Irreverent Coloring Books

Dragons Are Bastards

Fiction

GUNPOWDER AND MAGIC

The Outlier (As Drake Blackstone)

ONE LAST THING

Reviews are the lifeblood of any book on Amazon and especially for the independent author. If you would click five stars on your Kindle device or visit this special link at your convenience, that will ensure that I can continue to produce more books. A quick rating or review helps me to support my family and I deeply appreciate it.

Without stars and reviews, you would never have found this book. Please take just thirty seconds of your time to support an independent author by leaving a rating.

Thank you so much!

To leave a review go to ->

https://servenomaster.com/review

Sincerely,
Jonathan Green
ServeNoMaster.com

CPSIA information can be obtained
at www.ICGtesting.com
Printed in the USA
LVHW080353151019
634226LV00013B/849/P